Seventh Edition

W9-BNS-238

Human Relations

INTERPERSONAL, JOB-ORIENTED SKILLS

Andrew J. Dubrin

CUSTOM EDITION FOR THE CULINARY INSTITUTE OF AMERICA

Pearson
Custom
Publishing

Prentice
Hall

Taken from:

Human Relations: Interpersonal, Job-Oriented Skills, Seventh Edition,
by Andrew J. DuBrin
Copyright © 2001, 1997, 1992, 1988, 1984, 1981, 1978 by Prentice-Hall, Inc.
A Pearson Education Company
Upper Saddle River, New Jersey 07458

This special edition published in cooperation with Pearson Custom Publishing.

Printed in the United States of America

10 9 8 7 6 5 4

Please visit our web site at www.pearsoncustom.com

ISBN 0–536–63753–9

BA 993431

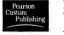

PEARSON CUSTOM PUBLISHING
75 Arlington Street, Suite 300, Boston, MA 02116
A Pearson Education Company

FRAMEWORK OF THE BOOK

The book is a blend of current and traditional topics dealing with interpersonal relations in organizations with a heavy component of skill development and self-assessment. The information is organized into chapters, all emphasizing interpersonal relations between two or more people. Chapter 1, "A Framework for Interpersonal Skill Development," sets the stage for improving one's interpersonal skills on the job. Chapter 2, "Understanding Individual Differences," presents information that is the foundation of effective interpersonal relations. Chapter 3, "Interpersonal Communications," deals with skills in sending and receiving messages.

Chapter 4, "Developing Teamwork Skills," sensitizes the reader to a vital set of skills in the workplace. Chapter 5, "Group Problem Solving and Decision Making," provides additional skill in collaborative effort. Chapter 6, "Cross-Cultural Relations and Diversity," is about developing cross-cultural skills in a diverse work force. Chapter 7, "Resolving Conflicts with Others," helps the reader develop skills in finding constructive solutions to differences of opinion and disputes with others.

Four consecutive chapters deal with exerting influence over others: Chapter 8, "Becoming an Effective Leader," presents information relevant to exercising leadership in the workplace; Chapter 9, "Motivating Others," emphasizes skills in getting others to work hard to achieve goals; Chapter 10, "Helping Others Develop and Grow," is about coaching, counseling, and teaching others; and Chapter 11, "Positive Political Skills," describes how to use power and influence for constructive purposes.

Chapter 12, "Customer Satisfaction Skills," describes several approaches to enhancing skills in satisfying customers, and thus lies at the heart of the quality revolution. Chapter 13, "Enhancing Ethical Behavior," translates ethical principles into usable skills. The rationale is that an ethical base is important for achieving career-long effectiveness in interpersonal relations. Chapter 14, "Personal Productivity and Stress Management," supports development of interpersonal skills in showing that productive people who have stress under control can relate more effectively to others. Chapter 15, "Job Search and Career Management Skills," includes information about the application of interpersonal skills (such as networking) to enhance one's career.

CHANGES IN THE NEW EDITION

This new edition of *Human Relations* is expanded and enlarged, in addition to including updated information wherever appropriate. Two new chapters have been added in response to requests by users of the previous edition. Chapter 14 deals with improving productivity and managing stress, and Chapter 15 is

Preface

Welcome to the new and expanded edition of *Human Relations: Interpersonal, Job-Oriented Skills*. Success in any position involving interaction with people requires two broad sets of competencies: functional skills and generic skills. The term *functional skills* refers to knowledge of one's discipline (or organizational function), technical skills, specialty skills, or simply details of the job. *Generic skills* refers to competencies important in a variety of jobs. Among these generic skills are good work habits and time management, computer skills, high ethics, and interpersonal skills.

My purpose in writing this book is to help readers enhance their interpersonal skills in the workplace. By enhancing interpersonal skills, a person has a better chance of capitalizing upon his or her other skills. Two primary approaches are used in this text to achieve the lofty goal of improving interpersonal skills. First, basic concepts are introduced to enhance understanding of key topics in interpersonal relations in organizations.

Second, skill-building suggestions, exercises, and cases are presented that are designed to improve interpersonal skills related to the topic. Chapter 4, for example, presents general information about the nature of teamwork, followed by suggestions for improving teamwork. The chapter also includes several exercises or experiential activities and a case—all designed to improve teamwork skills.

AUDIENCE FOR THE BOOK

The primary audience for this book is people taking courses that emphasize the development of interpersonal skills. Such courses typically include the term *human relations*. Because interpersonal relations contribute so heavily to effective leadership, the text is suited for participants in leadership and supervisory training courses.

CHAPTER 14 PERSONAL PRODUCTIVITY AND STRESS MANAGEMENT 290

Improving Personal Productivity 291
    Dealing with Procrastination 292
    Attitudes and Values That Enhance Personal Productivity 294
    Work Habits and Skills That Enhance Personal Productivity 297
    Overcoming Time Wasters 299
Understanding and Managing Stress 300
    Symptoms and Consequences of Stress 300
    Personality and Job Factors Contributing to Stress 304
    Methods and Techniques for Stress Management 307
Summary 308
Questions for Discussion and Review 311

CHAPTER 15   JOB SEARCH AND CAREER MANAGEMENT SKILLS   314

Conducting a Job Search 315
    Job-Hunting Tactics 315
    The Job Résumé and Cover Letter 321
    Performing Well in a Job Interview 324
The Vertical and Horizontal Career Paths 327
    The Vertical (Traditional) Career Path 327
    The Horizontal Career Path 328
Using Career Advancement Strategies and Tactics 330
Overcoming Career Barriers 336
    Coping with Job Loss 336
    Dealing with the Glass Ceiling 337
Summary 337
Questions for Discussion and Review 339

GLOSSARY 343

REFERENCES 347

INDEX 355

Techniques for Improving Cross-Cultural Relations and Valuing Differences   119
  Cultural Training   119
  Language Training   120
  Diversity Training (Training in Valuing Differences)   122
Summary   123
Questions for Discussion and Review   125

CHAPTER 7   RESOLVING CONFLICTS WITH OTHERS   127

Sources of Interpersonal Conflict in Organizations   128
  Competition for Limited Resources   128
  Role Conflict   131
  Building Stone Walls   132
  Personality Clashes   132
Aggressive Personalities, Including Bullies   133
Conflict-Management Styles   133
Guidelines and Techniques for Resolving Conflicts   135
  Confrontation and Problem Solving   136
  Constructive Handling of Criticism   137
  Image Exchanging   138
  Cognitive Restructuring   139
Negotiating and Bargaining   139
Combatting Sexual Harassment: A Special Type of Conflict   144
  Types and Frequency of Harassment   144
  Recent Supreme Court Rulings on Sexual Harassment   145
  The Adverse Effects of Sexual Harassment   146
  Guidelines for Preventing and Dealing with Sexual Harassment   146
Summary   148
Questions for Discussion and Review   151

CHAPTER 13   ENHANCING ETHICAL BEHAVIOR   269

Why Be Concerned About Business Ethics?   270
Common Ethical Problems   273
  A Survey of the Extent of Ethical Problems   273
  Frequent Ethical Dilemmas   274
  Choosing Between Two Rights: Dealing with Defining Moments   277
Guidelines for Behaving Ethically   280
  Developing the Right Character Traits   280
Using Corporate Ethics Programs   281
  Following a Guide to Ethical Decision Making   282
  Developing Closer Relationships with Work Associates   286
Summary   287
Questions for Discussion and Review   288

Collaborator   71
People Supporter   74
Challenger   74
Listener   75
Mediator   76
Gatekeeper   76
Guidelines for the Interpersonal Aspects of Team Play   77
Trusting Team Members   77
Displaying a High Level of Cooperation and Collaboration   77
Recognizing the Interests and Achievements of Others   79
Giving Helpful Criticism   80
Sharing the Glory   80
Taking Care Not to Rain on Another Person's Parade   80
Guidelines for the Task Aspects of Team Play   81
Technical Expertise (or Knowledge of the Task)   81
Assuming Responsibility for Problems   81
Seeing the Big Picture   81
Believing in Consensus   82
Helping Team Members Do Their Jobs Better   82
Summary   82
Questions for Discussion and Review   84

CHAPTER 5   GROUP PROBLEM SOLVING AND DECISION MAKING   86

Rational versus Political Decision Making in Groups   87
Guidelines for Using General Problem-Solving Groups   89
Guidelines for Brainstorming   92
Guidelines for Electronic Brainstorming   94
Limitations to Verbal Brainstorming   94
The Electronic Brainstorming Procedure   95
Guidelines for the Nominal Group Technique   96
Using Stand-Up Meetings to Facilitate Problem Solving   98
Using E-Mail and Groupware to Facilitate Group Decision Making   100
Using E-Mail to Facilitate Meetings   100
Using Groupware to Facilitate Group Problem Solving   101
Summary   101
Questions for Discussion and Review   104

CHAPTER 6   CROSS-CULTURAL RELATIONS AND DIVERSITY   105

The Diversity Umbrella   106
Understanding Cultural Differences   108
Competency Goals   108
Dimensions of Differences in Cultural Values   110
Cultural Bloopers   113
Overcoming Cross-Cultural Communication Barriers   115
Business Implications of Understanding Cultural Differences   118

Contents

PREFACE **xiii**

CHAPTER 1 A FRAMEWORK FOR INTERPERSONAL SKILL DEVELOPMENT 1

Plan of the Book 2
A Model for Improving Interpersonal Skills 3
Identification of Developmental Needs 6
    Universal Needs for Improving Interpersonal Relations 7
Developing Interpersonal Skills on the Job 10
    Informal Learning 10
    Specific Developmental Experiences 11
Summary 12
Questions for Discussion and Review 14

CHAPTER 2 UNDERSTANDING INDIVIDUAL DIFFERENCES 15

Personality 16
    Six Major Personality Factors and Traits 17
Cognitive Styles and Personality Types 19
    Cognitive Styles 19
    Guidelines for Dealing with Different Personality Types 21
Mental Ability 23
    Components of Traditional Intelligence 24
    Practical Intelligence 25
    Multiple Intelligences 27
    Emotional Intelligence 28
    Guidelines for Relating to People of Different Levels and Types
      of Intelligence 29

Values as a Source of Individual Differences   30
    How Values Are Learned   31
    Clarifying Your Values   31
    The Mesh Between Individual and Job Values   32
    Guidelines for Using Values to Enhance Interpersonal Relations   32
Summary   34
Questions for Discussion and Review   35

CHAPTER 3   INTERPERSONAL COMMUNICATIONS   39

Steps in the Communication Process   40
Nonverbal Communication in Organizations   42
Modes of Transmission of Nonverbal Communication   43
    Environment   43
    Interpersonal Distance   43
    Posture   43
    Gestures   44
    Facial Expressions   44
    Voice Quality   45
    Personal Appearance   45
Guidelines for Improving Nonverbal Communication   45
Guidelines for Overcoming Communication Problems and Barriers   48
    Understand the Receiver   48
    Discuss Differences in Paradigms   49
    Minimize Defensive Communication   50
    Use Multiple Channels   50
    Use Verbal and Nonverbal Feedback   50
    Display a Positive Attitude   51
    Use Persuasive Communication   51
    Engage in Active Listening   53
    Engage in Complementary Transactions with People   51
    Recognize Gender Differences in Communication Style   57
    Engage in Metacommunications   59
Summary   59
Questions for Discussion and Review   61

CHAPTER 4   DEVELOPING TEAMWORK SKILLS   63

Types of Teams   64
    Self-Managing Work Teams   65
    Cross-Functional Teams   67
    Virtual Teams   67
The Advantages and Disadvantages of Teams and Teamwork   68
    Advantages of Group Work and Teamwork   68
    Disadvantages of Group Work and Teamwork   69
Team Member Roles   70
    Knowledge Contributor   71
    Process Observer   71

about conducting a job search and career enhancement. Among the new topics in the text are:

- Informal learning by employees (Chapter 1)
- The triarchic theory of intelligence and multiple intelligences (Chapter 2)
- Metacommunication (Chapter 3)
- Virtual teams (Chapter 4)
- Groupware for decision making (Chapter 5)
- 360-degree feedback (Chapter 8)
- Self-efficacy as it contributes to motivation (Chapter 9)
- The integration of information technology into interpersonal skill development (Chapters 3, 6, and 14)

Most chapters contain at least one additional self-assessment quiz and one additional skill-building exercise. Many more references are made to the Internet and information technology, including using the Internet for developing cross-cultural skills (Chapter 6), enhancing personal productivity (Chapter 15), and conducting a job search (Chapter 15).

SUPPLEMENTAL MATERIALS

INSTRUCTOR'S MANUAL

The instructor's manual for this text contains 750 multiple choice and true/false test questions, chapter outlines and lecture notes, answers to discussion questions and case problems, and comments about the exercises.

PRENTICE HALL COMPUTERIZED TEST BANK

This testing software is available on 3.5-inch disk for the Windows platform. The program gives the instructor maximum flexibility in preparing tests. It can create custom tests and print up to 99 different scrambled versions of a test at one time; and build tests randomly by chapter, level of difficulty, or question type. The software also allows on-line testing and record keeping and the ability to add problems to the database.

PRENTICE HALL SELF-ASSESSMENT LIBRARY

A CD-ROM with a computerized assessment program that gives sudents insights into their skills, abilities, and interests. The Library includes 45 exercises to help students learn more about themselves and how they relate to others. It is easy to use and self-scoring.

MEETING WORKPLACE TRAINING GUIDELINES

The U.S. federal government guidelines recommend that postsecondary schools teach five competencies and a three-part foundation of skills and personal qualities needed for job performance. The competencies state that effective workers can productively use resources, interpersonal skills, information, systems, and technology. In addition, the foundation competence requires basic skills (such as reading, writing, and arithmetic), thinking skills (such as thinking creatively), and personal qualities (such as self-management and integrity).

Human Relations provides information and exercises that directly support components of six of the preceding eight requirements—use of resources, interpersonal skills, basic skills, personal qualities, and technology. Information and systems are ordinarily taught outside of an interpersonal skills or human relations curriculum. A guide to meeting the federal guidelines is presented next.

Effective workers can productively use the following:

- *Resources*
  Included are allocating time, money, materials, space, and staff. Chapter 2, about understanding individual differences, provides background information for doing an effective job of allocating staff.

- *Interpersonal Skills*
  Examples are working on teams, teaching others, serving customers, leading, negotiating, and working well with people from culturally diverse backgrounds. Interpersonal skills are taught throughout the book, and each of the skill areas just mentioned is covered by at least one chapter. Chapter 4 is about working on teams; Chapter 10, about helping others develop, covers teaching others; Chapter 12, about customer service skills, deals with serving customers. Leading others is the subject of Chapter 8; negotiating is explained in Chapter 7, about resolving conflicts with others; and Chapter 6, about cross-cultural relations, discusses working well with people from culturally diverse backgrounds.

- *Basic Skills*
  These include reading, writing, arithmetic and mathematics, speaking, and listening. Chapter 3, about communicating with people, provides suggestions for improved writing, speaking, and listening.

- *Thinking Skills*
  These consist of thinking creatively, making decisions, solving problems, seeing things in the mind's eye, knowing how to learn, and reasoning. Chapter 5, about group problem solving, deals directly with cre-

ative thinking, decision making, and problem solving. Chapter 13, about enhancing ethical behavior, deals with ethical reasoning.

- *Personal Qualities*
These encompass individual responsibility, self-esteem, sociability, self-management, and integrity. Chapter 13, about ethical behavior, discusses individual responsibility in the context of being ethical and having integrity, as well as constructive character traits. Chapter 8, about leadership, contains information about the importance of integrity. Personal qualities are also described in Chapter 2, on individual differences. Chapter 9 describes the role of self-efficacy in being motivated.

- *Technology*
Frequent mention is made of the Internet, including suggestions for its efficient use (Chapter 14), and using the Internet to enhance cross-cultural skills (Chapter 6).

ACKNOWLEDGMENTS

My appreciation goes to the many people who contributed to the development and production of this book. My primary thanks are due to my editorial and production team: Elizabeth Sugg, Mary Carnis, and Delia Uherec at Prentice Hall and Ann Mohan at WordCrafters Editorial Services. Appreciation is also expressed to the outside reviewers who made suggestions for shaping this edition of the text: H. Frederick Holmes, Ogeechee Technical Institute; Judy Bowie, DeVry Institute of Technology; Gary W. Piggrem, Ph.D., DeVry Institute of Technology; James E. Wetz, Central Florida Community College; Ruth V. Kellar, Ivy Tech State College; Lou Jean Peace, Valdosta Technical Institute; Patricia Lynn Anderson, Valdosta State University; and John Adamski II, Ivy Tech State College.

Andrew J. DuBrin
Rochester, New York

Chapter 1

A Framework for Interpersonal Skill Development

Learning Objectives

After reading and studying this chapter and doing the exercises you should be able to

➤ Explain how interpersonal skills are learned.

➤ Explain the model for interpersonal skill improvement.

➤ Pinpoint your needs for improvement in interpersonal relations.

➤ Describe potential opportunities for developing interpersonal skills on the job.

Sean, a credit analyst, was being considered for promotion to team leader. So far, Sean had not been informed of this development. Alison, Sean's manager, was discussing his pending promotion with his boss, the human resources director.

Alison spoke first: "I'm in Sean's corner. But the guy is just not ready for leadership responsibility. He's a fine credit analyst. Sean has wared off many bad credit risks. But he gets under people's skin. Time and time again, he rubs people the wrong way. If Sean just had better people skills, he would have a great future with our company. The way he deals with people now, he is not ready to manage them."

Scenarios similar to this one take place often in the workplace. Many people are held back from promotions and pay raises, and even lose their jobs, because of poor interpersonal relations. (**Interpersonal relations** is the technical term for relationships with people.) Effective interpersonal relations must be combined with technical knowledge and good work habits to achieve success in any job involving interaction with people. In Sean's case, his potential promotion to team leader was blocked by his poor interpersonal relations.

This chapter explains how people develop interpersonal skills and presents a model that can serve as a foundation for improving your interpersonal skills. In addition the chapter explains how the workplace can be a natural setting for developing interpersonal skills.

PLAN OF THE BOOK

This entire book is devoted to many different ways of improving interpersonal relations in organizations. A three part strategy is presented for achieving the high level of effectiveness in interpersonal relations required in today's workplace. First, each chapter presents key concepts required for understanding a particular aspect of interpersonal relations, such as resolving conflict. Second, the chapter provides specific suggestions or behavioral guidelines for improvement in the aspect of interpersonal relations under consideration.

Third, a variety of exercises give you the opportunity to work on and improve your skills. Among these exercises are self-assessment quizzes, skill-building exercises, and cases for analysis. In addition, the questions at the end of the chapter give you an opportunity to think through and apply the key ideas in each chapter.

Much of this book is concerned with **interpersonal skill training,** the teaching of skills in dealing with others so they can be put into practice. Interpersonal skill training is referred to as *soft-skills* training to differentiate it from technical training. (Technical skills are referred to as *hard skills*.) Soft-skill training builds interpersonal skills, including communication, listening, group problem solving, cross-cultural relations, and customer service. Soft-skills training is more important than ever as organizations realize that a combination of human effort and technology is needed to produce results.[1] For example, assume that a company establishes an elaborate Intranet system to enable

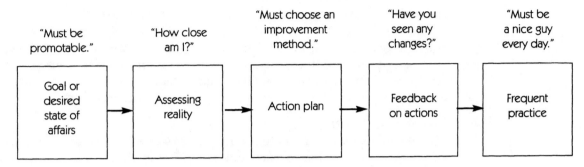

Figure 1-1 A Model for Improving Interpersonal Skills

employees to exchange work-related information with each other. The system will not achieve its potential unless employees are motivated to use it properly and they develop a spirit of cooperation.

A MODEL FOR IMPROVING INTERPERSONAL SKILLS

Acquiring and improving interpersonal skills is facilitated by following a basic model of learning as it applies to changing your behavior. Learning is a complex subject, yet its fundamentals follow a five-part sequence, as shown in Figure 1-1. To change your behavior, and therefore improve, you need a goal and a way to measure your current reality against this goal. You also need a way to affect that reality, and a way to obtain feedback on the impact of your new actions.[2]

Goal or Desired State of Affairs

Changing your behavior, including enhancing your interpersonal relations, requires a clear goal, or desired state of affairs. Your goal can also be regarded as what you want to accomplish as a result of your effort. As a concrete example, let us take the common problem of a person who nibbles his fingernails during tense situations, such as being called on in a meeting. The nibbler might say, "My hopes [a goal] are to be able to sit in a meeting and not nibble my nails even though I know I might be called on." This man's desired state of affairs (his goal) is to avoid putting his nails in his mouth in order to appear calm and professional. Having a goal helps provide motivation and makes it possible to exercise the self-discipline necessary to follow through on your plans. In short, the goal focuses your effort on acquiring the improvements in behavior you seek.

Here we return to Sean, the credit analyst who is being blocked from promotion because his manager perceives him as having poor interpersonal skills. After a discussion with his manager, Sean recognizes that he must improve his interpersonal relations if he wants to become a team leader.

Sean's goal is to be considered promotable to a leadership position. To achieve his goal, he will have to achieve the general goal of improving his interpersonal relations. By conferring with the human resources director, Sean learns that his broad goal of "improving my interpersonal relations" will have to be supported by more specific goals. Having poor interpersonal relations or "rubbing people the wrong way" includes many different behaviors. To begin, Sean selects one counterproductive behavior to improve: He is exceptionally intolerant of others and does not hide his intolerance. Sean's goal is to become less intolerant and more patient in his dealings with others on the job.

Assessing Reality

The second major requirement for a method of changing behavior is to assess reality. Sean needs a way to assess how far he is from his goal of being eligible for promotion and how intolerant he is perceived to be. Sean has already heard from his manager, Alison, that he is not eligible for promotion right now. Sean might want to dig for more information by finding answers to the following questions:

"If I were more tolerant, would I be promoted now?"

"How bad are my interpersonal relations in the office?"

"How many people in the office think I rub them the wrong way?"

"How many deficiencies do my manager and coworkers perceive me to have?"

A starting point in answering these questions might be for Sean to confer with Alison about his behavior. To be more thorough, however, Sean might ask a friend in the office to help him answer the questions. A coworker is some-times in an excellent position to provide feedback on how one is perceived by others in the office. Sean could also ask a confidant outside the office about his intolerance. Sean could ask a parent, a significant other, or both about the extent of his intolerance.

An Action Plan

The learning model needs some mechanism to change the relationship between the person and the environment. An **action plan** is a series of steps to achieve a goal. Without an action plan, a personal goal will be elusive. The person who sets the goal may not initiate steps to make his or her dream (a high-level goal) come true. If your goal is to someday become a self-employed business owner, your action plan should include saving money, establishing a good credit rating, and developing dozens of contacts.

Sean has to take some actions to improve his interpersonal relations, especially his intolerance. The changes should ultimately lead to the promotion he desires. Sean's action plan for becoming more tolerant includes the following:

➤ Pausing to attempt to understand why a person is acting the way he or she does. An example would be attempting to understand why a sales representative wants to extend credit to a customer with a poor credit rating.

➤ Learning to control his own behavior so he does not make intolerant statements just because he is experiencing pressure.

➤ Taking a course in interpersonal or human relations.

➤ Asking Alison to give him a quick reminder whenever she directly observes, or hears of him being intolerant toward customers or workmates.

In addition to formulating these action plans, Sean must have the self-discipline to implement them. For example, he should keep a log of situations in which he was intolerant and those in which he was tolerant. He might also make a mental note to attempt to be cooperative and flexible in most of his dealings at work. When a customer does not provide all the information Sean needs to assess his or her creditworthiness, Sean should remind himself to say, "I want to process your credit application as quickly as possible. To do this, I need some important additional information." Sean's reflex in the same situation had been to snap, "I can't read your mind. If you want to do business with us, you've got to stop hiding the truth."

Feedback on Actions

The fourth step in the learning model is to measure the effects of one's actions against reality. You obtain feedback on the consequences of your actions. When your skill-improvement goal is complex, such as becoming more effective at resolving conflict, you will usually have to measure your progress in several ways. You will also need both short- and long-term measures of the effectiveness of your actions. Long-term measures are important because skill-development activities of major consequence have long-range implications.

To obtain short-range feedback, Sean can consult with Alison to see whether she has observed any changes in his tolerance. Alison can also collect any feedback she hears from others in the office. Sean will also profit from feedback over a prolonged period of time, perhaps one or two years. He will be looking to see whether his image has changed from an intolerant person who rubs people the wrong way to a tolerant person who has cordial interactions with others.

Frequent Practice

The final step in the learning model makes true skill development possible. Implementing the new behavior and using feedback for fine-tuning is an excellent start in acquiring a new interpersonal skill. For the skill to be long lasting, however, it must be integrated into your usual way of conducting yourself. In Sean's case, he will have to practice being tolerant regularly until it becomes a positive habit.

After a skill is programmed into your repertoire, it becomes a habit. This is important because a skill involves many habits. For example, good customer service skills include the habits of smiling and listening carefully. After you attempt the new interpersonal skills described in this book, you will need to practice them frequently to make a noticeable difference in your behavior.

A sports analogy is appropriate here. Assume that Marty, a tennis player, takes a lesson to learn how to hit the ball with greater force. The instructor points out that the reason Marty is not hitting with much force is that he is relying too much on his arm and not enough on his leg and body strength. To hit the ball with more force, Marty is told that he must put one foot out in front of him when he strikes the ball.

Under the watchful eye of the coach, Marty does put a foot out in front when he strikes the ball. Marty is excited about the good results. But if Marty fails to make the same maneuver with his feet during his tennis matches, he will persist in hitting weakly. If Marty makes the effort to make better use of his legs on almost every shot, he will soon integrate the new movement into his game.

In summary, the basics of a model for learning skills comprises five steps: goal or desired state of affairs → assessing reality → an action plan → feedback on actions → frequent practice. You must exercise self-discipline to complete each step. If you skip a step, you will be disappointed with the results of your interpersonal skill-development program.

IDENTIFICATION OF DEVELOPMENTAL NEEDS

An important concept in skill development is that people are most likely to develop new skills when they feel the need for change. The importance of the perceived need for change is reflected in a variation of an old joke:

Question: How many psychologists does it take to change a lightbulb?

Answer: None, if the lightbulb wants to change.

As you read this book and do the experiential exercises, you will probably be more highly motivated to follow through with skill development in areas in which you think you need development. A specific area in which a person needs to change is referred to as a **developmental need**. For instance, some people may be too shy, some too abrasive, some too intolerant, and some may not give others the encouragement they need.

Developmental needs related to interpersonal skills can be identified in several ways. First, if you are candid with yourself you can probably point to areas in which you recognize that change is needed. You might reflect on your experiences and realize that you have had repeated difficulty in resolving conflict. Second, a related approach is to think of feedback you have received. If there has been consistency in asking you to improve in a particular area, you could hypothesize that the feedback has merit. Perhaps five different people have told you that you are not a good team player. "Becoming a better team player" might therefore be one of your developmental needs.

A third approach to assessing developmental needs is to solicit feedback. Ask the opinion of people who know you well to help you identify needs for improvement with respect to interpersonal skills. Present and previous managers are a valuable source of this type of feedback.

A fourth approach to pinpointing developmental needs is closely related to the previous three: feedback from performance appraisals or evaluations. If you have worked for a firm that uses performance appraisals to help people develop, you may have received constructive suggestions during the appraisal. For example, one manager told his assistant: "You need to project more self-confidence when you answer the phone. You sound so unsure and vague when you talk on the telephone. I have noticed this, and several customers have joked about it." The recipient of this feedback was prompted to participate in assertiveness training where she learned how to express herself more positively.

Self-Assessment Quiz 1-1 gives you the opportunity to identify your developmental needs. The same exercise is a first step in improving your interpersonal relations on the job, because identification of a problem is the first—and most important—step toward change. For example, if you cite improving your relationships with people from cultures different from your own, you have planted the seeds for change. You are then more likely to seek out people from other cultures in the workplace or at school and cultivate their friendship.

Now that you (and perhaps another person) have identified specific behaviors that may require change, you need to draw up an action plan. Proceed with your action plan even though you have just begun studying this text, but peek ahead to relevant chapters if you wish. Describe briefly a plan of attack for bringing about the change you hope to achieve for each statement that is checked. Ideas for your action plan can come from information presented anywhere in this text, from outside reading, or from talking to a person experienced in dealing with people. A basic example would be to study materials about customer service and observe an effective model if you checked "I feel awkward dealing with a customer."

UNIVERSAL NEEDS FOR IMPROVING INTERPERSONAL RELATIONS

We have just described how understanding your unique developmental needs facilitates improving your interpersonal skills. There are also areas for skill improvement in interpersonal relations that are shared by most managerial, professional, technical, and sales personnel. We refer to these common areas for improvement as **universal training needs**. Almost any professional person, for example, could profit from enhancing his or her negotiation and listening skills.

This book provides opportunity for skill development in a number of universal training needs. In working through these universal training needs, be aware that many of them will also fit your specific developmental needs. A given universal training need can be an individual's developmental need at the same time. It is reasonable to expect that you will be more strongly motivated to improve skills that relate closely to your developmental needs.

The major universal training needs covered in this text are as follows:

1. *Understanding individual differences.* To deal effectively with others in the workplace it is necessary to recognize that people have different capabilities, needs, and interests.

2. *Interpersonal communication.* Effective communication with people is essential for carrying out more than 50 percent of the work conducted by most professional and managerial workers.

WHAT ARE YOUR DEVELOPMENTAL NEEDS?

This exercise is designed to heighten your self-awareness of areas in which you could profit from personal improvement. It is not a test, and there is no scoring, yet your answers to the checklist may prove helpful to you in mapping out a program of improvement in your interpersonal relations.

Directions: Below are a number of specific aspects of behavior that suggest a person needs improvement in interpersonal skills. Check each statement that is generally true for you. You can add to the validity of this exercise by having one or two other people who know you well answer this form as they think it describes you. Then compare your self-analysis with their analysis of you.

Place check in this column

1. I'm too shy. _____
2. I'm too overbearing and obnoxious. _____
3. I intimidate too many people. _____
4. I have trouble expressing my feelings. _____
5. I make negative comments about people too readily. _____
6. I have a difficult time solving problems when working in a group. _____
7. I'm a poor team player. _____
8. Very few people listen to me. _____
9. My personality isn't colorful enough. _____
10. People say that I'm a clown. _____
11. When I'm in conflict with another person I usually lose. _____
12. I hog too much time in meetings or in class. _____
13. I'm very poor at office politics. _____
14. People find me boring. _____
15. It is difficult for me to criticize others. _____
16. I'm too serious most of the time. _____
17. I feel awkward working with a person from a culture quite different from mine. _____
18. I avoid controversy in dealing with others. __X__
19. It is difficult for me to find things to talk about with others. _____
20. I don't get my point across well. _____
21. I feel awkward dealing with a customer. _____
22. I don't get the point of the importance of ethics in business. _____
23. My attempts to lead others have failed. _____
24. Rarely have I been able to get somebody else to work hard on my behalf. _____
25. _____ (Fill in your own statement.) _____

3. *Developing teamwork skills.* The most sweeping change in the organization of work in recent years has been a shift to teams and away from conventional departments. Knowing how to be an effective team player therefore enhances your chances for success in the modern organization.

4. *Group problem solving.* As part of the same movement that emphasizes work teams, organizations now rely heavily on group problem solving. As a consequence, being an above-average contributor to group problem solving is a key part of effective interpersonal relations on the job.

5. *Cross-cultural relations.* The modern workplace has greater cultural diversity than ever before. Being able to deal effectively with people from different cultures, from within and outside your own country, is therefore an important requirement for success.

6. *Resolving conflicts with others.* Conflict in the workplace is almost inevitable as people compete for limited resources. Effective interpersonal relations are therefore dependent upon knowing how to resolve conflict successfully.

7. *Becoming an effective leader.* In today's organizations a large number of people have the opportunity to practice leadership, even if on temporary assignment. Enhancing one's leadership skills is therefore almost a universal requirement.

8. *Motivating others.* Whether you have the title of manager or leader or are working alone, you have to know how to motivate people whom you depend on to get your work accomplished. Given that few people are gifted motivators, most people can profit from skill development in motivation.

9. *Helping others develop.* As power is shared in organizations among managers and individual contributors (nonmanagers) alike, more people are required to help each other grow and develop. To carry out this role, most of us need skill development in coaching and mentoring.

10. *Positive political skills.* Whether you work in a small or large firm, part of having effective interpersonal relations is being able to influence others so your interests are satisfied. Positive political skills help you satisfy your interests without being unethical or devious.

11. *Customer service skills.* The current emphasis on customer satisfaction dictates that every worker should know how to provide good service to customers. Most people can benefit from strengthening their skills in serving both external and internal customers. (**Internal customers** are the people with whom you interact on the job.)

12. *Enhancing ethical behavior.* Although most workers in their heart know right from wrong, we can all sharpen our ability to make ethical decisions. By consistently making highly ethical decisions, people can improve their interpersonal relations.

13. *Personal productivity and stress management.* Having good work habits and time-management skills contributes to relating well to others even though they are not interpersonal skills themselves. By being efficient and productive and having your stress under control, you are in a better position to relate comfortably to others. Coworkers enjoy relating to a person who does not procrastinate and who is not visibly stressed.

14. *Job search and career-management skills.* Finding an outstanding job for yourself, holding onto the job, and moving ahead are not specifically interpersonal skills. However, both finding the right job for yourself and managing your career rely heavily on good interpersonal skills. Two basic examples are conducting yourself well in an interview and developing a network of contacts that can help you advance.

DEVELOPING INTERPERSONAL SKILLS ON THE JOB

The primary thrust of this book is to teach interpersonal skills that can be applied to the job. As part of enhancing your skills, it is essential to recognize that opportunities also exist in the workplace for developing interpersonal skills. This dual opportunity for learning soft skills is similar to the way hard skills are learned both inside and outside the classroom. Studying a text and doing laboratory exercises, for example, will help you learn useful information technology skills. On the job one day you might be asked to send a photo by e-mail. Having never performed this task before, you search a computer manual, ask questions of coworkers, telephone a help desk, and use trial and error. Within a few hours you have acquired a valuable new skill. The information technology skills you learned in the course facilitated learning new computer tasks. Yet the actual learning of how to send the photographs was done on the job.

Here we look at two related aspects of learning interpersonal skills on the job—informal learning and specific developmental experiences.

INFORMAL LEARNING

Business firms, as well as nonprofit organizations, invest an enormous amount of money and time in teaching interpersonal skills. Teaching methods include sending employees to courses, conducting training on company premises, video-conferencing, courses on video tape, and computer-assisted learning programs. (An Internet course, or *distance learning*, is an example of computer-assisted learning.) Workers also develop interpersonal skills by interacting with work associates and observing how other people deal with interpersonal challenges.

Informal learning is the acquisition of knowledge and skills that takes place naturally outside of a structured learning environment. In the context of the workplace, informal learning takes place without being designed by the organization. A study of more than 1,000 employees at seven companies in seven states found that up to 70 percent of learning takes place informally.[3] The director of the study in question emphasizes that formal training includes both a goal stated by the organization and a defined method or process. Informal learning can occur whether or not a goal is stated or the method defined.

Learning interpersonal skills informally can take place through such means as observing a coworker, manager, or team leader deal with a situation. A newly hired assistant store manager couldn't help seeing and overhearing a customer screaming at the store manager about a defective space heater. The manager said calmly, "It appears you are pretty upset about your heater that caused a short circuit in your house. What can I do to help you?" The customer calmed down as quickly as air being released from a balloon. The assistant store manager thought to herself, "Now I know how to handle a customer who has gone ballistic. I'll state what the customer is probably feeling, and then offer to help."

Informal learning can also occur when another person shows you how to handle a situation. The store manager might have said to the new assistant manager, "Let me tell you what to do in case you encounter a customer who goes ballistic. Summarize in a few words what he or she is probably feeling, and then offer to help. The effect can be remarkable." (This incident is classified as informal learning because it takes place outside of a classroom.)

Formal learning and informal learning of interpersonal skills are useful supplements to each other. If you are formally learning interpersonal skills your level of awareness for enhancing your interpersonal skills will increase. By formally studying interpersonal skills, you are likely to develop the attitude "What hints about dealing more effectively with people can I pick up on the job?" You may have noticed that if you are taking lessons in a sport, you become much more observant about watching the techniques of outstanding athletes in person or on television.

SPECIFIC DEVELOPMENTAL EXPERIENCES

Another perspective on developing interpersonal skills in the workplace is that certain experiences are particularly suited to such development. Coping with a difficult customer, as suggested above, would be one such scenario. Morgan W. McCall, Jr., an industrial psychologist, has studied for many years ways in which leaders develop on the job. Contending with certain challenges is at the heart of these key learning experiences. Several of the powerful learning experiences McCall has identified are particularly geared toward developing better interpersonal skills.[4]

➤ *Unfamiliar responsibilities.* The person has to handle responsibilities that are new, very different, or much broader than previous ones. Dealing with these unfamiliar responsibilities necessitates asking others for help and gaining their cooperation. For example, being assigned to supervise a group doing work unfamiliar to you would put you in a position of gaining the cooperation of group members who knew more about the work than you.

➤ *Proving yourself.* If you feel added pressure to show others that you can deal effectively with responsibilities, you are likely to develop skills in projecting self-confidence and persuading others.

➤ *Problems with employees.* If you supervise employees, or have coworkers, who lack adequate experience, are incompetent, or are poorly motivated, you need to practice such skills as effective listening and conflict resolution in order to work smoothly with them.

➤ *Influencing without authority.* An excellent opportunity for practicing influence skills is being forced to influence coworkers, higher management, company outsiders, and other key people over whom you have no control. Team leaders typically face the challenge of needing to influence workers whom they lack the authority to discipline or grant raises. (The reason is that a team leader usually does not have as much formal authority as a traditional manager.)

➤ *Difficult manager.* If you and your manager have different opinions on how to approach problems, or if your manager has serious shortcomings, you will have to use your best human relations skills to survive. You will need to develop such subtle skills as using diplomacy to explain to your manager that his or her suggestion is completely unworkable.

The general point to be derived from these scenarios is that certain on-the-job challenges require a high level of interpersonal skill. Faced with such challenges, you will be prompted to use the best interpersonal skills you have. Formal training can be a big help because you might remember a skill that should be effective in a particular situation. Assume that you are faced with an overbearing manager who belittles you in front of others. You might be prompted to try a conflict-resolution technique you acquired in class.

SUMMARY

Effective interpersonal relations must be combined with technical knowledge to achieve success in any job involving interactions with people. This book presents a three-part strategy for achieving a high level of interpersonal skill. Each chapter presents concepts related to an area of interpersonal skill, behavioral guidelines, and experiential exercises. Interpersonal skill training is also referred to as *soft-skill training* to differentiate it from technical training.

A five-part model of learning can be applied to improving interpersonal skills. First, state a goal or desired state of affairs. Second, assess the reality of how far you are from your goal. Third, develop an action plan to change the relationship between the person and the environment. Self-discipline is required to implement the action plan. Fourth, solicit feedback on actions to measure the effects of your actions against reality. Fifth, continue to practice your newly learned skill.

People are most likely to develop new skills when they feel the need for change. A developmental need is the specific area in which a person needs to change. Identifying your developmental needs in relation to interpersonal relations can be achieved through self-analysis and feedback from others. You can also solicit feedback and make use of the feedback you have received in performance appraisals.

CAN THE PRESIDENT OF MICROSOFT BE HELPED?

In 1998 Microsoft Corp. chairman and chief executive officer Bill Gates promoted Steven A. Ballmer as president of the software giant. Ballmer, who had been executive vice president of sales and support, filled a position that had been vacant for eight years.

A major purpose of the move was to enable Gates to focus on Microsoft's long-term vision and product strategy. Gates said in an interview, "I decided I wanted to spend more time with our product groups and drive the breakthroughs. Think of Steve as the business leader and customer champion." His formal role is to be in charge of sales and product development.

Ballmer has been a self-appointed cheerleader for Microsoft. During a company sales meeting several years ago, he vaulted on stage and shouted at the top of his lungs: "I love this company! I love this company! I love this company!" The 6,000-member sales team responded with a five-minute standing ovation. Shouting to cheer on employees, discipline them, and express disapproval is characteristic of Ballmer. Another motivational stunt he pulled at one time was to swim across a chilly Microsoft pond on a dare in front of dozens of company employees.

Ballmer, a college chum of Gates, has been copilot of Microsoft since 1980. Gates is thought of as the biggest brain in the company, whereas Ballmer is regarded as the biggest heart and inspiring sales leader. Another contrast is that Gates is seen as the company's technology visionary and Ballmer its top business strategist.

Ballmer's physical presence is imposing. He is six feet tall and built like a football linebacker. His shiny head is disproportionately large, and he has a booming voice. He is intensely devoted to his company and his family. His intensity, however, is often perceived negatively. He can become infuriated when facing conflict. He has been known to bawl out employees so violently that his voice can be heard through the air vents in company headquarters.

Ballmer has become well known for being outspoken with both company insiders and out-

siders. During a discussion of the Justice Department's investigation into Microsoft's business tactics, Ballmer blurted out, "To heck with Janet Reno." Later, however, Ballmer said he regretted making the comment. "That's the way I am," he said. "I have to work on being a better version of myself."

Gates, who can be undiplomatic himself, is not much concerned about Ballmer's roughness with people. "He's my best friend," says Gates. "We love working together on very hard problems. We trust each other and understand how the other thinks." Ballmer has equally warm comments about Gates. "Our friendship has grown much stronger as a result of working together. It's like a marriage," says Ballmer. [Both Gates and Ballmer are married with children.]

The Microsoft board deliberated six months before appointing Ballmer president. One concern was his fiery personality. A board member pointed out that "Steve's greatest strength can also be seen as a weakness." Ballmer shouts when he gets excited or angry (as mentioned above). His voice rises so suddenly that it shocks and intimidates many people. Most likely due to his shouting, Ballmer lost his voice during a business trip to Japan in the early 1980s and required vocal chord surgery to regain his speech.

Some of Ballmer's motivational techniques appear heavy handed to employees. When he directed the Microsoft Windows product group, he created fear in engineers by bellowing at them and pounding a baseball bat into his hand. In the last few years, Ballmer has made progress in becoming calmer in demanding business situations.

Gates cleared the way for Ballmer to be promoted by ensuring that each of the executives who would report to him was satisfied with the arrangement. Gates also convinced the board that he could modify Ballmer's behavior.

Despite his rough edges, Ballmer has many supporters. Many people who know Ballmer find

(Continued)

him joyful and refreshing and a good sport. He is willing to engage in publicity stunts such as participating in videos that mock the competition.

Case Questions

1. What needs for interpersonal skill development does Steven Ballmer appear to have?

2. To what extent do you believe that Bill Gates can modify Ballmer's behavior?

3. What positive interpersonal skills does Ballmer appear to have?

4. If it were your decision, would you have approved Steve Ballmer's appointment as president of Microsoft Corp?

Source: "Remaking Microsoft," *Business Week,* May 17, 1999, pp. 106–116; Steve Hamm, "Bill's Co-pilot," *Business Week,* September 14, 1998, pp. 76–90; "Microsoft Names President," http://cnnfn.com/digitaljam/9807/21/ballmer/.

Universal training needs are those areas for improvement that are common to most people. The major topics in this text reflect universal training needs because they are necessary for success in most positions involving interaction with people.

Opportunities exist in the workplace to develop interpersonal skill. A general approach to developing these skills is informal learning, whereby you acquire skills naturally outside of a structured work environment. Informal learning often takes place through such means as observing a coworker, manager, or team leader cope with a situation. Certain workplace experiences are particularly well suited to developing interpersonal skills. These include unfamiliar responsibilities, proving yourself, having problems with employees, influencing without authority, and having a difficult manager.

QUESTIONS FOR DISCUSSION AND REVIEW

1. One of the most prestigious business schools, the Wharton School, now places much more emphasis on "people" skills than previously. What do you suspect are the reasons for this change?

2. In your opinion, do high-ranking business executives rely more on soft skills or hard skills to accomplish their work?

3. Why do people need soft skills in an era of high technology?

4. In your own words, what does "assessing reality" mean in the model for improving interpersonal skills?

5. How does a person know whether or not the feedback he or she receives from another person is accurate?

6. Of the 14 universal training needs listed in this chapter, which two do you think would be the most difficult to improve? Explain.

7. Give an example of a skill you might have learned informally at any point in your life.

Chapter 2

Understanding Individual Differences

Billy Waxworth and Mary Lou Gold graduated from the Lincoln Institute in the same year, both majoring in business administration. The two met three years later at a class reunion. After exchanging hugs, Billy said, "Mary Lou, it's time we caught up with each other. What kind of work have you been doing?"

Mary Lou responded that she combined her interests in business and technical writing. Her job consisted of preparing technical manuals for electronic consumer products such as VCRs and TVs. She said she worked at her computer about 35 hours per week, preparing copy and diagrams. Billy explained that he sold office furniture and lighting fixtures to business firms.

"How boring that must be, preparing manuals all day long," said Billy. "You must get sick of such a grind." Mary Lou responded, "Quite the opposite, Billy, I intensely like work that requires concentration and produces tangible results. What would make me sick is what you do—knocking on doors and trying to convince strangers they should buy your product."

The exchange that took place between Billy and Mary Lou illustrates one of the most important factors influencing the behavior of people in the workplace. People show substantial **individual differences**, or variations, in how they respond to the same situation based on personal characteristics. Billy, an extrovert, is at his best away from the office, winning people over to his way of thinking. Mary Lou, in contrast, is introverted and analytical. She enjoys working on tasks that require prolonged concentration and attention to detail. In general, individual differences exert a profound effect on job performance and behavior.[1] One of hundreds of possible examples is that some people can concentrate longer and harder on their work, thereby producing more and higher quality work, than others.

This chapter describes several of the major sources of individual differences on the job. It also gives you the chance to measure your standing on several key dimensions of behavior and helps you develop skill in responding to individual differences. Knowing how to respond to such differences is the cornerstone of effective interpersonal relations.

PERSONALITY

"We're not going to promote you to department head," said the vice president to the analyst. "Although you are a great troubleshooter, you've alienated too many people in the company. You're too blunt and insensitive." As just implied, most successes and failures in people-contact jobs are attributed largely to interpersonal skills. And personality traits are important contributors to interpersonal, or human relations, skills. The subject of individual differences in personality must therefore be given consideration in any serious study of interpersonal relations in the workplace.

Personality refers to those persistent and enduring behavior patterns that tend to be expressed in a wide variety of situations. A person who is brash and insensitive in one situation is likely to behave similarly in many other situations.

Your personality is what makes you unique. Your walk, your talk, your appearance, your speech, and your inner values and conflicts all contribute to your personality. Have you ever noticed that when you know a person well you can identify that person by his or her footsteps even though you do not see the individual? This is true because many people have a distinctive gait.

We will illustrate the importance of personality to interpersonal relations in organizations by describing six key personality traits and psychological types related to cognitive styles. In addition, you will be given guidelines for dealing effectively with different personality types.

SIX MAJOR PERSONALITY FACTORS AND TRAITS

Many psychologists believe that the basic structure of human personality is represented by five broad factors, known as the Big Five: extraversion (the scientific spelling of *extroversion*), emotional stability, agreeableness, conscientiousness, and openness to experience. A sixth key personality factor, self-monitoring of behavior, has received much recent attention and is also included here.

Recent evidence has emphasized the contribution of genes, and strips of DNA in particular, in forming personality. The genes do not influence personality traits directly. Instead, they subtly bias the mind so that different individuals react to similar experiences in different ways. Another key speculation is that that genes affect the operation of brain chemicals such as dopamine and serotonin that influence our mood. For example, two experiences that release dopamine are seeing a person you perceive as physically attractive and eating chocolate. As a consequence of either ingesting chocolate or sighting the right person—or a combination of the two—you get a temporary high.

Genes appear to have their biggest impact on temperamental traits such as impulsiveness, openness, conservatism, and hostility. However, genes alone do not control the chemistry of the brain. The environment heavily influences how the genes will express themselves, such as one impulsive person becoming a day trader on the Internet and another becoming a shoplifter. Character helps control our personality traits.[2] A person of good moral character, for example, might channel her aggressiveness into being competitive rather than attacking other people verbally or physically.

All six factors have a substantial impact on interpersonal relations and job performance. The interpretations and meanings of these factors provide useful information because they can help you pinpoint important areas for personal development. Although these factors are partially inherited, most people can improve them providing they exert much conscious effort over a period of time. For example, it usually takes a minimum of three months of effort before a person is perceived to be more agreeable. The six factors, shown in Figure 2–1, are described in more detail in the following list.

1. *Extraversion.* Traits associated with the extraversion factor include being social, gregarious, assertive, talkative, and active. An outgoing person is often described as extraverted, while a shy person is described as being introverted.

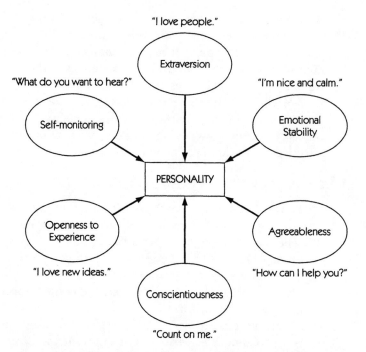

Figure 2-1 Six Major Personality Factors
The six major personality factors are the Big Five factors plus self-monitoring. Research has repeatedly shown that the Big Five factors are related to job performance. The most consistent finding is that job applicants who score high on the trait of conscientiousness perform well on a wide variety of jobs.

2. *Emotional stability.* A person with high emotional stability is calm, relaxed, and secure. Traits associated with the emotional stability factor include being anxious, depressed, angry, embarrassed, emotional, and worried. A person with low emotional stability is often referred to as neurotic or emotionally unstable.

3. *Agreeableness.* An agreeable person is friendly and cooperative. Traits associated with the agreeableness factor include being courteous, flexible, trusting, good-natured, cooperative, forgiving, softhearted, and tolerant.

4. *Conscientiousness.* A variety of meanings have been attached to the conscientiousness factor, but it generally implies being dependable. Traits associated with conscientiousness include being careful, thorough, responsible, organized, and purposeful. Honesty is also closely related to being conscientious. Other related traits include being hardworking, achievement oriented, and persevering.

5. *Openness to experience.* People who score high on the openness-to-experience factor have well-developed intellects. Traits commonly associated with this factor include being imaginative, cultured, curious, original, broad minded, intelligent, and artistically sensitive.

6. *Self-monitoring of behavior.* The self-monitoring trait refers to the process of observing and controlling how we are perceived by others. High self-monitors are pragmatic and even chameleon-like actors in social groups. They often say what others want to hear. Low self-monitors avoid situations that require them to adopt different outer images. In this way their outer behavior adheres to their inner values. Low self-monitoring can often lead to inflexibility. Do Self-Assessment Quiz 2-1 to measure your tendencies toward self-monitoring.

Depending on the job, any one of the preceding personality factors can be important for success. Conscientiousness relates to job performance for many different occupations. Another important research finding is that extraversion is associated with success for managers and sales representatives. The explanation is that managers and salespeople are required to interact extensively with other people.[3] Studies have shown that the Big Five personality factors are related to job performance in the European Community as well as in the United States and Canada. Conscientiousness and emotional stability were shown to be accurate predictors for job success for many different jobs and measures of success in Europe.[4] Different measures of success include objective information such as cost savings and sales figures, as well as ratings of performance by managers.

COGNITIVE STYLES AND PERSONALITY TYPES

COGNITIVE STYLES

Personality also influences a person's **cognitive style**, or the mental processes used to perceive and make judgments from information. A knowledge of these cognitive styles can help you relate better to people because you can better appreciate how they make decisions. According to psychiatrist Carl Jung, how people gather and evaluate information determines their cognitive style. Jung's analysis became the basis for a widely used test of personality and cognitive style called the Myers-Briggs Type Indicator.

Gathering Information

To solve problems it is necessary to gather information. Two different styles of information gathering are sensation and intuition. **Sensation-type individuals** prefer routine and order. They search for precise details when gathering information to solve a problem. Sensation-type individuals prefer to work with established facts rather than search for new possibilities. **Intuitive-type individuals** prefer an overall perspective—the "big picture." Such people enjoy solving new problems. They dislike routine and prefer to look for possibilities rather than work with facts.

Self-Assessment Quiz 2-1

THE SELF-MONITORING SCALE

Directions: Decide whether each of the following statements is more true or false for you. Circle T or F to indicate your answer.

1. I find it hard to imitate the behavior of other people.   T   F

2. My behavior is usually an expression of my true inner feelings, attitudes, and beliefs.   T   F

3. At parties and social gatherings, I do not attempt to say and do things that others will like.   T   F

4. I can only argue about ideas that I already have.   T   F

5. I can make impromptu speeches, even on topics about which I have almost no information.   T   F

6. I guess I put on a show to impress or to entertain people.   T   F

7. When I am uncertain how to act in a social situation, I look to the behavior of others for cues.   T   F

8. I'd make a good actor.   T   F

9. I rarely ask my friends' advice on movies, books, or music.   T   F

10. I sometimes appear to others to be experiencing deeper emotions than I actually am.   T   F

11. I laugh more when I watch a comedy with others than when alone.   T   F

12. In a group I am rarely the center of attention.   T   F

13. In different situations and with different people, I often act like very different persons.   T   F

14. I am not particularly good at making other people like me.   T   F

Scoring and Interpretation: To obtain your score, count one point for each False answer to statements 1, 2, 3, 4, 9, 12, and 14. Count one point for each True response to statements 5, 6, 7, 8, 10, 11, and 13. The higher your score, the stronger your tendencies toward self-monitoring. You are a high self-monitor if your score is 10 or higher; low if it is 5 or less. Refer to the text for the meaning of high and low self-monitoring.

Source: Adapted from Bernard Asbell, *What They Know About You* (New York: Random House, 1993).

When shopping for an automobile, a sensation-type individual would want to gather a large number of facts about such matters as miles or kilometers per gallon, warranty provisions, finance charges, and resale value. In contrast, the intuitive-type individual would be more concerned about the overall style of the car and how proud he or she would be as the owner.

Evaluating Information

The evaluation aspect of problem solving involves judging how to deal with information after it has been collected. Styles of information evaluation range from an emphasis on feeling to an emphasis on thinking. **Feeling-type individuals** have a need to conform and adapt to the wishes of others. Because of these tendencies, they try to avoid problems that might result in disagreements. **Thinking-type individuals** rely on reason and intellect to deal with problems. They downplay emotion in problem solving and decision making.

Assume that a team leader asks group managers their opinion of an idea for a new product. Feeling-type people in the group are likely to look for the good in the proposal and then express approval for the project. Thinking-type team members are likely to be more independent in their evaluation of the new-product idea. As a result they will express their opinion whether or not it is what the manager wants to hear. (Notice that feeling-type people are high self-monitors, and thinking types are the opposite.)

The Four Cognitive Styles

The two dimensions of information gathering and evaluation are combined to produce the following four-way classification of cognitive (or problem-solving) styles.

➤ Sensation/thinking

➤ Intuitive/thinking

➤ Sensation/feeling

➤ Intuitive/feeling

Figure 2-2 lists the four styles and occupations well suited to them.[5]

If you take the Myers-Briggs Type Indicator, often available in career centers, you will be presented with a diagnosis of your personality type. You can also study the four types and make a judgment as to your cognitive style. Recognizing your cognitive style can help you identify work that you are likely to perform well. For example, a person who is an intuitive/feeling type is likely to be skillful in resolving customer complaints. The same person might not be well suited by temperament to do bookkeeping.

GUIDELINES FOR DEALING WITH DIFFERENT PERSONALITY TYPES

A key purpose in presenting information about a sampling of various personality types is to provide guidelines for individualizing your approach to people. As a basic example, if you wanted to score points with an introvert, you would approach that person in a restrained, laid-back fashion. In contrast, a more gregarious, lighthearted approach might be more effective with an extravert. The purpose of individualizing your approach is to build a better working relationship or to establish rapport with the other person. To match your approach to dealing with a given personality type, you must first arrive at an approximate

Sensation/Thinking
Decisive, dependable, alert to details
➤ Accounting and bookkeeping
➤ Computer programming
➤ Manufacturing technology

Sensation/Feeling
Pragmatic, analytical, methodical, and conscientious
➤ Supervision
➤ Selling
➤ Negotiating

Intuitive/Thinking
Creative, progressive, perceptive
➤ Systems design
➤ Law, paralegal work
➤ Middle management

Intuitive/Feeling
Colorful, people-oriented, helpful
➤ Customer service
➤ Business communications
➤ Human resources

Figure 2-2 Four Problem-Solving Styles and Work Matchup

diagnosis of the individual's personality. The following suggestions are therefore restricted to readily observable aspects of personality.

1. When relating to an *extraverted* individual, emphasize friendliness, warmth, and a stream of chatter. Talk about people more than ideas, things, or data. Express an interest in a continuing working relationship.

2. When relating to an *introverted* individual, move slowly in forming a working relationship. Do not confuse quietness with a lack of interest. Tolerate moments of silence. Emphasize ideas, things, and data more heavily than people.

3. When relating to a person who appears to be *emotionally unstable* based on symptoms of worry and tension, be laid back and reassuring. Attempt not to project your own anxiety and fears. Be a good listener. If possible, minimize emphasis on deadlines and the dire consequences of a project's failing. Show concern and interest in the person's welfare.

4. When relating to an *agreeable* person, just relax and be yourself. Reciprocate with kindness to sustain a potentially excellent working relationship.

5. When relating to a *disagreeable* person, be patient and tolerant. At the same time, set limits on how much mistreatment you will take. Disagreeable people sometimes secretly want others to put brakes on their antisocial behavior.

6. When relating to a *conscientious* person, give him or her freedom and do not nag. The person will probably honor commitments without prompting. Conscientious people are often taken for granted, so remember to acknowledge the person's dependability.

7. When relating to a person of *low conscientiousness,* keep close tabs on him or her, especially if you need the person's output to do your job. Do not assume that because the person has an honest face and a pleasing smile he or she will deliver as promised. Frequently follow up on your requests, and impose deadlines if you have the authority. Express deep appreciation when the person does follow through.

8. When relating to a person who is *open to experience,* emphasize information sharing, idea generation, and creative approaches to problems. Appeal to his or her intellect by discussing topics of substance rather than ordinary chatter and gossip.

9. When relating to a person who is *closed to experience,* stick closely to the facts of the situation at hand. Recognize that the person prefers to think small and deal with the here and now.

10. When dealing with a person whom you suspect is a high *self-monitor,* be cautious in thinking that the person is really in support of your position. The person could just be following his or her natural tendency to appear to please others, but not really feel that way.

11. When dealing with a *sensation-type* person, emphasize facts, figures, and conventional thinking without sacrificing your own values. To convince the sensation type, emphasize logic more than emotional appeal. Focus on details more than the big picture.

12. When dealing with an *intuitive-type* individual, emphasize feelings, judgments, playing with ideas, imagination, and creativity. Focus more on the big picture than details.

To start putting these guidelines into practice, do the role plays in Skill-Building Exercise 2-1. Remember that a role player is an extemporaneous actor. Put yourself in the shoes of the character you play and visualize how he or she would act. Because you are given only the general idea of a script, use your imagination to fill in the details.

MENTAL ABILITY

Mental ability, or intelligence, is one of the major sources of individual differences that affects job performance and behavior. **Intelligence** is the capacity to acquire and apply knowledge, including solving problems. Abstract problems can best be solved by intelligent workers. In an exceedingly simple job, such as packing shoes into boxes, having below-average intelligence can be an advantage, because the employee is not likely to become bored.

Understanding the nature of intelligence contributes to effective interpersonal relations in organizations. Your evaluation of a person's intelligence can influence how you relate to that person. For example, if you think a person is intelligent you will tend to seek his or her input on a difficult problem. If you

---

Skill-Building Exercise 2-1

PERSONALITY ROLE PLAYS

The Extravert: One student assumes the role of a successful outside sales representative who has just signed a $3 million order for the company. The sales rep comes back to the office elated. The other student assumes the role of a member of the office support staff. He or she decides this is a splendid opportunity to build a good relationship with the triumphant sales rep. Run the role play for about 10 minutes. The people not involved in the role play will observe and then provide feedback when the role play is completed. (These directions regarding time, observation, and feedback also apply to the two other role plays in this exercise and throughout the book.)

Open to Experience: One student plays the role of an experienced worker in the department who is told to spend some time orienting a new co-op student. It appears that this new person is open to experience. Another student plays the role of the co-op student who is open to experience and eager to be successful in this new position.

Sensation and Intuitive Types: One student plays the role of a sensation-type individual who is responsible for reviewing the company expense accounts. The other student plays the role of a manager in whose department many expense account abuses (such as lack of documentation and high expenses) have been uncovered. This manager is an intuitive type. The person in charge of the accounts is visiting the manager in the latter's office to discuss this problem.

---

realize that different types of intelligence exist, you are more likely to appreciate people's strengths. You are thus less likely to judge others as being either good or poor problem solvers.

Here we describe four important aspects of mental ability: (1) the components of traditional intelligence, (2) practical intelligence, (3) multiple intelligences, and (4) emotional intelligence. Knowledge of the four aspects will enrich your understanding of other workers and yourself.

COMPONENTS OF TRADITIONAL INTELLIGENCE

Intelligence consists of more than one component. A component of intelligence is much like a separate mental aptitude. Evidence suggests that intelligence consists of a g **(general) factor** and s **(special) factors** that contribute to problem-solving ability. Scores of tests of almost any type (such as math, aptitude for computer programming, or reading skill) are somewhat influenced by the g factor. The g factor helps explain why some people perform well in so many different mental tasks. Another finding about g is that more intelligent people tend to rely less on g because they also have well-developed s factors. Less intelligent people tend to rely more heavily on g because they have a less diverse set of specific abilities.[6]

Over the years various investigators have arrived at different special factors contributing to overall mental aptitude. The following seven factors have been identified consistently:

1. *Verbal comprehension.* The ability to understand the meaning of words and their relationship to each other and to comprehend written and spoken information.

2. *Word fluency.* The ability to use words quickly and easily, without an emphasis on verbal comprehension.

3. *Numerical acuity.* The ability to handle numbers, engage in mathematical analysis, and to do arithmetic calculations.

4. *Spatial perception.* The ability to visualize forms in space and manipulate objects mentally, particularly in three dimensions.

5. *Memory.* Having a good rote memory for symbols, words, and lists of numbers, along with other associations.

6. *Perceptual speed.* The ability to perceive visual details, to pick out similarities and differences, and to perform tasks requiring visual perception.

7. *Inductive reasoning.* The ability to discover a rule or principle and apply it in solving a problem and to make judgments and decisions that are logically sound.

Being strong in any of the preceding mental aptitudes often leads to an enjoyment of work associated with that aptitude. The reverse can also be true: enjoying a type of mental activity might lead to the development of an aptitude for the activity. Self-Assessment Quiz 2-2 gives you the opportunity to measure your preferences for numerical information.

PRACTICAL INTELLIGENCE

Many people, including psychologists, are concerned that the traditional way of understanding intelligence inadequately describes mental ability. An unfortunate implication of intelligence testing is that intelligence as traditionally calculated is largely the ability to perform tasks related to scholastic work. Thus a person who scored very high on an intelligence test could follow a complicated instruction manual, but might not be street smart.

To overcome the limited idea that intelligence mostly involves the ability to solve abstract problems, the **triarchic theory of intelligence** has been proposed. The theory holds that intelligence is composed of three different subtypes: analytical, creative, and practical. The *analytical* subtype is the traditional intelligence needed for solving difficult problems. Analytical intelligence is required to perform well in most school subjects. The *creative* subtype is the type of intel-

ATTITUDES TOWARD NUMERICAL INFORMATION

Directions: Describe how well you agree with each of the following statements, using the following scale: disagree strongly (DS); disagree (D); neutral (N); agree (A); agree strongly (AS). Circle the number in the appropriate column.

	DS	D	N	A	AS
1. I enjoy work that requires the use of numbers.	1	2	3	4	5
2. I think quantitative information is difficult to understand.	5	4	3	2	1
3. I find it satisfying to solve day-to-day problems involving numbers.	1	2	3	4	5
4. Numerical information is very useful in everyday life.	1	2	3	4	5
5. I prefer not to pay attention to information involving numbers.	5	4	3	2	1
6. I think more information should be available in numerical form.	1	2	3	4	5
7. I don't like to think about issues involving numbers.	5	4	3	2	1
8. Numbers are not necessary for most situations.	5	4	3	2	1
9. Thinking is more enjoyable when it does not involve quantitative information.	5	4	3	2	1
10. I like to make calculations involving numerical information.	1	2	3	4	5
11. Quantitative information is vital for accurate decisions.	1	2	3	4	5
12. I enjoy thinking about issues that involve numerical information.	1	2	3	4	5
13. Understanding numbers is as important in daily life as reading or writing.	1	2	3	4	5
14. I easily lose interest in graphs, percentages, and other quantitative information.	5	4	3	2	1
15. I find numerical information to be relevant to most situations.	1	2	3	4	5
16. I think it is important to learn and use numerical information to make well-informed decisions.	1	2	3	4	5
17. Numbers are redundant for most situations.	5	4	3	2	1
18. It is a waste of time to learn information containing a lot of numbers.	5	4	3	2	1
19. I like to go over numbers in my mind.	1	2	3	4	5
20. It helps me think if I put down information as numbers.	1	2	3	4	5

Total Score _____

Scoring and Interpretation: Add the numbers you circled to obtain your total score.

85–100   You have strong positive attitudes toward numerical information and working with quantitative data.

55–84   You have moderately favorable attitudes toward numerical information and working with quantitative data.

20–54   You have very negative attitudes toward numerical information and working with quantitative data. Your dislike for quantitative solutions to problems is so strong that you are quick to distrust statistical analysis.

Source: Adapted with permission from Madhubalan Viswanathan, "Measurement of Individual Differences in Preference for Numerical Information," *Journal of Applied Psychology*, October 1993, p. 745.

ligence required for imagination and combining things in novel ways. The *practical* subtype is the type of intelligence required for adapting your environment to suit your needs.[7]

The idea of practical intelligence helps explain why a person who has a difficult time getting through school can still be a successful businessperson, politician, or athlete. Practical intelligence incorporates the ideas of common sense, wisdom, and street smarts. One major reservation some have about practical intelligence is the implication that people who are highly intelligent in the traditional sense are not practical thinkers. In truth, most executives and other high-level workers score quite well on tests of mental ability. These tests usually measure analytical intelligence.

MULTIPLE INTELLIGENCES

Another approach to understanding the diverse nature of mental ability is the theory of **multiple intelligences**. According to Howard Gardner, people know and understand the world in distinctly different ways and learn in different ways. Individuals possess the following eight intelligences, or faculties, in varying degrees:

1. *Linguistic.* Enables people to communicate through language, including reading, writing, and speaking.

2. *Logical-mathematical.* Enables individuals to see relationships between objects and solve problems, as in calculus and statistics.

3. *Musical.* Gives people the capacity to create and understand meanings made out of sounds and to enjoy different types of music.

4. *Spatial.* Enables people to perceive and manipulate images in the brain and to recreate them from memory, as is required in making graphic designs.

5. *Bodily/kinesthetic.* Enables people to use their body and perceptual and motor systems in skilled ways such as dancing, playing sports, and expressing emotion through facial expressions.

6. *Intrapersonal.* Enables people to distinguish among their own feelings and acquire accurate self-knowledge.

7. *Interpersonal.* Makes it possible for individuals to differentiate among, classify, and utilize various features of the physical external environment.

8. *Naturalist.* Enables individuals to differentiate among, classify, and utilize various features of the physcial external environment.

Your profile of intelligences influences how you best learn and to which types of jobs you are best suited. Gardner believes that it is possible to develop these separate intelligences through concentrated effort. However, any of these intelligences might fade if not used.[8] These separate types of intelligence might also be perceived as different talents or abilities. Having high general problem-solving ability *(g)* would contribute to high standing on each of the eight intelligences.

EMOTIONAL INTELLIGENCE

Later research has updated and expanded the idea of practical intelligence, suggesting that how effectively people use their emotions has a major impact on their success. **Emotional intelligence** refers to qualities such as understanding one's own feelings, having empathy for others, and regulating one's emotion to enhance living. A person with high emotional intelligence would be able to engage in such behaviors as sizing up people, pleasing others, and influencing them. In recent years, several different versions of emotional intelligence have been proposed. Five key factors included in a well-accepted analysis of emotional intelligence are as follows:[9]

1. *Self-awareness.* The ability to understand your moods, emotions, and needs as well as their impact on others. (A person with good self-awareness knows whether he or she is pushing other people too far.)

2. *Self-regulation.* The ability to control impulsiveness, calming down anxiety and reacting with appropriate anger to situations. (A person with low self-regulation would suddenly decide to drop a project because the work was frustrating.)

3. *Motivation.* A passion to work for reasons in addition to money or status. Also, drive, persistence, and optimism when faced with setbacks. (A person with this type of motivation would make the decision to keep trying when faced with a serious obstacle such as having lost a major account.)

4. *Empathy.* The ability to respond to the unspoken feelings of others. Also, the skill to respond to people according to their emotional reactions. (A manager with empathy would take into account the most likely reaction of group members before making a decision affecting them.)

5. *Social skill.* Competency in managing relationships and building networks of support, and having positive relationships with people. (A worker with social skill would use a method of persuasion that is likely to work well with a particular group or individual.)

Emotional intelligence thus incorporates many of the skills and attitudes necessary to achieve effective interpersonal relations in organizations. Most of the topics in this book, such as resolving conflict, helping others develop, and positive political skills, would be included in emotional intelligence. Self-Assessment Quiz 2-3 gives you an opportunity to measure your emotional intelligence, but you will need persistence to get the information.

Self-Assessment Quiz 2-3

WHAT IS YOUR ADVERSITY QUOTIENT (AQ)?

One of the many components to emotional intelligence is resiliency, or the ability to bounce back from adversity. Paul G. Stoltz has developed an Adversity Quotient, designed to measure your capacity to turn obstacles into opportunities.[10] He offers you an opportunity on the Internet to measure your Adversity Quotient. To make this self-assessment, go to www.doogee.com, where you will find complete instructions. If the Web site is not in operation, consult reference number 10 for a print version of the test to measure your AQ. To obtain a broader measure of your emotional intelligence, go to www.utne.com/cgi/bin/eq.

GUIDELINES FOR RELATING TO PEOPLE OF DIFFERENT LEVELS AND TYPES OF INTELLIGENCE

Certainly you cannot expect to administer mental ability and emotional intelligence tests to all your work associates, gather their scores, and then relate to associates differently based on their scores. Yet it is possible to intuitively develop a sense for the mental quickness of people and the types of mental tasks they perform best. For example, managers must make judgments about mental ability in selecting people for jobs and assigning them to tasks. Following are several guidelines worth considering to enhance your working relationships with others:

1. If you perceive another worker (your manager included) to be mentally quick, present your ideas in technical depth. Incorporate difficult words into your conversation and reports. Ask the person challenging questions.

2. If you perceive another worker to be mentally slow, present your ideas with a minimum of technical depth. Use a basic vocabulary, without going so far as to be patronizing. Ask for frequent feedback about having been clear.

3. If you perceive a workmate to relish crunching numbers, use quantitative information when attempting to persuade that person. Instead of using phrases such as "most people," say "about 65 percent."

4. If you perceive a work associate to have high creative intelligence, solicit his or her input on problems requiring a creative solution. Use statements such as "Here's a problem that requires a sharp, creative mind, so I've come to you."

5. If you perceive a work associate to have low emotional intelligence, explain your feelings and attitudes clearly. The person may not get the point of hints and indirect expressions.

Skill-Building Exercise 2-2

ADAPTING TO PEOPLE OF DIFFERENT MENTAL ABILITY

The Mentally Sharp Coworker: One person plays the role of a worker who needs to load a new software package onto the hard drive of his or her computer. You intend to approach a particular coworker who is known for having a sharp mind. You wonder whether this highly intelligent person will be interested in your problem. The other person plays the role of the computer whiz who ordinarily does not like to solve problems for people that they should be able to solve themselves. The first worker meets with the second to discuss loading the software.

The Mentally Average Team Member: One student plays the role of a supervisor who needs to explain to a team member how to calculate discounts for customers. To the supervisor's knowledge, the team member does not know how to calculate discounts, although it will be an important part of the team member's new job. The supervisor and the team member get together for a session on calculating discounts.

To start putting these guidelines into practice, do the role play in Skill-Building Exercise 2-2.

VALUES AS A SOURCE OF INDIVIDUAL DIFFERENCES

Another group of factors influencing how a person behaves on the job is that person's values and beliefs. A **value** refers to the importance a person attaches to something. Values are also tied to the enduring belief that one's mode of conduct is better than another mode of conduct. If you believe that good interpersonal relations are the most important part of your life, your humanistic values are strong. Similarly, you may think that people who are not highly concerned about interpersonal relations have poor values.

Values are closely tied in with **ethics**, or the moral choices a person makes. A person's values influence which kinds of behaviors he or she believes are ethical. An executive who strongly values profits might not find it unethical to raise prices higher than needed to cover additional costs. Another executive who strongly values family life might suggest that the company invest money in an on-premises child-care center. Ethics is such an important part of interpersonal relations in organizations that the topic receives separate mention in Chapter 13.

Differences in values among people often stem from age, or generational, differences. Workers over age 50, in general, may have different values than people much younger. These age differences in values have often been seen as a clash between Baby Boomers and members of Generation X. (Generation Y is just beginning to enter the workforce.) According to the stereotype, Boomers see Xers as disrespectful of rules, not willing to pay their dues, and being disloyal to employers. Generation Xers see Boomers as worshipping hierarchy (layers of authority), being overcautious, and wanting to preserve the status quo.

HOW VALUES ARE LEARNED

People acquire values in the process of growing up, and many values are learned by the age of four. One important way we acquire values is through observing others, or modeling. Models can be parents, teachers, friends, brothers, sisters, and even public figures. If we identify with a particular person, the probability is high that we will develop some of his or her major values.

> *Derek, a restaurant owner, was known for his ability to offer employment to troubled teenagers and then help them get back on their feet. Asked why he put so much effort into helping youths in trouble, he explained, "I was greatly influenced as a boy by my Uncle Clarence. I was going through troubled times—stealing from Woolworth and getting drunk on beer.*
>
> *"Uncle Clarence took me under his wing and spent hours listening to my problems. He would take me fishing and ask if there was anything he could do to help me. Finally, I straightened out. I decided that I would be like Uncle Clarence if someday I had a chance to help young people."*

Another major way values are learned is through the communication of attitudes. The attitudes that we hear expressed directly or indirectly help shape our values. Assume that using credit to purchase goods and services was considered an evil practice among your family and friends. You might therefore hold negative values about installment purchases.

Unstated but implied attitudes may also shape your values. If key people in your life showed no enthusiasm when you talked about work accomplishments, you might not place such a high value on achieving outstanding results. If, on the other hand, your family and friends centered their lives around their careers, you might develop similar values. (Or you might rebel against such a value because it interfered with a more relaxed life-style.) Many key values are also learned through religion and thus become the basis for society's morals. For example, most religions emphasize treating other people fairly and kindly. To "knife somebody in the back" is considered immoral both on and off the job.

CLARIFYING YOUR VALUES

The values that you develop early in life are directly related to the kind of person you are and to the quality of the relationships you form.[11] A recognition of this fact has led to exercises designed to help people clarify and understand some of their own values. Almost all of these value-clarification exercises ask you, in one way or another, to compare the relative importance you attach to different objects and activities. Self-Assessment Quiz 2-4 gives you an opportunity to clarify your values.

THE MESH BETWEEN INDIVIDUAL AND JOB VALUES

Under the best of circumstances, the values of employees mesh with those required by the job. When this state of congruence exists, job performance is likely to be higher. A national survey of managers investigated the fit between the values of managers and those of their organizations. (One such mesh would be a highly ethical person working for a highly ethical firm.) A major finding was that managers who experienced a good fit were more successful and more likely to believe they could reach their career goals. They were also more confident about remaining with their present firm and more willing to work long hours.[12]

When the demands made by the organization or a superior clash with the basic values of the individual, that person suffers from **person–role conflict.** The individual wants to obey orders, but does not want to perform an act that seems inconsistent with his or her values. A situation such as this might occur when an employee is asked to produce a product that he or she feels is unsafe or of no value to society.

> *A manager of a commercial weight-reduction center resigned after two years of service. The owners pleaded with her to stay, based on her excellent performance. The manager replied, "Sorry, I think my job is immoral. We sign up all these people with great expectations of losing weight permanently. Most of them do achieve short-term weight reduction. My conflict is that over 90 percent of our clientele regain the weight they lost once they go back to eating normal food. I think we are deceiving them by not telling them up front that they will most likely gain back the weight they lose."*

GUIDELINES FOR USING VALUES TO
ENHANCE INTERPERSONAL RELATIONS

Values are intangible and abstract, and thus not easy to manipulate to help improve your interpersonal relations on the job. Despite their vagueness, values are an important driver of interpersonal effectiveness. Ponder the following guidelines:

1. Establish the values you will use in your relationships with others on the job, and then use those values as firm guidelines in working with others. For example, following the Golden Rule, you might establish the value of treating others as you want to be treated. You would then not lie to others to gain personal advantage, and you would not backstab your rivals.

2. Establish the values that will guide you as an employee. When you believe that your values are being compromised, express your concern to your manager in a tactful and constructive manner. You might say to your manager, "Sorry, I choose not to tell our customers that our competitor's product is inferior just to make a sale. I choose not to say this because our competitor makes a fine product. But what I will say is that our service is exceptional."

Self-Assessment Quiz 2-4

CLARIFYING YOUR VALUES

Directions: Rank from 1 to 18 the importance of the following values to you as a person. The most important value on the list receives a rank of 1; the least important a rank of 18. Use the space next to "Other" if we have left out an important value in your life.

_____ Having my own place to live

_____ Having one or more children

_____ Having an interesting job and career

_____ Owning a car

_____ Having a good relationship with coworkers

_____ Having good health

_____ Watching my favorite television shows

_____ Participating in sports or other pastimes

_____ Following a sports team, athlete, music group, or other entertainer

_____ Being a religious person

_____ Helping people less fortunate than myself

_____ Loving and being loved by another person

_____ Having physical intimacy with another person

_____ Making an above-average income

_____ Being in good physical condition

_____ Being a knowledgeable, informed person

_____ Completing my formal education

_____ Other

1. Discuss and compare your ranking of these values with the person next to you.

2. Perhaps your class, assisted by your instructor, can arrive at a class average on each of these values. How does your ranking compare to the class ranking?

3. Look back at your own ranking. Does it surprise you?

4. Any surprises in the class ranking? Which values did you think would be highest and lowest?

Skill-Building Exercise 2-3

THE VALUE-CONFLICT ROLE PLAY

One student plays the role of a company president who makes an announcement to the group that the company must soon lay off 10 percent of the workforce in order to remain profitable. The president also points out that the company has a policy against laying off good performers. He or she then asks four of the company managers to purposely give below-average performance ratings to 10 percent of employees. In this way, laying them off will fit company policy.

Four other students play the role of the company managers who receive this directive. If such manipulation of performance evaluations clashes with your values, engage in a dialogue with your manager expressing your conflict. Remember, however, that you may not want to jeopardize your job.

Conduct this group role play for about 10 minutes, with other class members observing and being prepared to offer feedback.

To help you put these guidelines into practice, do Skill-Building Exercise 2-3. Remember, however, that being skilled at using your values requires day-by-day monitoring.

SUMMARY

Individual differences are one of the most important factors influencing the behavior of people in the workplace. Knowing how to respond to such differences is the cornerstone of effective interpersonal relations.

Personality is one of the major sources of individual differences. The six major personality factors described in this chapter are extraversion, emotional stability, agreeableness, conscientiousness, openness to experience, and self-monitoring of behavior. Depending on the job, any one of these personality factors can be important for success, and they also affect interpersonal relations.

Personality also influences a person's cognitive style, or the mental process used to perceive and make judgments from information. How people gather and evaluate information determines their cognitive style. Two different styles of gathering information are sensation and intuition. Sensation-type individuals prefer routine and order. Intuitive-type people prefer an overall perspective and enjoy solving new problems.

Styles for evaluating information tend to place emphasis on either feeling at one extreme or thinking at the other. Feeling-type people are conformists and avoid disagreement, whereas thinking-type individuals rely on intellect more than emotion in problem solving.

The two dimensions of information gathering and evaluation are combined to produce a four-way classification of cognitive styles: sensation/thinking; intuitive/thinking; sensation/feeling; and intuitive/feeling. Cognitive styles have implications for the types of work a person is best suited for (see Figure 2-2).

Mental ability, or intelligence, is one of the major sources of individual differences that affects job performance and behavior. Understanding the nature of intelligence contributes to effective interpersonal relations in organizations. For example, understanding that different types of intelligence exist will help a person appreciate the strengths of others.

Intelligence consists of many components. The traditional perspective is that intelligence includes a general factor along with special factors that contribute to problem-solving ability. A related perspective is that intelligence consists of seven components: verbal comprehension, word fluency, numerical acuity, spatial perception, memory, perceptual speed, and inductive reasoning.

To overcome the idea that intelligence involves mostly the ability to solve abstract problems, the triarchic theory of intelligence has been proposed. According to this theory, intelligence has three subtypes: analytical, creative, and practical (street smarts included). Another approach to understanding mental ability contends that people have multiple intelligences, or faculties, including linguistic, logical-mathematical, musical, spatial, bodily/kinesthetic, intrapersonal, interpersonal, and naturalist.

Emotional intelligence refers to factors other than traditional mental ability that influence a person's success. The five components of emotional intelligence are (1) self-awareness, (2) self-regulation, (3) motivation relating to task enjoyment and resiliency, (4) empathy, and (5) social skill.

Values and beliefs are another set of factors that influence behavior on the job, including interpersonal relations. Values are closely tied in with ethics, the moral choices a person makes. People acquire values in the process of growing up and modeling others. The values a person develops early in life are directly related to the kind of adult he or she becomes and to the quality of relationships formed. Values-clarification exercises help people identify their values. Person–role conflict occurs when the demands made by an organization or a superior clash with the basic values of an individual.

QUESTIONS FOR DISCUSSION AND REVIEW

1. Referring to the lead-in case illustration in the chapter, how effectively were Billy and Mary Lou relating to each other?

2. Why is responding to individual differences considered to be the cornerstone of effective interpersonal relations?

3. How can a knowledge of major personality factors help a person form better interpersonal relations on the job?

4. A coworker of yours who has a high standing on the personality factor "openness to experience" has an upcoming birthday. What would be an appropriate gift for the group to buy this person?

5. Suppose a high-self-monitoring person is attending a company-sponsored social event and that person dislikes such events. How is he or she likely to behave?

6. What kinds of problems would a sensation-type individual prefer to tackle?

7. Which of the seven components of intelligence represents your best mental aptitude? What is your evidence?

8. How could you use the concept of *multiple intelligences* to raise the self-esteem of people who did not consider themselves to be very smart?

9. Why is emotional intelligence so important for success in business?

10. How can you use information about a person's values to help you relate more effectively to him or her?

An Interpersonal Relations Case Problem

BAYER LAYS OUT ITS VALUES

The Bayer Group is a large business firm involved in a variety of businesses including chemicals, health-care (such as the familiar Bayer Aspirin), and photography supplies. Leadership at Bayer decided several years ago that for employees to be successful in their company they must accept company values such as customer loyalty, quality, and productivity.

Senior managers at Bayer wanted to make the message clear: No matter whether a person is a chemist, engineer, manufacturing technician, bookkeeper, salesperson, or customer service representative, the key to success is to embrace the company's values. One implication of this message was that employee performance would be measured against how well the individual's work reflected company values. An executive committee worked hard and long to develop a statement that would communicate company values clearly. Top management hoped that by

making these values explicit, employees would have a better understanding of how they should behave on the job. Exhibit 1 presents the Bayer values.

With the new values clearly spelled out for all workers, managers were now expected to guide employees toward behaving in a way consistent with the values. A production supervisor, for example, would devalue high productivity by an employee if he or she sacrificed safety to achieve a high production quota.

Dave Rapp, a packaging design specialist at a Bayer pharmaceutical plant, said to his supervisor, "I thought I was doing a great job helping design packages for medicine. If I designed an attractive package that protected the ingredients, I was rated highly. Now I have to figure out whether what I'm doing matches the company vision statement. Why are you making my job so difficult?"

(Continued)

Exhibit 1

THE VISION AND VALUES OF BAYER CORP., PITTSBURGH

The vision of Bayer Corp. Pittsburgh is to be a leader in the markets it serves and to be a major contributor to its worldwide parent company. The company will achieve its vision through a diversified, highly motivated workforce; by satisfying and retaining loyalties of its external and internal customers with an organization that fosters teamwork and is unencumbered by bureaucracy; by being environmentally responsible; and by being a good corporate citizen in the communities in which its workforce works and lives.

The following are Bayer Corp.'s Value statements:

OUR PEOPLE
➤ Rewarding people with fair and competitive compensation.
➤ Investing in employee professional development and growth.
➤ Achieving management diversity by gender, race and culture.
➤ Encouraging and recognizing outstanding accomplishments.

OUR BUSINESS
➤ Satisfying the requirements of external and internal customers.
➤ Maintaining high ethical standards in all business actions.
➤ Encouraging and supporting among employees, entrepreneurial attitudes, opportunity seeking and applied creativity.
➤ Managing for the long term.

OUR ORGANIZATION
➤ Assuring an organization unencumbered by bureaucracy.
➤ Delegating decision-making authority.
➤ Fostering teamwork and cooperation among organizational units worldwide.

OUR ENVIRONMENT AND COMMUNITIES
➤ Maintaining work environments in which employee health and safety are the highest priorities.
➤ Developing only products that can be manufactured, used, and disposed of in an environmentally friendly way.
➤ Taking an active role in the communities in which we work and live.

Source: Bayer Corp.

(Continued)

Nicole Berkshire, his team leader, responded: "Dave, be careful not to be too narrow-minded, or sell yourself short. Raise your sights. I think there are lots of things you're doing that fit the Bayer value statements. Just to get you started on the right track, think about that latest package you helped design. The one that will be used to hold arthritis medicine. Didn't you tell me the package was environmentally friendly?

"I've got some homework for you Dave. Come back to me next Monday morning with a list of at least five ways in which your work as a package designer fits the Bayer values. And don't forget to include how your personal values match the Bayer values."

"I'll give it a try," said Dave reluctantly. "But why can't I just go back to helping design packages and be evaluated on what I produce?"

Case Questions

1. How realistic is it for Bayer to expect employees to embrace the value statements?

2. Help Dave with his "homework." Describe as best you can how the work of a package designer might fit the value statements of Bayer.

3. What about you? Provide a brief analysis of how your values might fit the Bayer value statements.

Source: Much of the information in this case is based on Bayer Corp.; Jennifer J. Laabs, "Rating Jobs Against New Values," *Workforce*, May 1997, pp. 38–49.

Chapter 3

Interpersonal Communications

Learning Objectives

After reading and studying this chapter and doing the exercises you should be able to

➤ Explain the basic steps in the communication process.

➤ Understand nonverbal communication and improve your nonverbal communication skills.

➤ Understand barriers to communication, including gender differences, and know how to overcome them.

➤ Enhance your listening skills.

"Why isn't this project ready for shipment today?" barked the manager. "I told you to get it done as soon as you could get to it." "That's why it isn't done," replied the group member. "I was too busy to get to it."

The communication problem just described took place because the phrase "as soon as you can get to it" was interpreted differently by the two people involved. The mix-up that took place illustrates that communication breakdowns are responsible for many problems that take place on the job.

Communication is the sending, receiving, and understanding of messages. It is also the basic process by which managers, customer-contact workers, and professionals accomplish their work. For example, a customer service representative cannot resolve a thorny customer problem without carefully receiving and sending information. Communication is also important because communication skills are a success factor for workers in a wide variety of jobs. Figure 3-1 illustrates how important communication skills are to employers.

The information in this chapter is aimed at reducing communication problems among people and helping you enhance your communication effectiveness. The chapter approaches these ends in two ways. First, it explains the nature of a few key facets of interpersonal communication. Second, it presents guidelines for improving your effectiveness, along with skill-building exercises.

STEPS IN THE COMMUNICATION PROCESS

One way to understand how people communicate is to examine the steps involved in transmitting and receiving a message, as shown in Figure 3-2. For

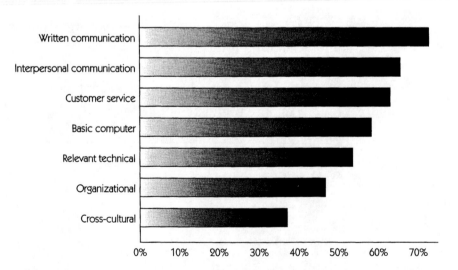

Figure 3-1 Employee Skills Companies Would Most Like to Enhance

Source: Based on data presented in *Human Resource Measurements,* Wonderlic Personnel Test, Inc., December 1991, and updated January 1995. See also Brien N. Smith, Carolee Jones, and Judy Lane, "Employers' Perceptions of Work Skills," *Business Education Forum,* April 1997, pp. 11–17.

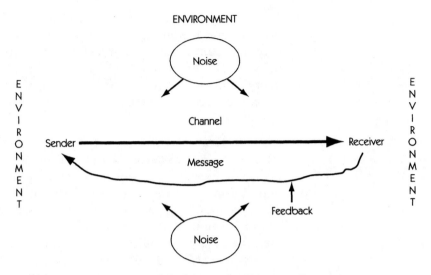

Figure 3-2   A Basic Model of the Communication Process

effective communication to take place, six components must be present: a sender, a message, a channel, a receiver, feedback, and the environment. In addition, the entire communication process is affected by a seventh component, noise. To help understand the communication process, assume that a production manager in a bicycle factory wants to inform a team leader that quality in her department slipped last month.

1. *Sender (or source).* The sender in a communication event is usually a person (in this case the production manager) attempting to send a spoken, written, sign language, or nonverbal message to another person or persons. The perceived authority and credibility of the sender are important factors in influencing how much attention the message will receive.

2. *Message.* The heart of the communication event is the **message**, a purpose or idea to be conveyed. Many factors influence how a message is received. Among them are clarity, the alertness of the receiver, the complexity and length of the message, and how the information is organized. The production manager's message will most likely get across if he says directly, "I need to talk to you about last month's below-average quality figures."

3. *Channel (medium).* Several communication channels, or media, are usually available for sending messages in organizations. Typically, messages are written (usually electronically), spoken, or a combination of the two. Some kind of nonverbal signal such as a smile or hand gesture accompanies most spoken messages. In the production manager's case, he has chosen to drop by the team leader's office and deliver his message in a serious tone.

4. *Receiver.* A communication event can be complete only when another party receives the message and understands it properly. In the example here, the team leader is the receiver. Perceptual distortions of various types act as filters that can prevent a message from being received as intended by the sender. If the team leader is worried that her job is at stake, she might get defensive when she hears the production manager's message.

5. *Feedback.* Messages sent back from the receiver to the sender are referred to as **feedback**. Without feedback it is difficult to know whether a message has been received and understood. The feedback step also includes the reactions of the receiver. If the receiver takes action as intended by the sender, the message has been received satisfactorily. The production manager will know his message got across if the team leader says, "Okay, when would you like to review last month's quality reports?" Effective interpersonal communication therefore involves an exchange of messages between two people. The two communicators take turns being receivers and senders.

6. *Environment.* A full understanding of communication requires knowledge of the environment in which messages are transmitted and received. The organizational culture (attitudes and atmosphere) is a key environmental factor that influences communication. It is easier to transmit controversial messages when trust and respect are high than when they are low.

7. *Noise.* Distractions such as noise have a pervasive influence on the components of the communication process. In this context, **noise** is anything that disrupts communication, including the attitudes and emotions of the receiver. Noise includes such factors as stress, fear, negative attitudes, and low motivation.

NONVERBAL COMMUNICATION IN ORGANIZATIONS

Our discussion so far has emphasized the use of words, or verbal communication. A substantial amount of communication between people, however, takes place at the nonverbal level. **Nonverbal communication** refers to the transmission of messages through means other than words. These messages accompany verbal messages or sometimes stand alone. The general purpose of nonverbal communication is to communicate the feeling behind a message. For instance, you can say no with either a clenched fist or a smile to communicate the intensity of your negative or positive feelings.

A classic study by Albert Mehrabian dramatizes the relevance of nonverbal communication. He calculated the relative weights of three elements of communication with respect to conveying emotion. The words we choose account for only about 7 percent of our emotional impact on others. Our voice tone accounts for 38 percent of the impact, and our facial expressions for 55 percent. Nonverbal behavior therefore accounts for 93 percent of the emotional impact of a message.[1] Merhabian's study is often interpreted to mean that 93 percent of communication is nonverbal. In truth, the study deals with the emotional impact of a message; it does not mean that the content of the message is unimportant.

The following paragraphs summarize the major modes of transmission of nonverbal communication and provide guidelines for improving nonverbal communication. Chapter 6, about cross-cultural relations, describes cultural differences in nonverbal communication.

MODES OF TRANSMISSION OF NONVERBAL COMMUNICATION

Nonverbal communication can be transmitted in many modes. You may be surprised that certain factors, such as dress and appearance are considered part of nonverbal communication.

ENVIRONMENT

The setting or environment in which you send a message can influence how that message is received. Assume that your manager invites you out to lunch at a fine restaurant to discuss a problem. You will think it is a more important topic under these circumstances than you would if the manager had lunch with you in the company cafeteria.

Other important environmental silent messages include room color, temperature, lighting, and furniture arrangement. A person who sits behind a large, uncluttered desk, for example, appears more powerful than a person who sits behind a small, messy desk.

INTERPERSONAL DISTANCE

The placement of one's body in relation to someone else *(proxemics)* is widely used to transmit messages. (See Figure 3-3.) In general, getting physically close to another person conveys a positive attitude toward that person. Putting your arm around someone is generally interpreted as a friendly act. (Some people, however, recoil when touched by someone other than a close friend. Touching others on the job can also be interpreted as sexual harassment.)

POSTURE

Posture communicates a variety of messages. Standing erect usually conveys the message that the person is self-confident and experiencing positive emotion. Slumping makes a person appear to be lacking in self-confidence or down in the dumps. Another interpersonal message conveyed by posture involves the direction of leaning. Leaning toward the sender suggests that you are favorably disposed toward his or her message; leaning backward communicates the opposite. Openness of the arms or legs serves as an indicator of liking or caring. In general, people establish closed postures (arms folded and legs crossed) when speaking to people they dislike.

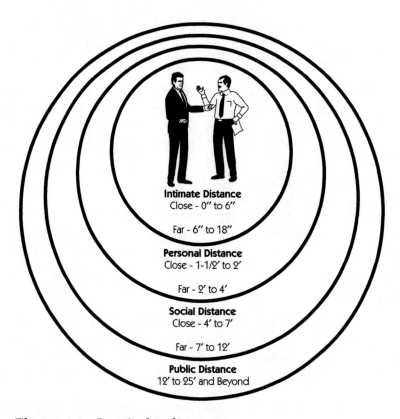

Figure 3-3 Four Circles of Intimacy

GESTURES

Positive attitudes toward another person are shown by frequent hand movements. In contrast, dislike or disinterest usually produces few gestures. An important exception is that some people wave their hands furiously while arguing. Gestures are also said to provide clues to a person's levels of dominance and submission. The gestures of dominant people are typically directed outward toward the other person. Examples include a steady, unwavering gaze and touching one's partner. Submissive gestures are usually protective, such as touching oneself or shrugging one's shoulders.

FACIAL EXPRESSIONS

Using your head, face, and eyes in combination provides the clearest indications of interpersonal attitudes. Looking at the ceiling (without tilting your head), combined with a serious expression, almost always communicates the message "I doubt what you're saying is true." Maintaining eye contact with another person improves communication. To maintain eye contact, it is usually necessary to move your face and eyes *with* the other person. Moving your face and eyes *away* from the other person is often interpreted as defensiveness or a lack of self-confidence.

Facial expressions are also important, because many people rely on them as indicators of whether or not a person is telling the truth. In general, fabrication is suggested by facial tics and nervous mannerisms that reveal how uncomfortable the sender is with telling something false. Looking away from a person is often interpreted as covering up a lie. Computer scientists at the Salk Institute in La Jolla, California, have documented the difference between a truthful smile and a lying smile. An authentic smile is most frequently characterized by crinkly eyes and a generally relaxed expression. A lying smile reveals itself in subtle ways, particularly eye wrinkles that resemble crow's feet more than laugh lines.[2]

VOICE QUALITY

Often more significance is attached to the *way* something is said than to *what* is said. A forceful voice, which includes a consistent tone without vocalized pauses, connotes power and control. Closely related to voice tone are volume, pitch, and rate of speaking. Anger, boredom, and joy often can be interpreted from voice quality. Anger is noted when the person speaks loudly, with a high pitch and at a fast rate. Boredom is indicated by a monotone. Joy is indicated by loud volume. Avoiding an annoying voice quality can make a positive impact on others. The research of voice coach Jeffrey Jacobbi provides some useful suggestions. He surveyed a nationwide sample of 1,000 men and women and asked, "Which irritating or unpleasant voice annoys you the most?" The most irritating was a whining, complaining, or nagging tone.

Jacobbi notes that we are judged by the way we sound. He also notes that careers can be damaged by voice problems such as those indicated in the survey. "We think about how we look and dress," says Jacobbi, "and that gets most of the attention. But people judge our intelligence much more by how we sound than how we dress."[3] Do Self-Assessment Quiz 3-1 to apply Jacobbi's findings to your development.

PERSONAL APPEARANCE

Your external image plays an important role in communicating messages to others. A current analysis confirms what has been known for a long time: A favorable personal appearance enhances a person's ability to persuade others, whether you are dealing with an individual receiver or an audience.[4] Job seekers show recognition of the personal appearance aspect of nonverbal communication when they carefully groom for a job interview. People pay more respect and grant more privileges to those they perceive as being well dressed and neatly groomed. Some research indicates that a favorable personal appearance leads to high starting salaries and later salary increases.[5]

GUIDELINES FOR IMPROVING NONVERBAL COMMUNICATION

Nonverbal communication, like verbal communication, can be improved. Here are six suggestions to consider:

Self-Assessment Quiz 3-1

VOICE-QUALITY CHECKUP

The voice-quality study cited in the text ranked voice quality in decreasing order of annoyance, as follows:

➤ Whining, complaining, or nagging tone—44.0 percent

➤ High-pitched, squeaky voice—15.9 percent

➤ Mumbling—11.1 percent

➤ Very fast talking—4.9 percent

➤ Weak and wimpy voice—3.6 percent

➤ Flat, monotonous tone—3.5 percent

➤ Thick accent—2.4 percent

Directions: Ask yourself and two other people familiar with your voice whether you have one or more of the preceding voice-quality problems. If your self-analysis and feedback from others does indicate a serious problem, get started on self-improvement. Record your voice on tape and attempt to modify the biggest problem. Another avenue of improvement is to consult with a speech coach or therapist.

1. *Obtain feedback on your body language by asking others to comment upon the gestures and facial expressions you use in conversations.* Be videotaped conferring with another individual. After studying your body language, attempt to eliminate those mannerisms and gestures that you think detract from your effectiveness. Common examples include nervous gestures such as moving knees from side to side, cracking knuckles, rubbing the eyes or nose, head scratching, and jingling coins.

2. *Learn to relax when communicating with others.* Take a deep breath and consciously allow your body muscles to loosen. Tension-reducing techniques should be helpful here. A relaxed person makes it easier for other people to relax. You are likely to elicit more useful information from other people when you are relaxed.

3. *Use facial, hand, and body gestures to supplement your speech, but don't overdo it.* A good starting point is to use hand gestures to express enthusiasm. You can increase the potency of enthusiastic comments by shaking the other person's hand, nodding approval, or smiling.

4. *Avoid using the same nonverbal gesture indiscriminately.* If you want to use nodding to convey approval, do not nod with approval when you dislike what somebody else is saying. Also, do not pat everybody on the back. Nonverbal gestures used indiscriminately lose their communication effectiveness.

Skill-Building Exercise 3-1

THE MIRRORING TECHNIQUE

To practice mirroring, during the next 10 days each class member schedules one mirroring session with an unsuspecting subject. An ideal opportunity would be an upcoming meeting on the job. Another possibility would be to ask a friend if you could practice your interviewing techniques with him or her—but do not mention the mirroring technique. A third possibility would be to sit down with a friend and conduct a social conversation.

While holding an interview or discussion with the other party, use the mirroring technique. Imitate the person's breathing pattern, rate of speech, hand movements, eye movements, leg movements, or any other noticeable aspect of behavior.

After the mirroring sessions have been conducted, hold a class discussion about the results. Questions include:

1. Did the other person notice the mirroring and comment on the behavior of the person doing the mirroring?

2. Was the rapport enhanced (or hindered) by the mirroring?

3. How many of the students intend to repeat the mirroring technique in the future?

5. *Use role playing to practice various forms of nonverbal communication.* A good starting point would be to practice selling your ideas about an important project or concept to another person. During your interchange, supplement your spoken messages with appropriate nonverbal cues such as posture, voice intonation, gestures, and so forth. Later, obtain the other person's perception of the effectiveness of your nonverbal communication.

6. *Use mirroring to establish rapport.* Nonverbal communication can be improved through **mirroring**, or subtly imitating someone. The most successful mirroring technique is to imitate the breathing pattern of another person. If you adjust your own breathing rate to match someone else's, you will soon establish rapport with that individual. Another effective mirroring technique is to adopt the voice speed of the person with whom you are communicating. If the other person speaks more slowly than you typically do, slow down to mirror him or her.

You can also use mirroring by imitating a manager to win favor. Many group members have a relentless tendency to copy the boss's mannerisms, gestures, way of speaking, and dress. As a consequence, without realizing why, your manager may think more favorably of you.

Caution: Do not use mirroring to the extent that you appear to be mocking another person, thereby adversely affecting rapport. To get started developing your mirroring skills, do Skill-Building Exercise 3-1.

```
    1.  Understand the receiver.
    2.  Discuss differences in paradigms.
    3.  Minimize defensive communication.
    4.  Use multiple channels.
    5.  Use verbal and nonverbal feedback.
    6.  Display a positive attitude.
    7.  Use persuasive communication.
    8.  Engage in active listening.
    9.  Engage in complementary transactions with people.
    10. Recognize gender differences in communication styles.
    11. Engage in metacommunications.
```

Figure 3-4   *Overcoming Communication Problems and Barriers*

GUIDELINES FOR OVERCOMING COMMUNICATION PROBLEMS AND BARRIERS

Communication problems in organizations are ever present. Some interference usually takes place between ideation and action, as suggested earlier by the noise factor in Figure 3-2. The type of message influences the amount of interference. Routine or neutral messages are the easiest to communicate. Interference is most likely to occur when a message is complex, emotionally arousing, or clashes with a receiver's mental set.

An emotionally arousing message deals with topics such as money or a relationship between two people. A message that clashes with a receiver's mental set requires the person to change his or her typical pattern of receiving messages. Try this experiment. The next time you visit a restaurant, order dessert first and the entrée second. The server probably will not receive your dessert order, because it deviates from the normal sequence.

Here we will describe strategies and tactics for overcoming some of the more frequently observed communication problems in organizations, as outlined in Figure 3-4.

UNDERSTAND THE RECEIVER

Understanding the person you are trying to reach is a fundamental principle of overcoming communication barriers. The more you know about your receiver, the better able you are to deliver your message effectively. Three important aspects of understanding the receiver are (1) developing empathy, (2) recognizing his or her motivational state, and (3) understanding the other person's frame of reference.

Developing **empathy** requires placing yourself in the receiver's shoes. To accomplish this you have to imagine yourself in the other person's role and assume the viewpoints and emotions of that individual. For example, if a supervisor were trying to communicate the importance of customer service to sales associates, the supervisor might ask himself or herself, "If I were a part-time employee being paid close to the minimum wage, how receptive would I be to messages about high-quality customer service?" To empathize you have to understand another person. *Sympathy* means that you understand and agree.

The receiver's **motivational state** could include any active needs and interests operating at the time. People tend to listen attentively to messages that show promise of satisfying an active need. Management usually listens attentively to a suggestion framed in terms of cost savings or increased profits.

People perceive words and concepts differently because their vantage points and perspectives differ. Such differences in **frame of reference** create barriers to communication. A frame of reference can also be considered a lens through which we view the world. A manager attempted to chastise a team member by saying, "If you keep up your present level of performance, you'll be a repair technician all your life." The technician replied, "That's good news," because he was proud of being the first person in his family to hold a skilled job. Understanding another person's frame of reference requires empathy.

DISCUSS DIFFERENCES IN PARADIGMS

Another way of understanding differences in frames of reference is to recognize that people often have different **paradigms** that influence how they interpret events. A paradigm is a model, framework, viewpoint, or perspective. When two people look at a situation with different paradigms, a communication problem may occur. For instance, one person may say, "Let's go to Las Vegas for the computer show." The other person may respond, "A ridiculous idea. It costs too much money and takes too much time. Besides, the company would never approve." These objections are based on certain unstated beliefs:

➤ Air travel is the most suitable mode of transportation.

➤ Traveling over 500 miles a day by auto is fatiguing and dangerous.

➤ Traveling over a weekend for business and using vacation days cannot be considered seriously.

➤ Paying for such a trip with personal money is out of the question.

The other person has a different set of unstated beliefs:

➤ It is possible, traveling on interstate highways and using two drivers, to cover 1,000 miles in one day.

➤ Traveling over a weekend and taking vacation days is sensible.

➤ Paying for the trip with personal money is a sound educational investment.

The solution to this communication clash is to discuss the paradigms. Both people live by different rules or guidelines (a major contributor to a paradigm). If the two people can recognize that they are operating with different paradigms, the chances for agreement are improved. Keep in mind that people can change their paradigms when the reasons are convincing.[6] For example, the second person in the preceding situation may never have thought about using personal funds for a trip as being an educational investment.

MINIMIZE DEFENSIVE COMMUNICATION

An important general communication barrier is defensive communication—the tendency to receive messages in such a way that our self-esteem is protected. Defensive communication is also responsible for people sending messages to make themselves look good. For example, when being criticized for low production, an investment banker might blame the advertising agency used by his or her firm.

Overcoming the barrier of defensive communication requires two steps. First, people have to recognize the existence of defensive communication. Second, they have to try not to be defensive when questioned or criticized. Such behavior is not easy because of the unconscious or semiconscious process of **denial**—the suppression of information we find uncomfortable. For example, the investment banker just cited would find it uncomfortable to think of himself or herself as being responsible for below-average performance.

USE MULTIPLE CHANNELS

Repetition enhances communication, particularly when different channels are used to convey the same message. Effective communicators at many job levels follow spoken agreements with written documentation. Since most communication is subject to at least some distortion, the chances of a message being received as intended increase when two or more channels are used.

Many firms have a policy of using a multiple-channel approach to communicate the results of a performance appraisal. The group member receives an oral explanation from the manager of the results of the review. The group member is also required to read the form and indicate by signature that he or she has read and understands the meaning of the review. Another useful way of using multiple channels is to follow up a telephone call or in-person conversation with an e-mail message summarizing key facts or agreements.

USE VERBAL AND NONVERBAL FEEDBACK

Ask for feedback to determine whether your message has been received as intended. A frequent managerial practice is to conclude a meeting with a question such as, "Okay, what have we agreed upon?" Unless feedback of this nature is obtained, you will not know whether your message has been received until the receiver carries out your request. If the request is carried out improperly, or if no action is taken, you will know that the message was received poorly.

Obtaining feedback is important because it results in two-way communication in which people take turns being sender and receiver, thereby having a dialogue. Dialogues take time because they require people to speak more slowly and listen more carefully. The results of having employees engage in dialogue are said to include a deeper sense of community (a feeling of belongingness) and greater trust among employees.[7] You might relate this finding to your own experiences. Do you trust people better when you both exchange ideas and listen to each other?

Feedback is also important because it provides reinforcement to the sender, and few people will continue to communicate without any reinforcement. The sender is reinforced when the receiver indicates understanding of the message. When the original receiver indicates that he or she understands the message, that person becomes the sender. A nod of approval would be an appropriate type of nonverbal reinforcement for the sender to receive.

DISPLAY A POSITIVE ATTITUDE

Being perceived as having a positive attitude helps melt communication barriers. This is true because most people prefer to communicate with a positive person. According to Sharon Lund O'Neil, you must establish credibility and trustworthiness if you expect others to listen, let alone get them to react positively to your communication.[8] Being positive helps make you appear more credible and trustworthy, whereas being consistently negative makes you less credible and trustworthy. As one coworker said about a chronic complainer in his office, "Why take Margot seriously? She finds something wrong with everybody and everything."

USE PERSUASIVE COMMUNICATION

A powerful tactic for overcoming communication barriers is to communicate so persuasively that obstacles disappear. *Persuasiveness* refers to the sender's convincing the receiver to accept his or her message. Persuasion thus involves selling to others. Hundreds of articles, books, audiotapes, and videos have been developed to help people become more persuasive. Following are some representative suggestions for becoming a more persuasive communicator, both in speaking and in writing.[9]

1. *Know exactly what you want.* Your chances of selling an idea increase to the extent that you have clarified the idea in your own mind. The clearer and more committed you are at the outset of a selling or negotiating session, the stronger you are as a persuader.

2. *Never suggest an action without telling its end benefit.* In asking for a raise, you might say, "If I get this raise, I'll be able to afford to stay with this job as long as the company likes."

3. *Phrase your proposition in terms of the receiver's interests.* The basic rule of selling is an extension of the communication strategy "understand the receiver." People are far more likely to accept your idea if it is clear how they will benefit. Most receivers want to know "What's in it for me?"

4 *Explore the reasons for people's objections.* Assume a potential customer says, "I like this model but I don't want it in my living room." An effective response would be "What is it that you don't like about it?" Another would be "Which features do you like in this product?"

5. *Get a yes response early on.* It is helpful to give the selling session a positive tone by establishing a "yes pattern" at the outset. Assume that an employee wanted to convince the boss to allow the employee to perform some work at home during normal working hours. The employee might begin the idea-selling questions with "Is it important for the company to obtain maximum productivity from all its employees?"

6. *Use power words.* An expert tactic for being persuasive is to sprinkle your speech with power (meaning *powerful*) words. Power words stir emotion and bring forth images of exciting events. Examples of power words include *decimating* the competition, *bonding* with customers, *surpassing* previous profits, *capturing* customer loyalty, and *rebounding* from a downturn.

7. *Minimize raising your pitch at the end of sentences.* Part of being persuasive is to not sound unsure and apologetic. In English and several other languages, a convenient way to ask a question or to express doubt is to raise the pitch of your voice at the end of a sentence or phrase. As a test, use the sentence "You like my ideas." First say *ideas* using approximately the same pitch and tone as with every other word. Then say the same sentence by pronouncing *ideas* with a higher pitch and louder tone. By saying *ideas* loudly, you sound much less certain and are less persuasive.

8. *Talk to your audience, not the screen.* Computer graphic presentations have become standard practice even in small-group meetings. Many presenters rely so heavily on computer-generated slides and transparencies that they basically read the slides and transparencies to the audience. Jean Mausehund and R. Neil Dortch remind us that in an oral presentation, the predominant means of connection between sender and receiver should be eye contact. When your audience is frequently distracted by movement on the screen, computer sounds, garish colors, or your looking at the screen, eye contact suffers. As a result the message is weakened, and you are less persuasive.[10]

9. *Avoid or minimize common language errors.* You will enhance your persuasiveness if you minimize common language errors, because you will appear more articulate and informed. Here are several common language errors:

   a. "Just between you and I" is wrong. "Just between you and me" is correct.

   b. *Irregardless* is not a word; *regardless* is correct.

   c. Avoid double negatives when you want to express the negative, despite the increasing popularity of double negatives. Common examples of double negatives are "I got no *nothing* from my best customer this week" and "We don't have *no money* in the budget for travel." If expressed with the right inflection, a double negative can be correct. For example to say "We don't have no money" with an emphasis on *no money* means that the budget is not completely depleted. Yet in general, double negatives make the sender appear so ill-informed that they fail to persuade.

d. "We are customer-oriented" is correct. "We are customer-orientated" is wrong.

If you can learn to implement most of the preceding nine suggestions you are on your way toward becoming a persuasive communicator. In addition, you will need solid facts behind you, and you will need to make skillful use of nonverbal communication.

ENGAGE IN ACTIVE LISTENING

Persuasion deals primarily with sending messages. Improving one's receiving of messages is another part of developing better communication skills. Unless you receive messages as they are intended, you cannot perform your job properly or be a good companion. Listening has even been described as our primary communication activity when engaged in face-to-face communication. Listening is a particularly important skill for anybody whose job involves troubleshooting, since one needs to gather information in order to solve problems.

Another reason that improving the listening skills of employees is important is that insufficient listening is extraordinarily costly. Listening mistakes lead to reprocessing letters, rescheduling appointments, reshipping orders, and recalling defective products. Effective listening also improves interpersonal relations because the people listened to feel understood and respected.

A major component of effective listening is to be an **active listener**. The active listener listens intensely, with the goal of empathizing with the speaker. As a result of listening actively, the listener can feed back to the speaker what he or she thinks the speaker meant. Feedback of this type relies on both verbal and nonverbal communication. Active listening also involves **summarization**. When you summarize, you pull together, condense, and thereby clarify the main points communicated by the other person. Here are two examples of summarization statements:

"What I heard you say during our meeting is that . . ."

"As I understand it, your position is that . . ."

Specific suggestions for improving active listening skills are summarized in Figure 3-5. These suggestions relate to good listening in general, as well as active listening. As with any other suggestions for developing a new skill, considerable practice (with some supervision) is needed to bring about actual changes in behavior. One of the problems a poor listener would encounter is the difficulty of breaking old habits in order to acquire new ones. Self-Assessment Quiz 3-2 gives you an opportunity to think about bad listening habits you may have acquired. To practice your listening skills, do Skill-Building Exercise 3-2 on page 56.

➤ *While your target is talking, look at him or her intently.* At the same time, maintain a steady eye contact.

➤ *Be patient about your turn to speak.* A common barrier to effective listening is to mentally prepare an answer while another person is speaking.

➤ *Nod your head in agreement from time to time.*

➤ *Mutter "mmh" or "uh-huh" periodically but not incessantly.*

➤ *Ask open-ended questions to encourage the other person to talk.* For example, you encourage more conversation by saying "What do you think of . . . " rather than asking "Do you agree that . . . ."

➤ *Reflect your target's content or meaning.* Rephrase and summarize concisely what the other person is saying.

➤ *Reflect the other person's feelings.* Reflection-of-feeling responses typically begin with "You feel that . . . ."

➤ *Keep your ratio of talking to listening down to about 1 to 5.* In other words, spend 20 percent of your time talking, and 80 percent listening to be perceived as a great listener.

➤ *Ask yourself whether anything the other person is saying could benefit you.* Maintaining this perspective will enable you to benefit from most listening episodes and will motivate you to listen intently.

Figure 3-5   Suggestions for Active Listening

ENGAGE IN COMPLEMENTARY TRANSACTIONS WITH PEOPLE

A specific technique for improving communications with people, and thereby breaking down barriers, is to engage in **complementary transactions**. A complementary transaction is an exchange of words between two people that reduces tension and moves the two people toward a positive resolution. The complementary transaction occurs when one person gets the kind of response he or she wants from the other. The skill of using complementary transactions involves adapting your response precisely to the actions and words of the other person, just as a complementary angle completes a circle.

According to the discipline called *transactional analysis,* transactions between people are classified as complementary or noncomplementary (crossed). Complementary transactions lead to effective interaction and *positive strokes,* or ego-building statements. Noncomplementary transactions lead to ineffective interactions and *negative strokes,* or ego-tearing insults.

Finding a complementary response is especially useful when attempting to keep communications running smoothly in a tense situation. You search for the type of response the person is seeking so you can keep the conversation positive. You then stand a reasonable chance of overcoming a communication barrier.

Assume that Dorothy is red in the face with anger because an important file she had been working on is erased from the personal computer she was using. Acting in a childlike manner, she goes into a tirade about how some fool must have been messing around with her computer files. By the tone of her voice, you get the impression she thinks you are the culprit.

One way you can engage in a complementary transaction is by acting in a controlling, parentlike manner in response to her childish state. You might

Self-Assessment Quiz 3-2

LISTENING TRAPS

Communication specialists at Purdue University have identified certain behavior patterns that interfere with effective hearing and listening. After thinking carefully about each trap, check how well the trap applies to you: Not a Problem, or Need Improvement. To respond to the statements accurately, visualize how you acted when you recently were in a situation calling for listening.

	Not a problem	Need improvement
➤ **Mind reader.** You will receive limited information if you constantly think "What is this person really thinking or feeling?"	☐	☐
➤ **Rehearser.** Your mental rehearsals for "Here's what I'll say next" tune out the sender.	☐	☐
➤ **Filterer.** You engage in selective listening by hearing only what you want to hear. (Could be difficult to judge because the process is often unconscious.)	☐	☐
➤ **Dreamer.** You drift off during a face-to-face conversation, which often leads you to an embarrassing "What did you say?" or "Could you repeat that?"	☐	☐
➤ **Identifier.** If you refer everything you hear to your experience, you probably did not really listen to what was said.	☐	☐
➤ **Comparer.** When you get sidetracked sizing up the sender, you are sure to miss the message.	☐	☐
➤ **Derailer.** You change the subject too quickly, giving the impression that you are not interested in anything the sender has to say.	☐	☐
➤ **Sparrer.** You hear what is said, but quickly belittle or discount it, putting you in the same class as the derailer.	☐	☐
➤ **Placater.** You agree with everything you hear just to be nice or to avoid conflict. By behaving this way you miss out on the opportunity for authentic dialogue.	☐	☐

Interpretation: If you checked "Need Improvement" for five or more of the above statements, you are correct—your listening needs improvement! If you checked only two or fewer of the above traps, you are probably an effective listener and a supportive person.

Source: Reprinted with permission from *Messages: The Communication Skills Book* (Oakland, CA: New Harbinger Publications, 1983).

respond, "Please calm down, Dorothy. I am good at finding lost files, and I will do my best to help you." Communication will probably continue, because Dorothy is receiving the type of helping response she wants.

Another way to engage in a complementary transaction with Dorothy is to respond in a childish manner to her childish tirade. You might respond, "Holy

Skill-Building Exercise 3-2

LISTENING TO A COWORKER

Before conducting the following role plays, review the 11 keys to effective listening presented in Figure 3-4. Suggestion 11 about restating what you hear (summarization) is particularly important when listening to a person who is talking about an emotional topic.

The Elated Coworker: One student plays the role of a coworker who has just been offered a promotion to supervisor of another department. She will be receiving a 10 percent raise in pay and be able to travel overseas twice a year for the company. She is eager to describe full details of her good fortune to a coworker. Another student plays the role of the coworker to whom the first worker wants to describe her good fortune. The second worker decides to listen intently to the first worker. Other class members will rate the second student on his or her listening ability.

The Discouraged Coworker: One student plays the role of a coworker who has just been placed on probation for poor job performance. His boss thinks that his performance is below standard and that his attendance and punctuality are poor. He is afraid that if he tells his girlfriend, she will leave him. He is eager to tell his tale of woe to a coworker. Another student plays the role of a coworker he corners to discuss his problems. The second worker decides to listen intently to his problems but is pressed for time. Other class members will rate the second student on his or her listening ability.

cats, what a mess. I bet some fool did mess up your files. Some of the temps we have working in this office are irresponsible. They have no respect for other people's work." Because a person acting like a child will also welcome a childish response in return, communication is likely to continue.

A crossed transaction occurs when a person does not get the type of response he or she sought. In Dorothy's situation, she is not looking for a response that will put her in her place and suggest she take responsibility for her own problems. You would engage in a crossed transaction with Dorothy if you responded, "Hey, Dorothy, don't yell at me in those accusatory tones. It's your responsibility to manage your own computer files. If you want to blame someone, look in the mirror."

In short, if another person is communicating to you in a childish, immature manner, transactional analysis suggests you can salvage the situation two ways. First, you can exert control in a firm, controlling manner, much like a parent. Second, you can respond in an immature manner, thus communicating on the same wavelength. Both responses result in complementary transactions. In a crossed transaction the second party is troubled or irritated by the message sent by the first party. As a result, the second party responds in a way that surprises and troubles the first party.[11] Skill-Building Exercise 3-3 gives you practice in identifying complementary versus crossed transactions.

Skill-Building Exercise 3-3

COMPLEMENTARY VERSUS CROSSED TRANSACTIONS

Following are alternative responses to the same statement. To the left of each response, indicate with a plus sign (+) if the response is a complementary and a minus sign (−) if it is a crossed transaction. Suggested answers may be found at the end of the chapter.

Situation A: A coworker says to you, "Why are you always late coming back from lunch?"

_____ "Look who's talking. You leave work early almost every day."

_____ "You're right. I take care of too many errands during lunch hour. Since it bothers you I will try to get back from lunch more promptly."

Situation B: Out of town on a company-sponsored trip, one worker says to the other, "Why don't we both eat at a sub shop tonight and then charge the company for a fancy dinner?"

_____ "I like the idea of having a little extra cash, but I am concerned that we would be violating company policy. Let's not do it."

_____ "Count me out. I dislike cheating, and I hate cheats."

RECOGNIZE GENDER DIFFERENCES IN COMMUNICATION STYLE

A trend in organizations for many years has been to move toward equality of the sexes. Despite this trend, substantial interest has arisen in identifying differences in communication styles between men and women. A book by linguist Deborah Tannen, *Talking from 9 to 5,* focuses especially on male–female differences in conversational style in the workplace. A book by John Gray, *Men Are from Mars, Women Are from Venus,* explores the same topic.

People who are aware of these differences face fewer communication barriers between themselves and members of the opposite sex. As we describe these differences, recognize that they are group stereotypes. Individual differences in communication style usually are more important than group (men versus women) differences. Here we will describe the major findings of gender differences in communication patterns.[12]

1. *Women prefer to use conversation for rapport building.* For most women, the intent of conversation is to build rapport and connections with people. Women are therefore more likely to emphasize similarities, to listen intently, and to be supportive.

2. *Men prefer to use talk primarily as a means to preserve independence and status by displaying knowledge and skill.* When most men talk they want to

receive positive evaluation from others and maintain their hierarchical status within the group. Men are therefore more oriented to giving a *report* while women are more interested in establishing *rapport.*

3. *Women want empathy, not solutions.* When women share feelings of being stressed out, they seek empathy and understanding. If they feel they have been listened to carefully, they begin to relax. When listening to the woman, the man may feel blamed for her problems or that he has failed the woman in some way. To feel useful, the man might offer solutions to the woman's problems.

4. *Men prefer to work out their problems by themselves, whereas women prefer to talk out solutions with another person.* Women look upon having and sharing problems as an opportunity to build and deepen relationships. Men are more likely to look upon problems as challenges they must meet on their own. The communication consequence of these differences is that men may become uncommunicative when they have a problem.

5. *Women are more likely to compliment the work of a coworker, whereas men are more likely to be critical.* A communication problem may occur when a woman compliments the work of a coworker and expects reciprocal praise.

6. *Men tend to be more directive in their conversation, whereas women emphasize politeness.* Women are therefore more likely to frequently use the phrases "I'm sorry" and "Thank you," even when there is no need to express apology or gratitude. For example, a supermarket manager notices that the store has suddenly become busy. She would therefore say to a store clerk unpacking boxes, "I'm sorry Pedro, but we've become busy all of a sudden. Could you please open up a new lane up front? Thank you." A manager who is a stereotyped male might say, "Pedro, we need you to open a line up front, pronto. Put down the boxes and get up there."

7. *Women tend to be more conciliatory when facing differences, whereas men become more intimidating.* Again, women are more interested in building relationships, whereas men are more concerned about coming out ahead.

8. *Men are more interested than women in calling attention to their accomplishments or hogging recognition.* In one instance a sales representative who had already made her sales quota for the month turned over an excellent prospect to a coworker. She reasoned, "It's somebody else's turn. I've received more than my fair share of bonuses for the month."

9. *Men tend to dominate discussions during meetings.* One study of college faculty meetings found that women's longest turns at speaking were, on the average, of shorter duration than men's shortest turns. A possible explanation here is that women are still less assertive than men in the workplace.

How can the information just presented help overcome communication problems on the job? As a starting point, remember that these gender differences often exist. Understanding these differences will help you interpret the communication behavior of people. For example, if a male coworker is not as effusive with praise as you would like, remember that he is simply engaging in gender-typical behavior. Do not take it personally.

A woman can remind herself to speak up more in meetings because her natural tendency might be toward diffidence. She might say to herself, "I must watch out to avoid gender-typical behavior in this situation." A man might remind himself to be more complimentary and supportive toward coworkers. The problem is that although such behavior is important, his natural tendency might be to skip the praise.

A woman should not take it personally when a male coworker or subordinate is tight-lipped when faced with a problem. She should recognize that he needs more encouragement to talk about his problems than would a woman. If the man persists in not wanting to talk about the problem, the woman might say, "It looks like you want to work out this problem on your own. Go ahead. I'm available if you want to talk about the problem."

Men and women should recognize that when women talk over problems, they might not be seeking hard-hitting advice. Instead, they might simply be searching for a sympathetic ear so they can deal with the emotional aspect of the problem.

A general suggestion for overcoming gender-related communication barriers is for men to improve communication by becoming more empathic (showing more empathy) listeners. Women can improve communication by becoming more direct.

ENGAGE IN METACOMMUNICATIONS

When confronted with a communication problem, one response is to attempt to work around the barrier, perhaps by using one of the methods already described. A more typical response is to ignore the barrier by making no special effort to deal with the problem—a "take-it-or-leave-it" approach to communication. Another possibility is to **metacommunicate**, or communicate about your communication, to help overcome barriers or resolve a problem.[13] If you as a team leader were facing heavy deadline pressures, you might say to a team member, "I might appear brusque today and tomorrow. Please don't take it personally. It's just that I have to make heavy demands on you because the team is facing a gruesome deadline."

SUMMARY

Communication is the basic process by which managers, customer-contact workers, and professionals accomplish their work, yet many communication problems exist in organizations. Communication among people is a complex

JUST CALL ME "KAT"

Katherine Matthews had worked for many years in a variety of retail positions, including a three-year assignment as an assistant manager at a woman's clothing store. Matthews was then involved in an automobile accident as the passenger in a friend's car. Although she was wearing a seat belt, Matthews was severely injured. Her right leg and ankle were broken as the door on her side caved in upon impact with a tree.

After four months of rehabilitation, Matthews walked well with the assistance of a cane. Yet she could not walk for long without enduring pain. Katherine and the team of medical specialists assisting her agreed that an on-the-feet job was not appropriate for her in the foreseeable future. Katherine assessed her financial situation and decided she needed to return to work soon. Her disability payments were ending soon, and her savings were depleted to $450.

To make the transition back to full-time employment, yet in another field, Katherine signed on with OfficeTemps, a well-established temporary placement agency. Katherine explained that she sought work that was mentally challenging but not physically demanding on her right leg and ankle. After carefully assessing Katherine's capabilities and experience, the employment interviewer, Jack Radison, created a computer file for her. Radison said, "I'll call you as soon as I find a suitable assignment."

One week later Radison called Katherine with good news. He had located a nine-month assignment for her as a telephone interviewer for a market research firm. The market research firm was hiring several people to conduct telephone interviews with dealers and retailers about the acceptability of a relatively new product, a personal air cooler. The cooler is about the size of the central processing unit on a personal computer, and it would easily fit on a desk or adjacent to a television set. The air cooler evaporates water, thereby lowering the temperature by 12° F (6.7° C) in a seven-foot area. Using an air cooler, a person would have less need for air conditioning. With the cooler operating, a person could either eliminate air conditioning or set it at a higher temperature. The manufacturer of the cooler was interested in estimating the potential market for the product, now being sold primarily by mail order.

Katherine's task was to telephone specific people (usually store managers or owners) from a long list of names. Completing an interview would require about 30 minutes, and it involved obtaining answers to 20 separate questions. Each market research interviewer was given a quota of six completed interviews per day.

As the interviewers perceived the task, a major challenge was to keep the interviewee on the line long enough to answer all the detailed questions. Quite often the interviewer had to dig for additional information (such as sales of room air conditioners and fans) or request that the interviewee search his or her files for appropriate information. The several interviewers also agreed that an even bigger challenge was to get the people on the list to cooperate. Among the problems were reaching a voice mail system instead of the actual person, excuses about being too busy to be interviewed, and outright rejection and rudeness.

Following closely the script provided by the market research firm, Katherine began her pitch in this manner: "Hello, this is Katherine from Garson Research Associates in Chicago. I'm asking for your cooperation to participate in an important study about an exciting new product, personal coolers. My interview should only take approximately 30 minutes. May we conduct the interview right now, or would you prefer another time in the next few days?"

Four weeks into the job, Katherine was behind quota by an average of two interviews per day. Feeling fatigued one day, she slipped into introducing herself as "Kat," the name used by family members and close friends. The interviewee prospect responded, "Oh sure, Kat, I can talk now."

(Continued)

Two days later, Katherine made a personal call to a friend and was thus prompted to think of herself as "Kat." She inadvertently introduced herself as "Kat" to the next person on her list. Again, the prospective interviewee responded with enthusiasm: "Hey Kat, I'm ready to talk."

Prompted by the second cooperative response, Katherine then shifted to introducing herself as "Kat." The percentage of prospects willing to be interviewed jumped from 30 percent to 50 percent. Katherine explained this unusual result to her supervisor, who said that using a nickname and achieving good results was probably just a coincidence, that maybe she had simply become more confident. The increased confidence was therefore responsible for the higher success ratio in obtaining interviews.

Katherine responded, "I'm not so sure. There must be some other reasons that Kat gets more interviews than Katherine."

Case Questions

1. How can information about overcoming communication barriers help explain why "Kat" gets more interviews than "Katherine"?

2. How might the sex of the receiver be related to the different success ratios of "Kat" and "Katherine" in obtaining interviews?

3. Based on Kat's good results, what recommendations can you offer the research firm to help them increase the percentage of people who agree to be interviewed?

process that can be divided into six components: sender or source, message, channel (or medium), receiver, feedback, and environment. Noise, or interference, can disrupt communication within any component.

Nonverbal communication plays an important part in sending and receiving messages and is especially important for imparting the emotional aspects of a message. The modes of nonverbal communication include the environment in which the message is sent, interpersonal distance, posture, gestures, facial expressions, voice quality, and personal appearance.

Nonverbal communication can be improved through such means as obtaining feedback, learning to relax, using gestures more discriminately, role playing, and mirroring. The latter refers to subtly imitating someone.

Methods of overcoming communication barriers include the following: (1) understand the receiver, (2) discuss differences in paradigms, (3) minimize defensive communication, (4) use multiple channels, (5) use verbal and nonverbal feedback, (6) display a positive attitude, (7) use persuasive communication, (8) engage in active listening, (9) engage in complementary transactions with people, (10) recognize gender differences in communication styles, and (11) engage in metacommunications (communicate about your communications).

QUESTIONS FOR DISCUSSION AND REVIEW

1. What are the reasons so many workers need improvement in communication skills?

2. How can knowing the steps in the communication process help a person become a more effective communicator?

Skill-Building Exercise 3-4

ENHANCING YOUR NONVERBAL COMMUNICATION E-MAIL SKILLS

Hi readers, The purpose of this assignment is to search the Internet for emoticoms [such as the ;-) for a wink and the :-) for a smile] and acronymns to incorporate nonverbal signals into your e-mail messages. Find a combination of 10 emoticoms and acronymns using the Internet. Compare your list with that of a few classmates, and look for a rare one. •IM [H]O it would be good to do it •ASAP. <G>

P.S. Your Internet search should help you decode the last two acronymns, and the last emoticom.

3. How can people use their automobiles to send nonverbal messages?

4. What type of voice quality do you think would be effective in most work situations?

5. What, if any, ethical problems are involved with mirroring?

6. Suppose your manager does not listen to your suggestions for job improvements. Explain this problem as a paradigm clash.

7. Should a person use power words when he or she is not in a powerful job? Explain.

8. Why is summarization such a powerful communication technique?

9. What are the implications of gender differences in communication for conducting meetings?

10. Describe an example from your work experience or personal life in which it would have been a good idea to metacomunicate.

Suggested Answers to Skill-Building Exercise 3-3

Situation A: The first response will most likely result in a crossed transaction (–) because the second person is revengeful and insulting. The second response will most likely result in a complementary transaction (+) because the second person submits to the parental approach of the first person in a submissive, obedient-child manner.

Situation B: The first response will most likely result in a complementary transaction (+) because the childlike behavior of the first person is being controlled in a parental way. The second response will probably result in a crossed transaction (–) because the first person is insulted by the second.

Chapter 4

Developing Teamwork Skills

Learning Objectives

After reading and studying this chapter and doing the exercises you should be able to

➤ Identify several types of teams in organizations.

➤ Understand the strengths and weaknesses of teams.

➤ Identify various team member roles.

➤ Be ready to apply people-related tactics for effective team play.

➤ Be ready to apply task-related tactics for effective team play.

Wilma Mankiller is principal chief of the Cherokee, the first woman to fill the top position in a major American tribe. While Mankiller has been chief, the tribe has blossomed economically. The Cherokee boast an annual operating budget of $86 million and 1,200 employees. New health centers have been established, along with children's programs and horticultural, motel, electronics, and livestock businesses. Instead of attributing these successes to her individual leadership, Mankiller contends that "the growth is the result of teamwork. Here we call it management by workgroup."[1]

The words of Wilma Mankiller underscore a major shift in the way in which work is accomplished in organizations. Many firms rely more on teamwork than on individuals acting alone to accomplish work. To be successful in the modern organization, it is therefore necessary to be an effective team player. You have to work smoothly with other members of the team to accomplish your goals.

The challenges a team member faces come to light when the true nature of a team is recognized. Two experts on the subject define a **team** as "a small number of people with complementary skills who are committed to a common purpose, set of performance goals, and approach for which they hold themselves mutually accountable."[2] In other words, members of a team work together smoothly, and all pull in the same direction. A workplace team should be more like an effective athletic team than a group of individuals out for individual glory.

This chapter gives you the information, insights, and preliminary practice necessary to develop effective teamwork skills. Self-Assessment Quiz 4-1 will help you assess your current mental readiness to be a contributing team member.

TYPES OF TEAMS

All teams in the workplace have the common element of people working together cooperatively and members possessing a mix of skills. Nevertheless, many specific types of work teams can be identified. Successful people will usually have an opportunity to be a member of several different types of teams.

Three representative work teams are self-managing work teams, cross-functional teams, and virtual teams. Projects, task forces, and committees are similar in design to cross-functional teams, so they do not receive separate mention here. No matter what label the team carries, its broad purpose is contribute to a *collaborative workplace* in which people help each other achieve constructive goals. The idea is for workers to collaborate (a high level of cooperation) rather than compete with or prevent others from getting their work done.

As teams have become more common in the workplace, much effort has been directed toward specifying the skills and knowledge a person needs to function effectively on a team, particularly a self-managing work team. Self-Assessment Quiz 4-2 presents a representative listing of team skills as perceived by employers.

Self-Assessment Quiz 4-1

TEAM PLAYER ATTITUDES

Directions: Describe how well you agree with each of the following statements, using the following scale: Disagree strongly (DS); Disagree (D); Neutral (N); Agree (A); Agree strongly (AS).

	DS	D	N	A	AS
1. I am at my best when working alone.	5	4	3	2	1
2. I have belonged to clubs and teams ever since I was a child.	1	2	3	4	5
3. It takes far too long to get work accomplished with a group.	5	4	3	2	1
4. I like the friendship of working in a group.	1	2	3	4	5
5. I would prefer to run a one-person business than to be a member of a large firm.	5	4	3	2	1
6. It's difficult to trust others in the group on key assignments.	5	4	3	2	1
7. Encouraging others comes to me naturally.	1	2	3	4	5
8. I like the give-and-take of ideas that is possible in a group.	1	2	3	4	5
9. It is fun for me to share responsibility with other group members.	1	2	3	4	5
10. Much more can be accomplished by a team than by the same number of people working alone.	1	2	3	4	5

Total Score _____

Scoring and Interpretation: Add the numbers you circled to obtain your total score.

41–50 You have strong positive attitudes toward being a team member and working cooperatively with other members.

30–40 You have moderately favorable attitudes toward being a team member and working cooperatively with other members.

10–29 You much prefer working by yourself to being a team member. To work effectively in a company that emphasizes teamwork, you may need to develop more positive attitudes toward working jointly with others.

SELF-MANAGING WORK TEAMS

The best-known work team is a group of workers who take over much of the responsibility for managing their own work. The same type of team is referred to as a self-managing work team, a production work team, a work team, or a team. A **self-managing work team** is a small group of employees responsible for managing and performing technical tasks to deliver a product or service to an external or internal customer.[3] According to one survey, about 80 of the largest companies have half of their employees assigned to work teams.[4] Work teams in a wide variety of activities including producing motorcycles, telephone directories, or a major component for a large computer.

TEAM SKILLS

A variety of skills are required to be an effective member of various types of teams. Several different business firms use the skill inventory here to help guide team members toward the competencies they need to become high-performing team members. Review each team skill listed and rate your skill level for each one using the following classification:

S = strong (capable and comfortable with effectively implementing the skill)

M = moderate (demonstrated skill in the past)

B = basic (minimum ability in this area)

N = not applicable (not relevant to the type of work I do)

Communication skills	*Skill level (S, M, B, or N)*
Speak effectively	_____
Foster open communications	_____
Listen to others	_____
Deliver presentations	_____
Prepare written communication	_____

Self-management skills	
Act with integrity	_____
Demonstrate adaptability	_____
Engage in personal development	_____
Strive for results	_____
Display a commitment to work	_____

Thought process skills	
Innovate solutions to problems	_____
Use sound judgment	_____
Analyze issues	_____
Think "outside the box"	_____

Organizational skills	
Know the business	_____
Use technical/functional expertise	_____
Use financial/quantitative data	_____

Strategic (broad business perspective) skills	
Recognize "big picture" impact	_____
Promote corporate citizenship	_____
Focus on customer needs	_____
Commit to quality	_____
Manage profitability	_____

Interpretation: We do not have a scoring key for this questionnaire. Its purpose is to raise your awareness of the types of skills that are required to be a successful team member in business.

Members of a self-managing work team typically work together on an ongoing, day-by-day basis, thus differentiating it from a task force or a committee. The work team is often given total responsibility for or "ownership" of an entire product or service, such as producing a telephone directory. At other times, the team is given responsibility for a major chunk of a job, such as building an airplane engine (but not the entire airplane).

CROSS-FUNCTIONAL TEAMS

It is common practice for teams to be composed of workers from different specialties. A **cross-functional team** is a work group composed of workers from different specialties, and about the same organizational level, who come together to accomplish a task. The purpose of the cross-functional team is to get workers from different specialties to blend their talents toward accomplishing a task that requires such a mix. A typical application of a cross-functional team would be to develop a new product such as a Net TV. Among the specialties needed on such a team would be computer science, engineering, manufacturing, industrial design, marketing, and finance. (The finance person would help guide the team toward producing a Net TV that could be sold at a profit.) When members from different specialties work together, they can take into account each other's perspectives when making their contribution. For example, if the manufacturing representative knows that a Net TV must sell for about one-half the price of a personal computer, then he or she will have to build the device inexpensively. A major advantage of cross-functional teams for product development is that they enhance communication across groups, thereby saving time.

In addition to product development, cross-functional teams are used for such purposes as improving quality, reducing costs, and running a company (in the form of a top management team).

To perform well on a cross-functional team a person would have to think in terms of the good of the larger organization, rather than in terms of his or her own specialty. For example, a manufacturing technician might say, "If I proposed using expensive components for the Net TV, would the product cost too much for its intended market?"

VIRTUAL TEAMS

Some teams conduct most of their work by sending electronic messages to each other rather than conducting face-to-face meetings. A **virtual team** is a small group of people who conduct almost all of their collaborative work by electronic communication rather than face-to-face meetings. In the language of information technology, they engage in "cybercollaboration" by conducting "cybermeetings." E-mail is the usual medium for sharing information and conducting meetings. *Groupware* is another widely used approach to conducting a cybermeeting. Using groupware, several people can edit a document at the same time, or in sequence. Desktop videoconferencing is another technological advance that facilitates the virtual team.[5] Electronic brainstorming, as described in Chapter 5, is well suited for a virtual team.

Most high-tech companies make some use of virtual teams and cybermeetings. Strategic alliances in which geographically dispersed companies work with each other are a natural for virtual teams. It is less expensive for the field technician in Iceland to hold a cybermeeting with her counterparts in South Africa, Mexico, and California than it is to bring them all together in one physical location. IBM makes some use of virtual teams in selling information-technology systems, partially because so many IBM field personnel work from their homes and vehicles.

Despite the efficiency of virtual teams, there are times when face-to-face interaction is necessary to deal with complex and emotional issues. Negotiating a new contract between management and a labor union, for example, is not well suited to a cybermeeting.

THE ADVANTAGES AND DISADVANTAGES OF TEAMS AND TEAMWORK

Groups have always been the building blocks of organizations. Yet groups and teams have recently grown in importance as the basic unit for organizing work. In an attempt to cope with numerous changes in the outside world, many organizations have granted teams increased independence and flexibility. Furthermore, teams are often required to work more closely with customers and suppliers.

The increased acceptance of teams suggests that group work offers many advantages. Nevertheless, it is useful to specify several of these advantages and also examine the potential problems of groups. Being aware of these potential pitfalls can often help a person avoid them. These same advantages and disadvantages also apply to group decision making, to be described in Chapter 5.

ADVANTAGES OF GROUP WORK AND TEAMWORK

Group work and group decision making offer several advantages over individual effort. If several knowledgeable people are brought into the decision-making process, a number of worthwhile possibilities may be uncovered. It is also possible to gain **synergy**, whereby the group's total output exceeds the sum of each individual's contribution. For example, it would be a rare person working alone who could build a racing car. Dozens of case histories have been collected about successes with work teams, as illustrated next.

> Teams at Monarch Marking Systems, a Dayton, Ohio, manufacturer of labeling, identification and tracking equipment, trimmed the square footage of an assembly area by 70 percent, reduced past-due shipments 90 percent and doubled productivity. In one year alone, they identified 1,400 areas of waste in the organization.[6]

Group decision making is also helpful in gaining acceptance and commitment. The argument is that people who contribute to making a decision will feel some ownership about implementing the decision. Team members often evaluate each other's thinking, so the team is likely to avoid major errors. An advertising specialist was developing an advertising campaign to attract seniors to live in a retirement community. The proposed ads had photographs of senior citizens engaged in playing shuffleboard, visiting the pharmacy, and sleeping in a hammock. Another team member on the project pointed out that many seniors perceive themselves to be energetic and youthful. Ads emphasizing advanced age might therefore backfire. A successful advertising campaign was then developed that featured seniors in more youthful activities such as jogging and dancing.

Working in teams and groups also enhances the job satisfaction of members. Being a member of a work group makes it possible to satisfy more needs than working alone. Among these needs are affiliation, security, self-esteem, and self-fulfillment. (See Chapter 9 for details about psychological needs.)

DISADVANTAGES OF GROUP WORK AND TEAMWORK

Group activity has some potential disadvantages for both individuals and the organization. Teams and other groups often waste time because they talk too much and act too little. Committees appear to suffer from more inaction than teams. Abigail Johnson, a top executive at Fidelity Corp., the financial services giant, says that committees are not effective decision makers. "They have tended to be slow and overly risk averse. Even worse, I believe, they can drain an organization of talent, because the group can only be as good as the average."[7]

A major problem is that members face pressures to conform to group standards of performance and conduct, as just implied. Some teams might shun a person who is much more productive than his or her coworkers. Shirking of individual responsibility is another problem frequently noted in groups. Unless work is assigned carefully to each team member, an undermotivated person can often squeeze by without contributing his or her fair share to a group effort.

Social loafing is the psychological term for shirking individual responsibility in a group setting. The social loafer risks being ostracized (shunned) by the group but may be willing to pay the price rather than work hard. Loafing of this type is sometimes found in groups such as committees and project teams. Have you ever encountered a social loafer on a group project at school?

At their worst, teams and other groups foster conflict on the job. People within the work group often bicker about such matters as doing a fair share of the undesirable tasks within the department. Cohesive work groups can also become xenophobic (fearful of outsiders). As a consequence, they may grow to dislike other groups and enter into conflict with them. A customer service group might put considerable effort into showing up a sales group because the latter makes promises to customers that the customer service group cannot keep. For example, a sales representative might promise that a customer can get a loaner if his or her equipment needs repair, although customer service has no such policy.

A well-publicized disadvantage of group decision making is **groupthink**, a deterioration of mental efficiency, reality testing, and moral judgment in the interest of group solidarity. Simply put, groupthink is an extreme form of consensus. The group atmosphere values getting along more than getting things

> ➤ The team has clear-cut goals linked to organizational goals so that group members feel connected to the entire organization.
> ➤ Members learn to think for themselves rather than expecting a supervisor to solve all the difficult problems.
> ➤ Members learn to think "outside of the box" (be creative).
> ➤ Members receive extensive training in technical knowledge, problem-solving skills, and interpersonal skills.
> ➤ Members inspect their own work for quality.
> ➤ Members receive part of their pay related to team or group incentives rather than strictly based on individual performance.
> ➤ Group size is generally about 6 people, rather than 10 or more.
> ➤ Team members have good intelligence and personality factors, such as conscientiousness and pride, that contribute to good performance.
> ➤ There is honest and open communication among group members and with other groups in the organization.
> ➤ Members have the philosophy of working as a team—25 brains, not just 50 hands.

Figure 4-1   Key Characteristics of Effective Teams and Work Groups

Source: Ben Nagler, "Recasting Employees into Teams," *Workforce,* January 1998, p. 104; Carla Johnson, "Teams at Work," *HR Magazine,* May 1999, pp. 30–36; Dale E. Yeatts and Cloyd Hyten, *High-Performing Self-Managed Work Teams: A Comparison of Theory and Practice* (Thousand Oaks, CA: Sage, 1998).

done. The group thinks as a unit, believes it is impervious to outside criticism, and begins to have illusions about its own invincibility. As a consequence, the group loses its powers of critical analysis.[8]

Groupthink took place at one of the failed savings and loan associations. The senior management group voted themselves extraordinary salaries and bought art collections that they frequently borrowed for personal use. In addition, they purchased corporate jets to fly around the country looking for investments and to use for vacations for themselves and their families. Not one of the savings and loan association executives expressed a dissenting opinion.

Two conditions are important for overcoming the potential disadvantages of teams and groups. First, the members must strive to act like a team,[9] following some of the suggestions given in the pages ahead. Second, the task given to the group should require collective effort instead of being a task that could better be performed by individuals. For example, an international business specialist would probably learn to conjugate verbs in a foreign language better by working alone than in a team. What is your opinion on this issue?

Figure 4-1 presents more information about key factors associated with effective work teams and groups. The more of these factors present, the more likely it is that a given team or groups will be productive.

TEAM MEMBER ROLES

A major challenge in learning to become an effective team member is to choose the right roles to occupy. If you carry out positive roles, you will be perceived as a contributor to team effort. If you neglect carrying out these roles, you will be perceived as a poor contributor. Self-Assessment Quiz 4-3 will help you evaluate your present inclinations toward occupying effective roles as a team member. In this section we describe a number of the most frequently observed positive roles played by team members.[10] The description will be followed by an activity in which the roles can be practiced.

KNOWLEDGE CONTRIBUTOR

A technically knowledgeable team member, the *knowledge contributor,* gravitates toward the role of providing the group with useful and valid information. (In this sense, *technical* refers to knowledge about the group task.) He or she is a facts-and-figures person who is intent upon helping the team with task accomplishment. The knowledge contributor believes it is important to share technical expertise with team members. He or she does not ignore the human element in a team setting but pays attention to it primarily to help get the task accomplished. Being a knowledge contributor is especially important for virtual teams, because much of the activity in such teams consists of sharing information. A financial specialist on a cross-functional team explains how the human factor can enter into working with facts and figures:

> As the financial expert on the team, I had to explain the reasoning behind a sales forecast I developed. To really understand this forecast, a person has to know basic calculus. Unfortunately, the person I was explaining the forecast to had zero knowledge of calculus. I had to calm him down enough so he could listen to me. I explained that very few people in customer service understood calculus. He then stopped being so defensive, and I was able to explain the value of my forecast.

PROCESS OBSERVER

Dealing with knowledge, technology, and methodology is indispensable for group achievement—the *hard side* of collective effort. Another key aspect of a team's work is the processes within the group. This *soft side* of teamwork includes the transactions that take place among and between members of the team. Among the many processes within a team are soothing each other's feelings, forming coalitions, communicating problems, and complimenting each other.

The *process observer* forces the group to look at how it is functioning with a statement such as: "Look, gang. We've been at it for two and one-half hours, and we have only taken care of one agenda item. Shouldn't we be doing better?" The process observer might point to excellent progress that the team has made.

COLLABORATOR

Another key role is the person who pitches in to do whatever is necessary to achieve team goals and is not constrained by his or her official statement of responsibilities. The *collaborator* keeps the team focused on its goal and fre-

TEAM PLAYER ROLES

Directions: For each of the following statements about team activity, check Mostly agree or Mostly disagree. If you have not experienced such a situation, imagine how you would act or think if placed in that situation. In responding to the statements, assume that you are taking the questionnaire with the intent of learning something about yourself.

	Mostly agree	*Mostly disagree*
1. It is rare that I ever miss a team meeting.	_____	_____
2. I regularly compliment team members when they do something exceptional.	_____	_____
3. Whenever I can, I avoid being the notetaker at a team meeting.	_____	_____
4. From time to time, other team members come to me for advice on technical matters.	_____	_____
5. I like to hide some information from other team members so I can be in control.	_____	_____
6. I welcome new team members coming to me for advice and learning the ropes.	_____	_____
7. My priorities come first, which leaves me with very little time to help other team members.	_____	_____
8. During a team meeting, it is not unusual for several other people at a time to look toward me for my opinion.	_____	_____
9. If I think the team is moving in an unethical direction, I will say so explicitly.	_____	_____
10. Rarely will I criticize the progress of the team even if I think such criticism is deserved.	_____	_____
11. It is not unusual for me to summarize the progress in a team meeting, even if not asked.	_____	_____
12. To conserve time, I attempt to minimize contact with my teammates outside of our meetings.	_____	_____
13. I intensely dislike going along with a consensus decision if the decision runs contrary to my thoughts on the issue.	_____	_____
14. I rarely remind teammates of our mission statement as we go about our work.	_____	_____
15. Once I have made up my mind on an issue facing the team, I am unlikely to be persuaded in another direction.	_____	_____
16. I am willing to accept negative feedback from team members.	_____	_____
17. Just to get a new member of the team involved, I will ask his or her opinion.	_____	_____

(Continued)

18. Even if the team has decided on a course of action, I am not hesitant to bring in new information that supports another position. _____ _____

19. Quite often I talk negatively about one team member to another. _____ _____

20. My teammates are almost a family to me, because I am truly concerned about their welfare. _____ _____

21. When it seems appropriate, I joke and kid with teammates. _____ _____

22. My contribution to team tasks is as important to me as my individual work. _____ _____

23. From time to time I have pointed out to the team how we can all improve in reaching our goals. _____ _____

24. I will fight to the last when the team does not support my viewpoint and wants to move toward consensus. _____ _____

25. I will confront the team if I believe that the members are thinking too much alike. _____ _____

Total Score _____

Scoring and Interpretation: Give yourself one point (+1) for each statement you gave in agreement with the keyed answer. The keyed answer indicates carrying out a positive, as opposed to a negative, role.

Question number	Positive role answer	Question number	Positive role answer
1.	Mostly agree	14.	Mostly disagree
2.	Mostly agree	15.	Mostly disagree
3.	Mostly disagree	16.	Mostly agree
4.	Mostly agree	17.	Mostly agree
5.	Mostly disagree	18.	Mostly agree
6.	Mostly agree	19.	Mostly disagree
7.	Mostly disagree	20.	Mostly agree
8.	Mostly agree	21.	Mostly agree
9.	Mostly agree	22.	Mostly agree
10.	Mostly disagree	23.	Mostly agree
11.	Mostly agree	24.	Mostly disagree
12.	Mostly disagree	25.	Mostly agree
13.	Mostly disagree		

20–25 You carry out a well above average number of positive team roles. Behavior of this type contributes substantially to being an effective team player. Study the information in this chapter to build upon your already laudable sensitivity to occupying various positive roles within the team.

10–19 You carry out an average number of positive team roles. Study carefully the roles described in this chapter to search for ways to carry out a greater number of positive roles.

0–9 You carry out a substantially above average number of negative team roles. If becoming an effective team player is important to you, you will have to assiduously search for ways to play positive team roles. Study the information in this chapter carefully.

quently reminds the group to do whatever is necessary to stay on track. A collaborator's typical behavior during a team meeting would be to indicate how much progress the team has made toward goal attainment. A representative comment would be, "We are halfway through our time budget, and we have achieved one-fourth of our goals. We are behind schedule, but catching up is doable."

The collaborator works for the good of the group and does not care who gets recognition as long as the job gets done. He or she often works quietly behind the scenes and does not look for individual recognition.

PEOPLE SUPPORTER

The *people supporter* on the team assumes some of the leader's responsibility for providing emotional support to teammates and resolving conflict. He or she serves as a model of active listening when others are presenting. The people supporter helps others relax by smiling, making humorous comments, and appearing relaxed. However, the people supporter is not the team clown who attempts to defuse the seriousness of a situation. In contrast, he or she is a model of etiquette and professionalism.

The people supporter reinforces the views of other team members with whom he or she agrees. Most team players find this to be a comfortable role. What distinguishes people supporters is their willingness to also support and encourage team members with whom they disagree. The people supporter believes that anybody who is serious about his or her position on an issue deserves encouragement. By receiving encouragement now, the person is more likely to contribute ideas in the future.

CHALLENGER

To prevent complacency and groupthink, a team needs one or more members who confront and challenge bad ideas. The *challenger* fills this role if he or she has effective enough interpersonal skills to fill the role successfully. Antagonistic, attack-style people who attempt the challenger role lose their credibility quickly. A challenger will criticize any decision or preliminary thinking of the team that is deficient in any way, including being ethically unsound. An accomplished challenger will even criticize the methods and decision-making process of a team.

Here is a transcript of a portion of a team meeting in which Ruth is the challenger. Carlos is the team leader. The team was formed within a service organization to develop suggestions for reducing costs throughout the organization.

Carlos: We've been gathering information for a month now. It's about time we heard some of the specific suggestions.

Jack: At the top of my list is cutting pension benefits. Our pension payments are higher than those required by law. Our medical benefits are way above average. If we cut back on pension benefits, no current employees would be adversely affected.

Melissa: I like your analysis, Jack. No sense risking laying off employees just to keep retirees happy.

Jordan: We should first make absolutely certain there are no legal complications here. Then we can sharpen our cost-cutting knives and dig right in.

Gunther: I'll support cutting pension benefits. It will probably reduce expenses more dramatically than the smaller ways to reduce expenses that I have uncovered.

Carlos: There seems to be consensus so far that we should look toward making recommendations about cutting pension benefits. Ruth, what do you think?

Ruth: I think it is much too early to reach consensus on such a sensitive issue. Cutting pension benefits would create panic in our retirees. Our older employees would also be screaming. We'll have an avalanche of negative publicity in the media.

Jordan: Hold on, Ruth. I said the team would first check out this idea with the legal department.

Ruth: Just because cutting pension benefits could squeeze by legally doesn't mean it's a good idea. We haven't studied enough of the negative ramifications of cutting pension benefits. Let's study this issue further before word leaks out that we're taking away the golden egg.

Carlos: Maybe Ruth has a point. Let's investigate this issue further before making a recommendation.

LISTENER

Listening to others is an important aspect of several team-player roles, including the people supporter. Nevertheless, listening contributes so substantially to team success that it comprises a separate role. If other people are not heard, the full contribution of team effort cannot be realized. Listening takes hard work and commitment, with the *listener* serving as a model for the rest of the group.

Some people neglect slipping into the listener role when appropriate and required because they are so preoccupied with their own points of view and agendas. Think back to recent meetings you have attended. Do you remember how some people start their counterargument before the speaker has finished his or her sentence? Another reason some team members do not listen is that they become closed-minded and defensive when their views are challenged.

The team leader must shift frequently into the listener role, as did Carlos when he listened carefully to Ruth's concerns about cutting the pension benefits. Other members of the team also must seize the opportunity to occupy the role of listener—one who listens intently to elicit information, understand the opinion or data being presented, and increase the satisfaction of another member.

As a result of being a listener, a team member or team leader is able to summarize discussion and progress for the team. So many details and varied points arise during team meetings that confusion may result. Members may ask themselves *"Where are we?"* or *"What's going on here?"* At other times, several group members may forget the purpose of the meeting.

MEDIATOR

Despite the good intentions of team effort, disputes within the group may become so intense or prolonged that two people no longer listen or respond to each other. The two antagonists develop such polarized viewpoints that they are unwilling to move toward each other's point of view. In addition, they have moved beyond the point that conciliation is effective. Instead, it becomes necessary for the team leader or a team member to mediate the dispute. The *mediator* attempts to resolve the conflict following (approximately) these steps:

1. Ask permission to interpret each position.

2. Interpret each side, and then ask both parties whether the interpretation is accurate.

3. Give each side the opportunity to edit or correct the statement of his or her position.

The mediator's intervention helps clarify for each side what the other side has said. In the heat of the dispute, each side may not have listened carefully to the other side. After the three-point intervention is completed, other members of the team can discuss the differences in viewpoints. Mediation makes a contribution because it can move a group away from being stuck and on to more productive activity.

GATEKEEPER

A recurring problem in group effort is that some members may fail to contribute because most of the time has been taken up by dominant team members. Even when the viewpoints of the timid team members have been expressed, they may not be remembered because one or two other members contribute so frequently to discussion. When the opportunity gate is closed to several members, the *gatekeeper* in the group intentionally opens the gate. The gatekeeper requests that a specific team member be allowed to contribute, or that his or her past contribution be recognized, with comments such as the following:

➤ "Alice has been trying for 15 minutes to make a point. We've all been talking so much that she hasn't found room to talk. I think it's Alice's turn."

➤ "Tom, you've been using much more than your share of our discussion time. Since this is a team effort, we need to hear from other people on the team also."

The many roles just presented overlap somewhat. For example, the process observer might engage in gatekeeper activities. Do not be concerned about the overlap. Instead, pick and choose from the many roles as the situation dictates—whether or not overlap exists. Skill-Building Exercise 4-1 gives you an opportunity to observe these roles in action.

The behavior associated with the roles just described is more important than remembering the labels. For example, remembering to help others resolve conflict in meetings is more important than remembering the specific label *mediator role*.

GUIDELINES FOR THE INTERPERSONAL ASPECTS OF TEAM PLAY

The purpose of this and the following section is to help you enhance your effectiveness as a team player by describing the skills, actions, and attitudes required to be an effective team player. You can regard these *behaviors* (the collective term for skills, actions, and attitudes) as goals for personal improvement. Identify the actions and attitudes for which you need the most improvement, and proceed accordingly with self-development. Apply the model for skill-development presented in Chapter 1.

One convenient method for classifying team activities in pursuit of goals is to categorize them as people-related or task-related. Remember, however, that the categorization of people- versus task-related activities is not entirely accurate. For example, if you are challenging your teammates with a difficult goal, are you focusing more on the people (offering them a motivational challenge) or the task (achieving the goal)? We begin first with people-related actions and attitudes, followed in the next section by task-related actions and attitudes.

TRUSTING TEAM MEMBERS

The cornerstone attitude of an outstanding team player is to trust team members, including the leader. Working on a team is akin to a small-business partnership. If you do not believe that the other team members have your best interests at heart, it will be difficult for you to share opinions and ideas. You will fear that others will make negative statements behind your back.

Trusting team members also includes believing that their ideas are technically sound and rational until proven otherwise. Another manifestation of trust is taking risks with others. You can take a risk by trying out one of their unproved ideas. You can also take a risk by submitting an unproved idea and not worrying about being ridiculed. Skill-Building Exercise 4-2 is a widely used trust-building exercise.

DISPLAYING A HIGH LEVEL OF COOPERATION AND COLLABORATION

Cooperation and collaboration are synonymous with teamwork. If you display a willingness to help others by working cooperatively with them, you will be

TEAM MEMBER ROLES

A team of approximately six people is formed to conduct a 20-minute meeting on a significant topic of their choosing. Possibilities include (a) a management team deciding on whether to lay off one-third of the workforce in order to increase profits, (b) a group of fans who have volunteered to find a new team mascot name to replace "Redskins," and (c) a community group attempting to launch an initiative to help battered adults and children.

While the team members are conducting their heated discussion, other class members make notes on which team members carry out which roles. Watching for the eight different roles can be divided among class members. For example, the people in the first row might look for examples of knowledge contributor. Use the role worksheet that follows to help make your observations. Summarize the comment that is indicative of the role. An example would be noting in the challenger category: "Linda said naming the team the 'Washington Rainbows' seems like too much of an attempt to be politically correct."

Knowledge contributor: _____

_____

_____

Process observer: _____

_____

_____

Collaborator: _____

_____

_____

People supporter: _____

_____

_____

Challenger: _____

_____

_____

Listener: _____

_____

_____

Mediator: _____

_____

_____

Gatekeeper: _____

_____

_____

Skill-Building Exercise 4-2

THE TRUST FALL

A standard part of outdoor training for team building and leadership is for people to experience being dependent upon other team members for their physical safety. One such trust builder is for a person to fall backward into the arms of teammates. If the person is not caught, he or she will sustain serious physical injury. (*Caution:* Excuse yourself from this exercise if you are currently injured, are suffering from circulatory or eye disease, or are pregnant.)

The class organizes into groups of six. Each group member takes a turn standing on a chair (a blindfold is optional). At the appropriate signal from a team member, the person falls backward into the arms of teammates. The fall can take place outdoors on a lawn, on the beach, or in the snow, or inside the classroom. After each person has taken a turn, discuss among yourselves the impact of this exercise on the development of trust. If time allows, conduct a class discussion of the advantages and disadvantages of the trust fall.

regarded as a team player. If you do not cooperate with other team members, the team structure breaks down. Collaboration at a team level refers to working jointly with others to solve mutual problems. Although working with another person on a given problem may take longer than working through a problem yourself, the long-term payoff is important. You have established a climate favorable to working on joint problems where collective action is necessary.

Achieving a cooperative team spirit is often a question of making the first move. Instead of grumbling about poor teamwork, take the initiative and launch a cooperative spirit in your group. Target the most individualistic, least cooperative member of the group. Ask the person for his or her input on an idea you are formulating. Thank the person, then state that you would be privileged to return the favor.

RECOGNIZING THE INTERESTS AND ACHIEVEMENTS OF OTHERS

A fundamental tactic for establishing yourself as a solid team player is to actively recognize the interests and achievements of others. Let others know you care about their interests. After you make a suggestion during a team meeting, ask: "Would my suggestion create any problems for anybody else?" or "How do my ideas fit into what you have planned?"

Recognizing the achievements of others is more straightforward than recognizing interests. Be prepared to compliment any tangible achievement. Give realistic compliments by making the compliment commensurate with the achievement. To do otherwise is to compromise your sincerity. For example, do not call someone a genius just because he or she showed you how to compute an exchange rate from one currency to another. Instead, you might say, "Thank you. I am very impressed by your knowledge of exchange rates."

GIVING HELPFUL CRITICISM

The outstanding team player offers constructive criticism when needed, but does so diplomatically. To do otherwise is to let down the team. A high-performance team demands sincere and tactful criticism among members. No matter how diplomatic you are, keep your ratio of criticism to praise small. Keep two time-tested principles in mind. First, attempt to criticize the person's work, not the person. It is better to say, "The conclusion is missing from your analysis" than "You left out the conclusion." (The latter statement hurts because it sounds like your teammate did something wrong.)

Another key guideline for criticism is to ask a question rather than to make a declarative statement. By answering a question, the person being criticized is involved in improving his or her work. In the example at hand, it would be effective to ask, "Do you think your report would have a greater impact if it contained a conclusion?" In this way, the person being criticized contributes a judgment about the conclusion. The person has a chance to say, "Yes, I will prepare a conclusion."

SHARING THE GLORY

An effective team player shares praise and other rewards for accomplishment even if he or she is the most deserving. Shared praise is usually merited to some extent because teammates have probably made at least some contribution to the achievement that received praise. For example, if a team member comes up with a powerful suggestion for cutting costs, it is likely that somebody else in the group sparked his or her thinking. Effective examples of sharing glory are easy to find. Think back to watching athletes and other entertainers who win a title or an award. Many of them are gracious enough to share the glory. Shortly after he retired, hockey legend Wayne Gretzky told a television reporter, "I never would have accomplished what I did if I hadn't played with such a great group of guys."

TAKING CARE NOT TO RAIN
ON ANOTHER PERSON'S PARADE

As teamwork specialist Pamela Lovel observes, we all have achievements and accomplishments that are sources of pride. Belittling the achievements of others for no legitimate reason brings about tension and anger. Suppress your feelings of petty jealousy.[11] An example would be saying to someone who is proudly describing an accomplishment, "Don't take too much credit. It looks to me like you were at the right place at the right time." If you support teammates by acknowledging their accomplishments, you are more likely to receive their support when needed.

GUIDELINES FOR THE TASK ASPECTS OF TEAM PLAY

The task aspects of team play also make a key contribution to becoming an effective team player. Here we describe five major task-related tactics. As mentioned earlier, a task aspect usually has interpersonal consequences.

TECHNICAL EXPERTISE (OR KNOWLEDGE OF THE TASK)

Most people are selected for a work team primarily because of their technical expertise. *Technical* refers to the intimate details of any task, not just tasks in engineering, physical science, and information technology. The sales promotion specialist on a product development team has technical expertise about sales promotion, whether or not sales promotion requires knowledge of engineering or computers.

As team consultant Glenn Parker observes, to use your technical expertise to outstanding advantage you must have the willingness to share that expertise.[12] Some experts perceive their esoteric knowledge as a source of power. As a consequence, they are hesitant to let others share their knowledge for fear of relinquishing power. It is also necessary for the technical expert to be able to communicate with team members in other disciplines who lack the same technical background. The technical person who cannot explain the potential value of his or her contribution may not receive much attention.

ASSUMING RESPONSIBILITY FOR PROBLEMS

The outstanding team player assumes responsibilities for problems. If a problem is not yet assigned to anybody, he or she says, "I'll do it." One team member might note that true progress on the team's effort is blocked until the team benchmarks (compares itself) with other successful teams. The effective team player might say, "You are right, we need to benchmark. If it's okay with everybody else, I'll get started on the benchmarking project tomorrow. It will be my responsibility." Taking responsibility must be combined with dependability. The person who takes responsibility for a task must produce, time after time.

SEEING THE BIG PICTURE

Effective team players need to think conceptually, or see the big picture. A trap in team effort is that discussion can get bogged down in small details and the team might lose sight of what it is trying to accomplish. The team player (including the team leader) who can help the group focus on its broader purpose plays a vital role. The following case history illustrates what it means to see the big picture.

A sales process improvement team was asked to make it easier for customers to purchase office equipment when they visited the company's retail center. Under the existing process, five different people had to handle the sales transaction. The customer was often kept waiting for up to an hour. During its second meeting, the team vented its hostility toward the warehouse specialists. As the conversation became more heated, several team members discussed documenting all the problems created by the warehouse personnel and then reporting them to the vice president of marketing. As emotions intensified, several team members ridiculed the warehouse workers.

Beth, the store manager and one of the team members, helped the group step back and see the big picture. She challenged the group in these words: "Hold on. Why are we here? Is our purpose to improve the sales process or to attack the very people who keep items for sale in stock?" The team accepted the suggestion and praised Beth for her contribution. The team then refocused its effort on reducing the paperwork required to complete a sales transaction.

BELIEVING IN CONSENSUS

A major task-related attitude for outstanding team play is to believe that consensus has merit. **Consensus** is general acceptance of a decision by the group. Every member may not be thrilled about the decision, yet they are not opposed and are willing to support the decision. Believing that consensus is valuable enables you to participate fully in team decisions without thinking that you have sacrificed your beliefs or the right to think independently. To believe in consensus is to believe that the democratic process has relevance for organizations and that ideal solutions are not always possible.

HELPING TEAM MEMBERS DO THEIR JOBS BETTER

Your stature as a team player will increase if you take the initiative to help coworkers make needed work improvements. Helping other team members with their work assignments is a high-level form of cooperation. Make the suggestions in a constructive spirit rather than displaying an air of superiority. Identify a problem that a coworker is having, and then suggest alternatives he or she might be interested in exploring. Avoid saying to team members that they "should" do something, because many people become defensive when told what they should do. The term *should* is usually perceived as a moral judgment given to one person by another, such as being told that you should save money, should learn a second language, or should improve your math skills.

Skill-Building Exercise 4-3 will help you integrate the many suggestions presented here for developing teamwork skills.

SUMMARY

To be successful in the modern organization it is necessary to be an effective team player. Team members have complementary skills and are committed to a common purpose. All teams have some elements in common, but three key types of teams are self-managing work teams, cross-functional teams, and virtu-

Skill-Building Exercise 4-3

HABITAT FOR THE HOMELESS

Organize the class into teams of about six people. Each team takes on the assignment of formulating plans for building temporary shelters for the homeless. The task will take about one hour and can be done inside or outside of class. The dwellings you plan to build, for example, might be two-room cottages with electricity and indoor plumbing.

During the time allotted to the task, formulate plans for going ahead with Habitat for the Homeless. Consider dividing up work by assigning certain roles to each team member. Sketch out tentative answers to the following questions:

1. How will you obtain funding for your venture?
2. Which homeless people will you help?
3. Where will your shelters be located?
4. Who will do the actual construction?

After your plan is completed, evaluate the quality of the teamwork that took place within the group. Specify which teamwork skills were evident and which ones did not surface. Search the chapter for techniques you might use to improve teamwork.

al teams. (A virtual team does most of its work electronically instead of in face-to-face meetings.)

Groups and teams offer such advantages as synergy, avoiding major errors, and increased acceptance of and commitment to decisions. Working in groups can also enhance job satisfaction. Groups and teams also have disadvantages, such as more talk than action, conformity in thinking and action, social loafing, and the creation of conflict. A serious potential problem is groupthink, whereby bad decisions are made as a by-product of strong consensus. Key characteristics of effective work groups are outlined in Figure 4-1.

An important part of being an effective team player is to choose effective roles. The roles studied here are knowledge contributor, process observer, collaborator, people supporter, challenger, listener, mediator, and gatekeeper.

Guidelines for effectively contributing to the interpersonal aspects of team play include (a) trusting team members, (b) displaying a high level of cooperation and collaboration, (c) recognizing the interests and achievements of others, (d) giving helpful criticism, (e) sharing the glory, and (f) taking care not to rain on another person's parade.

Guidelines for effectively contributing to the task aspects of team play include (a) providing technical expertise, (b) assuming responsibility for problems, (c) seeing the big picture, (d) believing in consensus, and (e) helping team members do their jobs better.

QUESTIONS FOR DISCUSSION AND REVIEW

1. Part of being a good team player is helping other members. How can members of a workplace team help each other?

2. How do team members know when they have achieved synergy?

3. What should the other team members do when they uncover a social loafer?

4. What is the potential downside of heavily emphasizing the knowledge contributor role?

5. Explain the difference between the hard side and soft side of contributing to team effort.

6. How can the challenger role backfire for a person?

7. Why is it important for the team leader to frequently occupy the listener role?

8. How effective do you think the "trust fall" really is in building trust among team members?

9. The "little picture" in studying this chapter is learning details about teamwork skills. What is the "big picture"?

10. How can a person achieve individual recognition yet still be a team player?

THE UNBALANCED TEAM

Fidelity Protection Systems is one of the largest home and small-business security system distributors in its city, with annual sales of $18 million. Two years ago, Jim Maxwell, the vice president of marketing and sales, reorganized the sales force. Previously the sales force consisted of inside sales representatives (who took care of phone-in orders) and outside sales representatives (who called on accounts). The reorganization divided the outside sales force into two groups: direct sales and major accounts. The direct-sales representatives were made responsible for small commercial customers and individual homeowners. As before, they would service existing customers and prospect for new accounts. Servicing existing customers usually involves adding fire protection to burglary protection and upgrading the burglary systems.

Three of the people who were direct-sales representatives were promoted to major account executives. The account executives would service Fidelity's largest accounts, including prospecting for new business within those accounts. An example would be expanding the security system to other stores of a retailer. To promote teamwork and cooperation, Maxwell assigned group sales quotas to the account representatives. Collectively, their goal was to bring in 21 new large accounts per month.

Given that the sales quota was a group quota, the account representatives were supposed to work together on strategy for acquiring new accounts. If a particular account executive did not have the expertise to handle his or her customer's problems, another account executive was supposed to offer help. Brian Jones, for example, was the resident expert on the unique security problems of warehouses. If invited, Brian would join one of the two other account executives to call on a customer who owned a warehouse.

After the new sales organization had been in place 19 months, Karen Klein, an account executive, was having lunch with Larry Starks, the manufacturing director at Fidelity. "I've about had it," said Karen, "I'm tired of single-handedly carrying the team."

"What do you mean you are single-handedly carrying the team?" asked Larry.

"You're a trusted friend, Larry. So let me lay out the facts. Each month the group is supposed to bring in 21 new sales. If we don't average those 21 sales per month, we don't get our semi-annual bonus. That represents about 25 percent of my income. So a big chunk of my money comes from group effort.

"My average number of new accounts brought in for the last 12 months has been 11. And we are averaging about 18 new sales per month. This translates into the other account execs averaging about 7 sales among them. I'm carrying the group, but overall sales are still below quota. This means I didn't get my bonus last month.

"The other account execs are friendly and helpful in writing up proposals. But they just don't bring in their share of accounts."

Larry asked, "What does your boss say about this?"

"I've had several conversations with him about the problem. He tells me to be patient and to remember that the development of a fully balanced team requires time. He also tells me that I should develop a stronger team spirit. My problem is that I can't pay my bills with team spirit."

Case Questions

1. What does this case illustrate about teamwork?

2. What role or roles is Karen Klein occupying in the group?

3. What teamwork behaviors is Karen demonstrating?

4. What teamwork behaviors is Karen not demonstrating?

5. To what extent are Karen's complaints justifiable?

Chapter 5

Group Problem Solving and Decision Making

Learning Objectives

After reading and studying this chapter and doing the exercises you should be able to

➤ Understand the difference between rational and political decision making.

➤ Use the general approach to problem-solving groups.

➤ Make effective use of brainstorming.

➤ Recognize the potential contribution of electronic brainstorming.

➤ Make effective use of the nominal group technique.

➤ Understand how to increase the efficiency of group problem solving through e-mail and groupware.

The vice president of human resources at a consumer products company announced to the human resources staff that they would be receiving an average raise of 5 percent for the year. "Sounds great," said Melissa Olsten, the director of training. "But how is management deciding who gets how much? I take it we are not all going to receive the same 5 percent raise."

With an excited expression, the vice president replied, "You people are an empowered group of professionals. You will decide how to divide up the pool of money available for raises." Surprised but delighted with the answer to her question, Melissa took the initiative to ask the group to set aside time for a three-hour meeting. The goal of the problem-solving session would be to decide how to divide up the money allocated for the raises. Several of the group members were apprehensive, but they realized that here was a chance to engage in meaningful group decision making.

The case example just presented illustrates an increasingly important aspect of interpersonal relations in organizations: Many key problems are solved by groups. Part of having high-level interpersonal skills is the ability to work closely with others in solving problems and making decisions. This chapter will enhance your group problem-solving and decision-making skills. You will receive guidelines for applying several major group problem-solving methods. As a starting point in studying these techniques, first think through your present level of receptiveness toward group problem solving by doing Self-Assessment Quiz 5-1.

RATIONAL VERSUS POLITICAL DECISION MAKING IN GROUPS

Group decision making is the process of reaching a judgment based on feedback from more than one individual.[1] Most people involved in group problem solving may share the same purpose in agreeing on a solution and making a decision. Nevertheless, they may have different agendas and use different methods. Two such different approaches to group decision making are the rational model and the political model.

The *rational decision-making model* is the traditional, logical approach to decision making, based on the scientific method. It is grounded in establishing goals, establishing alternatives, examining consequences, and hoping for optimum results. The search for optimum results is based on an economic view of decision making—the idea that people hope to maximize gain and minimize loss when making a decision. For example, a work team would choose the lowest cost/highest quality supplier even though the team leader was good friends with the sales representative of a competitor.

The rational model also assumes that each alternative is evaluated in terms of how well it contributes to reaching the goals involved in making the decision. For example, if one of the goals in relocating a factory was to reduce energy costs and taxes, each alternative would be carefully examined in terms of its

Self-Assessment Quiz 5-1

MY PROBLEM-SOLVING TENDENCIES

Directions: Describe how well you agree with the following statements. Use the following scale: Disagree strongly (DS); Disagree (D); Neutral (N); Agree (A); Agree strongly (AS).

	DS	D	N	A	AS
1. Before reaching a final decision on a matter of significance, I like to discuss it with one or more other people.	1	2	3	4	5
2. If I'm facing a major decision, I like to get away from others to think it through.	5	4	3	2	1
3. I get lonely working by myself.	1	2	3	4	5
4. Two heads are better than one.	1	2	3	4	5
5. A wide range of people should be consulted before an executive makes a major decision	1	2	3	4	5
6. To arrive at a creative solution to a problem it is best to rely on a group.	1	2	3	4	5
7. From what I've seen so far, group decision making is a waste of time.	5	4	3	2	1
8. Most great ideas stem from the solitary effort of great thinkers.	5	4	3	2	1
9. Important legal cases should be decided by a jury rather than by a judge.	1	2	3	4	5
10. Individuals are better suited than groups to solve technical problems.	5	4	3	2	1

Total Score _____

Scoring and Interpretation: Add the numbers you circled to obtain your total score.

46–50   You have strong positive attitudes toward group problem solving and decision making. You will therefore adapt well to the decision-making techniques widely used in organizations. Be careful, however, not to neglect your individual problem-solving skills.

30–45   You have neutral attitudes toward group problem solving and decision making. You may need to remind yourself that group problem solving is well accepted in business.

10–29   You much prefer individual to group decision making. Retain your pride in your ability to think independently, but do not overlook the contribution of group problem solving and decision making. You may need to develop more patience for group problem solving and decision making.

tax and energy consequences. A team member might say, "Setting up a factory in the Phoenix area sounds great. It's true that taxes are low, the labor market is wonderful, and we won't lose any days to snow emergencies. But did you know that the energy costs are very high because of the amount of air conditioning required?"

The *political decision-making model* assumes that people bring preconceived notions and biases into the decision-making situation. Because the decision makers are politically motivated (a focus on satisfying one's own interests), the individuals often do not make the most rational choice. In the relocation example at hand, two of the members may say "Thumbs up to Phoenix" for reasons that satisfy their own needs. One team member might be fascinated with the American Indian culture so prevalent in Arizona and therefore want to move to Phoenix. Another member might have retired parents living in Phoenix and be interested in living near them.

People who use the political model may operate on the basis of incomplete information. Facts and figures that conflict with personal biases and preferences might get blocked out of memory or rationalized away. A team member might say, "Those air conditioning costs are exaggerated. I have heard that if you use thermal pumps in a factory, the cooling costs go way down."

In practice, it is sometimes difficult to determine whether a decision maker is being rational or political. Have you ever noticed that many hotels do not have a 13th floor? The reason is both rational and political. The hotel manager might say rationally, "Many people are superstitious about the number 13, so they will refuse to take a room on the 13th floor. So if we want to maximize room use, the rational decision for us is to label the 13th floor as 14. In this way we will avoid the irrational (political) thinking of guests."

Whether groups approach their decisions rationally or politically, it is helpful to look at a sampling of the problems work groups tackle. Figure 5-1 presents a list of the specific types of decisions often made by self-managing work teams. Group problem solving is the rule in carrying out these activities, because work teams are designed to be democratic. For example, a highly empowered work team might decide which one of its members should be the next team leader.

GUIDELINES FOR USING GENERAL PROBLEM-SOLVING GROUPS

When team members get together to solve a problem, they typically hold a discussion rather than rely on formal problem-solving techniques. Several team members might attempt to clarify the true nature of the problem, and a search then begins for an acceptable solution. Although this technique can be effective, the probability of solving the problem well (and therefore making the right decision) increases when the team follows a systematic procedure. The following guidelines represent a time-tested way of solving problems and making decisions within a group.[2] You may recognize these steps as having much in common with the scientific method. The same steps are therefore ideal for following the rational decision making.

Assume that you are a team member of a small business that distributes food supplies to hospitals, nursing homes, and schools. Your business volume is adequate, but you have a cash-flow problem because some of your customers

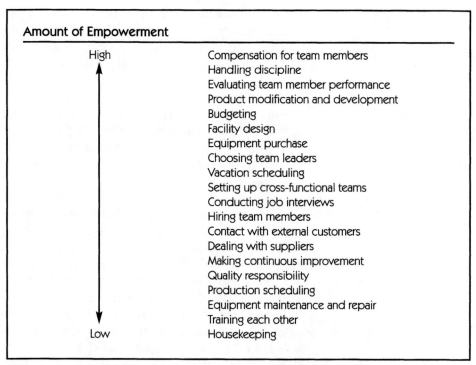

Figure 5-1 Problem-Solving and Decision-Making Topics for Work Teams

Source: Based on information in Richard S. Wellins, William C. Byham, and Jeanne M. Wilson, *Empowered Teams: Creating Self-Directed Work Groups That Improve Quality, Productivity, and Participation* (San Francisco: Jossey-Bass, 1991), p. 26; Carla Johnson, "Teams at Work," *HR Magazine*, May 1999, pp. 30–36.

take over 30 days to pay their bills. Here is how problem solving would proceed following the steps for effective group problem solving and decision making:

1. *Identify the problem.* Describe specifically what the problem is and how it manifests itself. The surface problem is that some customers are paying their bills late. Your company's ultimate problem is that it does not have enough cash on hand to pay expenses.

2. *Clarify the problem.* If group members do not see the problem the same way, they will offer divergent solutions to their own individual perceptions of the problem. To some team members, late payments may simply mean the company has less cash in the bank. As a result, the company earns a few dollars less in interest. Someone else on the team might perceive the problem as mostly an annoyance and inconvenience. Another person may perceive late payers as being immoral and therefore want to penalize them. The various perceptions of the problem solvers contribute to their exercising a political model of decision making. It is important for the group to reach consensus that the ultimate problem is not enough cash on hand to run the business, as explained in Step 1.

3. *Analyze the cause.* To convert what exists into what they want, the group must understand the cause of the specific problems and find ways to overcome the causes. Late payment of bills (over 30 days) can be caused by several factors. The customers may have cash-flow problems of their own, they may have slow-moving bureaucratic procedures, or they may be understaffed. Another possibility is that the slow-paying customers are dissatisfied with the service and are holding back on payments in retaliation. Research, including interviewing customers, may be needed to analyze the cause or causes.

4. *Search for alternative solutions.* Remember that multiple alternative solutions can be found to most problems. The alternative solutions you choose will depend on your analysis of the causes. Assume that you did not find customers to be dissatisfied with your service, but that they were slow in paying bills for a variety of reasons. Your team then gets into a creative mode by developing a number of alternatives. Among them are offering bigger discounts for quick payment, dropping slow-paying customers, sending out your own bills more promptly, and using follow-up phone calls to bring in money. Another possibility would be to set up a line of credit that would enable your firm to make short-term loans to cover expenses until your bills were paid.

5. *Select alternatives.* Identify the criteria that solutions should meet; then discuss the pros and cons of the proposed alternatives. No solution should be laughed at or scorned. Specifying the criteria that proposed solutions should meet requires you to think deeply about your goals. For example, your team might establish the following criteria for solutions: that they (a) improve cash flow, (b) do not lose customers, (c) do not cost much to implement, and (d) do not make the company appear desperate. The pros and cons of each proposed alternative can be placed on a flip chart, chalkboard, or computer screen.

6. *Plan for implementation.* Decide what actions are necessary to carry out the chosen solution to the problem. Suppose your group decides that establishing a bank line of credit is the most feasible alternative. The company president or the chief financial officer might then meet with a couple of local banks to apply for a line of credit at the most favorable rate. Your group also chooses to initiate a program of friendly follow-up telephone calls to encourage more rapid payment.

7. *Clarify the contract.* The contract is a restatement of what group members have agreed to do and deadlines for accomplishment. In your situation, several team members are involved in establishing a line of credit and initiating a system of follow-up phone calls.

8. *Develop an action plan.* Specify who does what and when to carry out the contract. Each person involved in implementing alternatives develops an action plan in detail that stems logically from the previous step.

9. *Provide for evaluation and accountability.* After the plan is implemented, reconvene to discuss progress and to hold people accountable for results that have not been achieved. In the situation at hand, progress will be measured in at least two objective ways. You can evaluate by accounting measures whether the cash-flow problem has improved and whether the average cycle time on accounts receivable has decreased.

The steps for effective group problem solving are best applied to complex problems. Straightforward problems of minor consequence (such as deciding on holiday decorations for the office) do not require all the steps. Nevertheless, remember that virtually every problem has more than one feasible alternative. For practice in using the steps just described, do Skill-Building Exercise 5-1.

GUIDELINES FOR BRAINSTORMING

In many work situations, groups are expected to produce creative and imaginative solutions to problems. When the organization is seeking a large number of alternatives for solving the problems, **brainstorming** is often the technique of choice. Brainstorming is a group problem-solving technique that promotes creativity by encouraging idea generation through noncritical discussion. The basic technique is to encourage unrestrained and spontaneous participation by group members. The term *brainstorm* has become so widely known that it is often used as a synonym for a clever idea.

Brainstorming is used both as a method of finding alternatives to real-life problems and as a creativity-training program. In the usual form of brainstorming, group members spontaneously call out alternative solutions to a problem facing them. Any member is free to enhance or "hitchhike" upon the contribution of another person. At the end of the session, somebody sorts out the ideas and edits the more unrefined ones.

Brainstorming is widely used to develop new ideas for products, find names for products, develop advertising slogans, and solve customer problems. For instance, the idea for luxury sport utility vehicles (SUVs) emerged from a brainstorming session. Brainstorming has also been used to develop a new organization structure in a government agency, and it is now widely used in developing software.

Adhering to a few simple rules or guidelines helps ensure that creative alternative solutions to problems will be forthcoming. The brainstorming process usually falls into place without frequent reminders about guidelines. Nevertheless, here are eight rules to improve the chances of having a good session:

1. *Group size should be about five to seven people.* If there are too few people, not enough suggestions are generated; if there are too many people, the session becomes uncontrolled. However, brainstorming can be conducted with as few as three people.

2. *Everybody is given the chance to suggest alternative solutions.* Members spontaneously call out alternatives to the problem facing the group. (Another approach is for people to speak in sequence.)

3. *No criticism is allowed.* All suggestions should be welcome; it is particularly important not to use derisive laughter.

4. *Freewheeling is encouraged.* Outlandish ideas often prove quite useful. It's easier to tame a wild idea than to originate one.

5. *Quantity and variety are very important.* The greater the number of ideas put forth, the greater the likelihood of a breakthrough idea.

6. *Combinations and improvements are encouraged.* Building upon the ideas of others, including combining them, is very productive. "Hitchhiking" or "piggybacking" is an essential part of brainstorming.

7. *Notes must be taken during the session by a person who serves as the recording secretary.* The session can also be taped, but this requires substantial time to retrieve ideas.

8. *Do not overstructure by following any of the seven ideas too rigidly.* Brainstorming is a spontaneous group process.

Brainstorming is an effective technique for finding a large number of alternatives to problems, particularly when the list of alternatives is subsequently refined and edited. Brainstorming in groups is also valuable, because it contributes to job satisfaction for many people. Skill-Building Exercise 5-2 gives you an opportunity to practice a commercially useful application of brainstorming.

Skill Building Exercise 5-2

1-800-INSIGHT

Using conventional brainstorming, huddle in small groups. Your task is to develop 800, 888, or 900 numbers for firms in various enterprises. Keep in mind that the best 800, 888, or 900 numbers are easy to memorize and have a logical connection to the goods or services provided. After each group makes up its list of telephone numbers (approximately five for each firm on the list), compare results with the other groups. Here is the list of nationwide enterprises:·

➤ A chain of funeral homes

➤ A heating and air-conditioning firm

➤ A software problem help line for Microsoft Corp.

➤ A used-car chain

➤ A dial-a-laugh service (a 900 number)

➤ An introduction (dating) service (a 900 number)

A curious feature of brainstorming is that individuals working alone typically produce more useful ideas than those placed in a group. Brainstorming by individuals working alone is referred to as **brainwriting**. When electronic brainstorming is described in the next section, we will analyze why some people generate fewer ideas in a group setting. Skill-Building Exercise 5-3 gives you a chance to compare brainstorming with brainwriting.

GUIDELINES FOR ELECTRONIC BRAINSTORMING

A promising electronic procedure has been developed to overcome the limitations of conventional brainstorming in groups. First, we will examine problems with brainstorming more carefully; then we will describe electronic brainstorming.

LIMITATIONS TO VERBAL BRAINSTORMING

The full potential of brainstorming has been held back by three forces that block production of ideas: evaluation apprehension, free riding, and inhibiting procedures.[3] Being aware of these production-blocking mechanisms can help you improve your skill in brainstorming.

Evaluation apprehension means that many people are unwilling to come forth with some of their ideas because they fear being critically evaluated. This fear may be intensified when people are told that the group is being observed and rated or that experts are in the group. (Did you notice any evaluation apprehension in the brainstorming exercise?) When people work by themselves—and do not have to present their ideas to the larger group—they will have less evaluation apprehension.

Skill Building Exercise 5-3

BRAINSTORMING VERSUS BRAINWRITING

Half the class is organized into brainstorming groups of about six people. The rest of the class work by themselves. Groups and individuals then work on the same problems for 10 minutes. The brainstorming groups follow the aforementioned guidelines. Individuals jot down as many alternatives as come to mind without interacting with other people. After the problem-solving sessions are completed, compare the alternatives developed by the groups and individuals.

Groups and individuals choose one of the following problems so that solutions can be compared to the same problems:

1. How might we effectively utilize the senior citizens in our community?

2. How can we earn extra money, aside from holding a regular job?

3. How can we find new people to date?

4. How can we save money on food costs?

5. How can we save money on gasoline?

Free riding is just about the same behavior as social loafing. Free riders do not work as hard in a group as they would if they worked alone. They are willing to let the next person do the heavy thinking. A reason offered for free riding is that being an outstanding contributor in a group carries no larger reward than being a noncontributor. A person generating ideas alone would not have the opportunity to free ride.

An *inhibiting procedure* in verbal brainstorming is that only one person can speak at a time. This limits the idea generation and production time available to group members. As a result some people forget what they wanted to say because they were listening to others. They might also ignore the ideas of others because they are rehearsing what they want to say. Furthermore, they will hold back on ideas that are redundant.

THE ELECTRONIC BRAINSTORMING PROCEDURE

A recent development designed to overcome the problem of production blocking in brainstorming is **electronic brainstorming**. Using this method, group members simultaneously enter their suggestions into a computer, and the ideas are distributed to the screens of other group members. Although the group members do not talk to each other, they are still able to build on each other's ideas and combine ideas.

Electronic brainstorming allows members to enter their ideas whenever they want, while sending along their ideas anonymously. These two features reduce the inhibitions caused by waiting for other people and by fear of negative evaluations.

During electronic brainstorming, individuals work in face-to-face groups, typically seated around a U-shaped table. Each group member has a computer terminal connected to all the other terminals and a monitor. *Electronic Brainstorming* is the title of representative software for this activity. The software enables individuals to enter their ideas anonymously as those ideas occur to them. (Good keyboarding skills are essential to keep up with the group.)

Every time an individual enters an idea, a random set of the group's ideas is entered on the individual's monitor. Individuals can access other random sets of ideas by pressing a specified function key. Accessing the other ideas can stimulate the person's own generation of new ideas and also allows for piggybacking.

An experiment with electronic brainstorming indicated that, with large groups, the method produces more useful ideas than does verbal brainstorming (the usual type). In the study, a four-person electronic brainstorming group produced more nonredundant ideas than verbal groups (traditional brainstorming). The group also produced more ideas than nonelectronic groups who did not interact with people.[4]

Electronic brainstorming researcher Keng L. Siau suggests that brainstorming via e-mail can increase both the quantity and quality of ideas. When participants do not face each other directly, they can concentrate more on the creativity task at hand and less on the interpersonal aspects of interaction.[5]

If your school or employer is equipped with an electronic brainstorming capability, you are encouraged to try the procedure. Setting up such a capability is costly, however. Next, we describe a low-cost manual (nonelectronic) procedure that offers many of the advantages of electronic brainstorming. In addition, you will be able to test the procedure yourself.

GUIDELINES FOR THE NOMINAL GROUP TECHNIQUE

A team leader or other manager who must make a decision about an important issue sometimes needs to know what alternatives are available and how people would react to them. In such cases, group input may be helpful. Verbal brainstorming is not advisable, because the problem is still in the exploration phase and requires more than a list of alternative solutions.

A problem-solving technique called the **nominal group technique (NGT)** has been developed to fit the situation. The NGT is a group problem-solving technique that calls people together in a structured meeting with limited interaction. The group is called *nominal* (in name only) because people first present their ideas without interacting with each other, as they would in a *real* group. (This aspect of the nominal group technique is incorporated into electronic brainstorming.) However, group discussion does take place at a later stage in the process.

A problem that is an appropriate candidate for NGT is a decision about which suppliers or vendors should be eliminated. Many companies are shrinking their number of suppliers because they believe that working with a smaller number of suppliers can lead to higher quality components. It is easier to train a small number of suppliers, and it is also possible to build better working relationships when fewer people are involved.

A decision of this type can lead to hurt feelings and breaking up of old friendships. Suppose Pedro Ortiz, the team leader, is empowered to make this decision about reducing the number of suppliers. The nominal group technique is followed by using a six-step decision process.

1. Work-team members are assembled because they will all participate in the decision to reduce the number of companies that serve as suppliers to the team. All team members are told in advance of the meeting and the agenda. The meeting is called, and an office assistant is invited to help take care of the administrative details of the meeting.

2. The team leader presents a specific question. Ortiz tells the group, "Top management says we have to reduce our number of suppliers by two-thirds. It's too difficult to keep track of all these different suppliers and train them to meet our quality specs. I dislike terminating a supplier as much as anybody, but I can understand the logic of top management. Right now our team is doing business with 12 suppliers, and we should shrink that number to 4. Your assignment is to develop criteria for choosing which suppliers to eliminate. I also need to know how you feel about the decision you make on supplier reduction and how it might affect the operations of our team."

3. Individual team members write down their ideas independently, without speaking to other members. Using notepads, the five team members write down their ideas about reducing the number of suppliers by two-thirds.

4. Each team member in turn presents one idea to the group. The group does not discuss the ideas. The office assistant summarizes each idea by writing it on a flip chart. Here are the ideas submitted by each team member:

Alternative A. We'll carefully study the prices offered by all 12 suppliers. The 8 suppliers with the highest average prices for comparable goods are given the boot. I like this idea because our team will save the company a bundle of money.

Alternative B. Let's keep the 4 suppliers who have the best quality record. We'll ask each supplier if they have won a quality award. If a supplier has won a quality award, the company is put on the retained list. We'll include awards from their customers or outside standards such as ISO 9000. If we find more than 4 of the suppliers have won awards, we'll retain those with the most impressive awards.

Alternative C. I say we reward good service. We keep the 4 suppliers among the 12 who have been the most prompt with deliveries. We'll also take into account how good the suppliers have been about accepting returns of damaged or defective merchandise.

Alternative D. Here's an opportunity to get in good with top management. Stop kidding each other. We know that the plant's general manager [Jake] has his favorite suppliers. Some of them are his fishing and golfing buddies. The suppliers who are friends with Jake get our vote. In this way, Jake will think our team shows really good judgment.

Alternative E. Let's reward the suppliers who have served us best. We'll rate each supplier on a 1 to 10 scale on three dimensions: the quality of goods they have provided us, price, and service in terms of prompt delivery and returns policy. We could do the ratings in less than one hour.

5. After each team member has presented his or her idea, the group clarifies and evaluates the suggestions. The length of the discussion for each of the ideas varies substantially. For example, the idea about rating suppliers on three criteria might precipitate a 30-minute discussion. The discussion about retaining the plant manager's political connections might last only 5 minutes.

6. The meeting ends with a silent, independent rating of the alternatives. The final group decision is the pooled outcome of the individual votes. The team members are instructed to rate each alternative on a 1 to 10 scale, with 10 being the most favorable rating. The ratings that follow are the *pooled ratings* (the sum of the individual ratings) received for each alternative. The maximum score is 50 (10 points $\times$ 5 raters).

Alternative A, price alone: 35

Alternative B, quality-award record: 30

Alternative C, good service: 39

Alternative D, plant manager's favorites: 14

Alternative E, combination of quality, price, and service: 44

Team leader Ortiz agrees with the group's preference for choosing the four suppliers with the best combination of quality, price, and service. He schedules a meeting to decide which suppliers meet these standards. Ortiz brings the team's recommendations to the plant manager, and they are accepted. Although the team is empowered to make the decision, it is still brought to management for final approval. To practice the nominal group technique, do Skill-Building Exercise 5-4.

USING STAND-UP MEETINGS TO FACILITATE PROBLEM SOLVING

Problem solving and decision making can sometimes be improved by conducting meetings while standing up instead of sitting down. The general idea is that participants standing up in the problem-solving group are likely to be more alert and will come to a decision more quickly. Some people solve problems bet-

Skill Building Exercise 5-4

THE NOMINAL GROUP TECHNIQUE

With a clear understanding of the mechanics of the NGT as described in the text, the technique can be demonstrated in about 30 minutes. The class is divided into groups of about seven. One person plays the role of the team leader, who can also assume the responsibility of the office assistant (recording information on flip charts).

You are the key members of a motion picture and television film production company. You have a contract to produce a series of four action films. The problem you face is which North American (U.S., Canadian, or Mexican) city to choose as the film site. The president has ruled out Hollywood because expenses are too high. Solve this problem using the NGT, and make a decision about which city to choose for your film site.

ter when standing because they literally "think well on their feet." Few people would be willing to stand for several hours, so they reach a decision quickly.

Many meeting leaders who use stand-up meetings are pleased with the results in terms of reaching high-quality decisions rapidly. For example, a team of researchers decided to investigate the validity of their observations.[6] Study participants were 555 students in an introduction to management course who were offered extra credit for participating in the study. The students were randomly assigned to five-person groups, producing 111 groups. They were divided almost equally into stand-up and sit-down groups.

All groups were assigned the Lost on the Moon exercise, which presents a scenario involving a crash on the moon. Participants were asked to rank 15 pieces of equipment that survived the crash in terms of their importance for survival. Correct answers to the problem were the ranking of the equipment given by NASA astronauts and scientists. The major results of the experiment were as follows:

1. Sit-down meetings lasted about 34 percent longer than the stand-up meetings (788 seconds versus 589 seconds).

2. Sit-down and stand-up meetings made decisions of equal quality.

3. More suggestions about task accomplishment were used by groups in the sit-down than in the stand-up meetings.

4. Participants in the sit-down meetings were more satisfied than participants in the stand-up meetings.

One implication for this study is that people make decisions more quickly when standing up, without sacrificing decision quality. However, people prefer to sit down. In general, if you think that a task can be performed in 30 minutes or less, a stand-up meeting is likely to be effective.

USING E-MAIL AND GROUPWARE TO FACILITATE GROUP DECISION MAKING

The presence of so many teams in the workplace means that people must work collectively and that they must make decisions together. An obvious require-ment of group decision making is that group members have to engage in col-lective effort. Collective effort usually translates into meetings. Without any meetings, people are working primarily on their own and thus are not benefit-ing from working in teams. Yet with too many meetings it is difficult to accom-plish individual work such as making telephone calls, analyzing information, and preparing reports.

Appropriate use of e-mail and groupware can facilitate interaction among team members and group decision making, while at the same time minimizing the number of meetings. (**Groupware** is technology designed to facilitate the work of groups.) Such use of e-mail and other electronic tools makes possible the virtual teams described earlier in the chapter.

USING E-MAIL TO FACILITATE MEETINGS

By using e-mail, team members can feed important information to all other members of the team without the ritual of entering a meeting and passing around handouts.[7] The typical use of e-mail is to send brief memos to people on a distribution list. A more advanced use of e-mail is to distribute word pro-cessing documents as well as spreadsheets and graphics, including photo-graphs, as attachments.

Think back to the decision reached by the team using the nominal group technique. As a follow-up to the meeting, the team was to get together to rate all 12 suppliers on quality, price, and service. Using e-mail, the group could cut down substantially on the amount of time they would have to spend in a group meeting. They might even be able to eliminate a group meeting. Pedro Ortiz might instruct the team members to send their ratings and explanations to each other within 10 working days.

Each team member would then rate all 12 suppliers on quality, service, and price. The ratings would then be sent to all other team members by e-mail. Pedro could tally the results and report the final tally to each team member by e-mail. Since all team members could have performed the same calculation themselves, there would be no claims of a biased decision. A team meeting could be called to discuss the final results if Pedro or the other team members thought it was necessary.

Pushing the use of e-mail too far can inhibit rather than enhance group decision making and teamwork. If people communicate with each other almost exclusively by e-mail, the warmth of human interaction and facial expressions is lost. Piggybacking of ideas is possible by reading each other's ideas on a com-puter monitor. Nevertheless, the wink of an eye, the shared laughter, and the encouraging smiles that take place in a traditional meeting make an important contribution to team effort, including group problem solving.

USING GROUPWARE TO FACILITATE
GROUP PROBLEM SOLVING

The application of e-mail just described can be considered part of groupware because e-mail was used to facilitate work in groups. Electronic brainstorming also relies on groupware because software is applied to facilitate group decision making. At its best, groupware offers certain advantages over single-user systems. Some of the most common reasons people use groupware are as follows:[8]

➤ To facilitate communication by making it faster, clearer, and more persuasive.

➤ To communicate when it would not otherwise be possible.

➤ To enable telecommuting (working from home).

➤ To reduce travel costs.

➤ To bring together multiple perspectives and expertise.

➤ To assemble groups with common interests where it would not be possible to gather a sufficient number of people face to face.

➤ To facilitate group problem solving.

Another example of groupware is a *shared whiteboard* that allows two or more people to view and draw on a shared drawing surface even when they are at a distance. The link to group decision making is that drawing sketches and diagrams might be an important part of the decision making. An example would be a sales team suggesting ways of dividing a geographic territory for selling.

A shared whiteboard can be used during a telephone call, with each person jotting down notes or several participants working together on a visual problem. Typical shared whiteboards are designed for informal conversation, but they can also service more technical applications such as collaborative graphic design and working out a manufacturing problem. The various drawings, or modifications of an existing drawing, submitted by group members are indicated by telepointers, color-coded to identify each person.

Despite all these potential applications and benefits of groupware, the system will break down unless almost all the parties involved use the software successfully. For example, all members of the virtual team must be willing to get online at the same time to have a successful meeting.

SUMMARY

An important aspect of interpersonal relations in organizations is that many key problems are solved by groups. Group problem solvers and decision makers often use the rational model or the political model. The rational decision-making model is the traditional, logical approach to decision making based on the scientific method. The model assumes that each alternative is evaluated in terms of how well it contributes to reaching the goals involved in making the decision.

The political decision-making model assumes that people bring preconceived notions and biases into the decision-making situation. Because the decision makers are politically motivated, the individuals often do not make the most rational choice. Instead, the decision makers attempt to satisfy their own needs.

General problem-solving groups are likely to arrive at better decisions when they follow standard guidelines for group problem solving. The guidelines are as follows: (a) identify the problem; (b) clarify the problem; (c) analyze the cause; (d) search for alternative solutions; (e) select alternatives; (f) plan for implementation; (g) clarify the contract; (h) develop an action plan; and (i) provide for evaluation and accountability.

When the organization is seeking a large number of alternatives to problems, brainstorming is often the technique of choice. Brainstorming is used as a method of finding alternatives to real-life problems and as a creativity-training program. Using the technique, group members spontaneously call out alternative solutions to the problem. Members build on the ideas of each other, and ideas are not screened or evaluated until a later stage. Brainstorming by working alone, or brainwriting, is also effective in generating alternative solutions.

Electronic brainstorming is a recent development designed to overcome the problem of production blocking in brainstorming, such as free riding. Using electronic brainstorming, group members simultaneously enter their suggestions into a computer, and the ideas are transmitted to the screens of other group members. Building on each other's ideas is allowed. Experiments with electronic brainstorming have been favorable.

The nominal group technique (NGT) is recommended for a situation in which a leader needs to know what alternatives are available and how people will react to them. In the NGT, a small group of people contribute written solutions to the problem. Other members respond to their ideas later. Members rate each other's ideas numerically, and the final group decision is the sum of the pooled individual votes.

Problem solving and decision making can sometimes be improved by conducting meetings while standing up instead of sitting down. The general idea is that participants who are standing up are more likely to be alert and come to a decision quickly. An experiment with management students indicated that stand-up groups made decisions more quickly, but that decision makers who sat down were more satisfied.

Electronic mail can be used to facilitate group decision making because members can feed information to each other without having to meet as a group. Memos, spreadsheet analyses, and graphics can be distributed through the network. Too much emphasis on e-mail, however, results in losing the value of face-to-face human interaction.

Various types of groupware, including e-mail and electronic brainstorming, can facilitate group decision making. Also, a shared whiteboard allows two or more people to view and draw on a shared drawing surface even when they are at a distance.

An Interpersonal Relations Case Problem

THE GREAT WIPER BLADE MYSTERY

It was a mystery—a mystery with millions of dollars and hundreds of jobs riding on the answer. A huge 6.5 percent of the windshield wiper systems being manufactured at an ITT automotive plant in upstate New York for DaimlerChrysler's minivans were defective. Nobody could figure out why the defect existed. All the parts met specifications; they were assembled correctly, and engineers found no fault with the design. Yet, in a test run, many wipers failed to make a complete sweep across the windshield—a potential disaster for Chrysler and for the 3,800 automotive workers in the upstate plant.

Plant management assembled a six-person team including engineers, union members, and manufacturing experts to become a detective force to find the answers. The team felt a lot of pressure to resolve the problem because the livelihood of the plant was threatened. If its major product was defective, the plant might be shuttered.

Technical Aspects of the Problem

The new wiper system was the biggest and most complex ever assembled in the plant. Instead of just delivering wiper blades, the local plant was given "black box responsibility" to deliver a perfectly functioning windshield system that Chrysler workers could just snap into place.

The blades, instead of moving right and left in tandem, came together in the center of the windshield and spread apart again, making timing a crucial issue. "The number of things that could go wrong was exponentially greater than for anything we had ever done before," said Rob Price, manufacturing general supervisor. Just one thing did go wrong, but it was enough to threaten the project.

In 6.5 percent of the wipers, the blade's swing was up to 2.5 degrees short. That's equivalent to less than half a second on the face of a clock. But it was enough to make the blade fall short of sweeping the full area in front of the driver's face—an area that federal regulators insist be kept clear of rain and ice.

The Cross-Functional Team Tackles the Problem

Responsibility for solving the problem fell to the Chrysler cross-functional team: leader of the plant's Chrysler team Craig Hysong, manufacturing general supervisor Rob Price, quality technician Rick Fisher, quality analyst Jeannine Marciano, engineer Mike Kinsky, and Ron Maor, an engineer from a sister plant in Ontario, Canada. Each new ITT automotive product has its cross-functional team, drawn from the different departments. The team's goal was to make sure the product was launched flawlessly.

The Chrysler team picked the best and worst of the wipers—called "Bob" and "Wow" for the best of the best and the worst of the worst. They thought that by comparing the best with the worst, they might somehow isolate and fix the problem.

The team felt the pressure to perform, because unless they solved the mystery Chrysler would have to find a new supplier for windshield wiper systems. Finally, Fisher, the technician, and Maor, the engineer from the plant that supplies the motors, found the answer. It was in the serrations (rough marks, like those on a serrated knife) on the motor's drive shaft that are meant to hold the crank in place.

Case Questions

1. Which approach to (or method of) group problem solving did the plant team use?

2. To what extent did management make the right move in assigning the flawed windshield wiper problem to a team instead of to one engineer or technician?

(Continued)

3. Where would the windshield wiper problem fit on Figure 5-1 of this chapter in terms of degree of empowerment?

4. If by chance you happen to have the right expertise, what would you guess was the problem with the windshield wiper system?

Case excerpted and paraphrased from Phil Ebersole, "ITT Automotive Sleuths Solve a Design Mystery," Rochester, New York, *Democrat and Chronicle*, May 4, 1997, pp. 1E, 4E.

QUESTIONS FOR DISCUSSION AND REVIEW

1. Why are group decision-making skills so important for members of a work team?

2. Based on any experience you have had at school or at work, what process or method is usually followed in making group decisions?

3. Most textbook mentions of brainstorming are neutral to unfavorable. What do you suppose the textbook authors tend to dislike about brainstorming?

4. Identify several problems on or off the job for which you think brainstorming would be effective.

5. What, if any, accommodations should be made in electronic brainstorming for group members who have poor keyboarding skills?

6. Identify two work-related problems for which the nominal group technique is particularly well suited?

7. Companies have known about stand-up meetings for many years, and the results have been favorable in terms of productivity. Why, then, are stand-up meetings still not very popular?

8. What advantage does e-mail offer over paper memos and telephone calls as a contributor to group decision making?

9. How can a team leader apply groupware to help the group become more productive?

10. Which group decision-making technique described in this chapter do you think members of top management are the most likely to use? Why?

Chapter 6

Cross-Cultural Relations and Diversity

Stella, who is Puerto Rican, receives excellent performance reviews as a teller at an East Harlem branch of a major bank. East Harlem is a Latino section of New York City. Stella has been taking college courses and continuing education courses offered by the bank, which will qualify her for a position in the bank's central operations department in midtown Manhattan.

Her boss, John, is surprised and annoyed when Stella asks to be recommended for the operations job. He tells Stella that she won't fit in with others and that her style of dress is too flamboyant for the bank's midtown customers. He also encourages Stella to stay at the branch where her Spanish skills are helpful with Latino customers. He says, "Stella, we really need you here to work with our customers. Don't you want to help serve your people? They need you, and I don't think you should let them down."

Stella is discouraged about her career and resents the comments about the community. She knows many other bank people who could do her job as a teller and also speak Spanish.[1]

The brewing conflict between Stella and her manager, John, points out the need for better cross-cultural understanding. John appears to be stereotyping Stella in terms of what he thinks her role should be. Stella wants to break through the limited view of her potential contribution to the bank. Conflicts based on misunderstandings of this nature are frequent because today's workplace is so diverse. Minority group members in the United States are growing seven times as fast as the majority population. According to the Bureau of Labor Statistics, women make up about 47 percent of the workforce. Minorities and workers from other countries occupy 26 percent of jobs. Furthermore, white males constitute only 15 percent of new entrants to the workforce.

Not only is the workforce becoming more diverse, but business has become increasingly international. Small- and medium-size firms, as well as corporate giants, are increasingly dependent on trade with other countries. An estimated 10 to 15 percent of jobs in the United States depend on imports or exports. Furthermore, most manufactured goods contain components from more than one country.

All this workplace diversity has an important implication for the career-minded individual. To succeed in today's workplace a person must be able to relate effectively to people from different cultural groups from within and outside his or her country. Being able to relate to a culturally diverse customer base is also necessary for success.

This chapter presents concepts and techniques you can use to sharpen your ability to work effectively with people from diverse backgrounds. To get you started thinking about your readiness to work in a culturally diverse environment, take Self-Assessment Quiz 6-1.

THE DIVERSITY UMBRELLA

Improving cross-cultural relations includes understanding the true meaning of appreciating diversity. To appreciate diversity a person must go beyond toler-

Self-Assessment Quiz 6-1

CROSS-CULTURAL SKILLS AND ATTITUDES

Listed below are various skills and attitudes that various employers and cross-cultural experts think are important for relating effectively to coworkers in a culturally diverse environment.

	Applies to me now	Not there yet
1. I have spent some time in another country.	_____	_____
2. At least one of my friends is deaf, blind, or uses a wheel chair.	_____	_____
3. Currency from other countries is as real as the currency from my own country.	_____	_____
4. I can read in a language other than my own.	_____	_____
5. I can speak in a language other than my own.	_____	_____
6. I can write in a language other than my own.	_____	_____
7. I can understand people speaking in a language other than my own.	_____	_____
8. I use my second language regularly.	_____	_____
9. My friends include people of races different from my own.	_____	_____
10. My friends include people of different ages.	_____	_____
11. I feel (or would feel) comfortable having a friend with a sexual orientation different from mine.	_____	_____
12. My attitude is that although another culture may be very different from mine, that culture is equally good.	_____	_____
13. I would be willing to (or already do) hang art from different countries in my home.	_____	_____
14. I would accept (or have already accepted) a work assignment of more than several months in another country.	_____	_____
15. I have a passport.	_____	_____

Interpretation: If you answered "Applies to me now" to 10 or more of the preceding questions, you most likely function well in a multicultural work environment. If you answered "Not there yet" to 10 or more of the questions, you need to develop more cross-cultural awareness and skills to work effectively in a multicultural work environment. You will notice that being bilingual gives you at least five points on this quiz.

Source: Several ideas for statements on this quiz are derived from Ruthann Dirks and Janet Buzzard, "What CEOs Expect of Employees Hired for International Work," *Business Education Forum*, April 1997, pp. 3–7; and Gunnar Beeth, "Multicultural Managers Wanted," *Management Review*, May 1997, pp. 17–21.

ating and treating people from different racial and ethnic groups fairly. The true meaning of valuing diversity is to respect and enjoy a wide range of cultural and individual differences. To be diverse is to be different in some measurable way.

Eva Hall, a diversity consultant, helps employees recognize that everybody is different. As she mentions in her seminars, "I'm different in many ways. I'm a middle-aged woman of color, and everyone in this room is different in at least one important way."[2] To be highly skilled in interpersonal relations, one must recognize and appreciate these differences. Some people are more visibly diverse than others because of physical features or disabilities. Yet the diversity umbrella is supposed to include everybody in an organization. To value diversity is therefore to appreciate individual differences among people.

The diversity umbrella continues to include more people as the workforce encompasses a greater variety of people. The goal of a diverse organization is for persons of all cultural backgrounds to achieve their full potential, not restrained by group identities such as sex, nationality, or race.[3]

Figure 6-1 presents a broad sampling of the ways in which workplace associates can differ from one another. Studying this list can help you anticipate the types of differences to understand and appreciate in a diverse workplace. The differences include cultural as well as individual factors. Individual factors are also important because people can be discriminated against for personal characteristics as well as group factors. Many people, for example, believe they are held back from promotion because of their weight-to-height ratio.

UNDERSTANDING CULTURAL DIFFERENCES

The groundwork for developing effective cross-cultural relations is to understand cultural differences. The information about different communication patterns between men and women presented in Chapter 3 is relevant here. Some researchers think that men and women represent different cultures! One cultural difference between the two groups is that women tend to speak indirectly and soften criticism. Men, in contrast, tend to be more direct in giving criticism. Here we feature three aspects of understanding cultural differences: (1) competency goals, (2) dimensions of differences in cultural values, and (3) cultural bloopers.

COMPETENCY GOALS

Setting competency goals will improve your chances of understanding cultural differences. As shown in Figure 6-2, three such goals are cultural sensitivity, respect for diverse groups, and cultural fluency. All three goals are closely related.

Cultural Sensitivity

In order to relate well to someone from a foreign country, a person must be alert to possible cultural differences. When working in another country a person must be willing to acquire knowledge about local customs and learn how

- Race
- Sex (or gender)
- Religion
- Age (young, middle-aged, and old)
- Ethnicity (country of origin)
- Education
- Abilities
- Mental disabilities (including attention deficit disorder)
- Physical disabilities (including hearing status, visual status, able-bodied, wheelchair user)
- Values and motivation
- Sexual orientation (heterosexual, homosexual, bisexual)
- Marital status (married, single, cohabitating, widow, widower)
- Family status (children, no children, two-parent family, single parent, grandparent)
- Personality traits
- Functional background (area of specialization)
- Technology interest (high-tech, low-tech, technophobe)
- Weight status (average, obese, underweight, anorexic)
- Hair status (full head of hair, bald, wild hair, tame hair, long hair, short hair)
- Tobacco status (smoker versus nonsmoker, chewer versus nonchewer)
- Styles of clothing and appearance (dress up, dress down, professional appearance, casual appearance)

Figure 6-1   The Diversity Umbrella

Understanding cultural differences   {   Cultural sensitivity

Respect for all

Cultural fluency

Figure 6-2   Competency Goals for Understanding Cultural Differences to speak the native language at least passably. When working with people from different cultures, even from his or her own country, the person must be patient, adaptable, flexible, and willing to listen and learn. The characteristics just mentioned are part of **cultural sensitivity**, an awareness of and willingness to investigate the reasons why people of another culture act as they do.[4] A person with cultural sensitivity will recognize certain nuances in customs that will help build better relationships from cultural backgrounds other than his or her own.

Respect for All Workers and Cultures

An effective strategy for achieving cross-cultural understanding is to simply respect all others in the workplace, including their cultures. An important component of respect is to believe that although another person's culture is different from yours, it is equally good. Colgate-Palmolive Company, the consumer products giant, conducts a program for managers called "Valuing Colgate People." The program's key objective is to teach managers to respect all workers. Respect comes from valuing differences.

Respecting other people's customs can translate into specific attitudes, such as respecting one coworker for wearing a yarmulke on Friday or another for wearing an African costume to celebrate Kwanza. Another way of being respectful would be to listen carefully to the opinion of a senior worker who says the company should never have converted to voice mail in place of assistants answering the phone (even though you disagree).

An aspect of respecting all workers that has achieved attention recently is the importance of respecting the rights of majorities, particularly white males. Gillian Flynn, a human resource professional, states the problem in this way: "These days things aren't so easy for white males. They've been under attack for a long time, en masse, for the problems of women and minorities. And some should be, certainly. But it's ironic that a movement that demands equal treatment for individuals often lumps all men into one troublesome bundle."[5] Following this logic, a true multicultural person would not have negative attitudes toward a person just because that person is a white male.

Cultural Fluency

A high-level goal in understanding cultural differences is to achieve **cultural fluency**, the ability to conduct business in a diverse, international environment.[6] Achieving cultural fluency includes a variety of skills, such as relating well to people from different cultures and knowing a second language. Cultural fluency also includes knowledge of the international business environment, such as how the exchange rate can affect profits.

Skill-Building Exercise 6-1 is a warm-up activity for achieving cultural sensitivity, and perhaps respect for all workers.

DIMENSIONS OF DIFFERENCES IN CULTURAL VALUES

One way to understand how national cultures differ is to examine their values. Table 6-1 presents an introduction to the subject by comparing values in the United States to the collective values of many Western and Eastern countries.

Skill-Building Exercise 6-1

DEVELOPING CULTURAL SENSITIVITY

Carefully observe products and services such as tennis shoes, notebooks, bicycles, and banking services, and attempt to find out how they are marketed and sold in other countries. For a convenient reference source, interview foreign students and foreigners outside of class about these products and services. Your digging for information might uncover such nuggets as the following:

➤ In India, cricket champions are celebrities comparable to U. S. basketball stars who endorse soft drinks like Coca-Cola and Pepsi.

➤ In Hungary, peanut butter is considered a luxury food item.

➤ In some countries in warm climates, meat is freshly killed and hung on hooks for sale—without refrigeration or freezing.

After conducting these product and service interviews, arrive at some kind of interpretation or conclusion. Share your insights with other class members.

Source: "Teaching International Business," *Keying In* (The Newsletter of the National Business Education Association), January 1999, p. 1.

You can use this information as a general stereotype of how Americans are likely to differ from people in many other countries.

The focus of our attention is a more detailed look at eight different values and how selected nationalities relate to them, based on the work of several researchers.[7] A summary of these values follows.

    1. *Individualism versus collectivism.* At one end of the continuum is **individualism**, a mental set in which people see themselves first as individuals

TABLE 6-1 Comparison of United States Values with Those in Many Other Countries

In the United States	In many other countries
Time is to be controlled	Time is fluid, malleable
Emphasis on change	Tradition, continuity
Individualism	Group orientation
Personal privacy	Openness, accessibility
Informality	Formality
Individual competition	Cooperation
Equality/egalitarianism	Hierarchy/authority
Short-term emphasis	Long-term emphasis
Work emphasis ("One lives to work.")	Leisure + work emphasis ("One works to live.")
Task emphasis	People emphasis
Direct/explicit communication style	Indirect/implicit communication style
Action bias or emphasis	Planning and preparation emphasis

Source: Adaptation of chart prepared by International Orientation Resources.

and believe that their own interests take priority. **Collectivism**, at the other end of the continuum, is a feeling that the group and society receive top priority. Members of a society who value individualism are more concerned with their careers than with the good of the firm. Members of a society who value collectivism, in contrast, are typically more concerned with the organization than with themselves.

Highly individualistic cultures include the United States, Canada, Great Britain, Australia, and the Netherlands. Japan, Taiwan, Mexico, Greece, and Hong Kong are among the countries that strongly value collectivism.

> An example of collectivistic thinking took place during South Korea's economic crisis in 1997. Worried about the crisis, employees in a Seoul government office gathered up spare change from their desk drawers and donated it to their country. Banks encouraged people to open accounts with their hoarded foreign currencies. Furthermore, collection boxes were placed on the streets for donation of spare bills and coins. Many citizens brought foreign currency to banks to exchange it for Korean currency.[8]

2. *High power distance versus low power distance.* The extent to which employees accept the idea that members of an organization have different levels of power is referred to as **power distance**. In a high-power-distance culture, the boss makes many decisions simply because he or she is the boss. Group members readily comply because they have a positive orientation toward authority. In a low-power-distance culture, employees do not readily recognize a power hierarchy. They accept directions only when they think the boss is right or when they feel threatened. High-power-distance cultures include France, Spain, Japan, Mexico, and Brazil. Low-power-distance cultures include the United States, Israel, Germany, and Ireland.

3. *Low uncertainty avoidance versus high uncertainty avoidance.* People who accept the unknown and tolerate risk and unconventional behavior are said to have low **uncertainty avoidance**. In other words, these people are not afraid to face the unknown. A society ranked high in uncertainty avoidance contains a majority of people who want predictable and certain futures. Low-uncertainty-avoidance cultures include the United States, Canada, Australia, and Singapore. Workers in Israel, Japan, Italy, and Argentina are more motivated to avoid uncertainty in their careers.

4. *Materialism versus concern for others.* In this context, **materialism** refers to an emphasis on assertiveness and the acquisition of money and material objects. It also means a deemphasis on caring for others. At the other end of the cotinuum is **concern for others**, an emphasis on personal relations and a concern for the welfare of others. Materialistic countries include Japan, Austria, and Italy. The United States is considered to be moderately materialistic. Scandinavian nations all emphasize caring as a national value. (In the original, the same dimension was referred to as *masculinity* versus *femininity*. Such terms are considered to be sexist today.)

5. *Long-term orientation versus short-term orientation.* Workers from a culture with a **long-term orientation** maintain a long-range perspective, thus being thrifty and not demanding quick returns on their investments. A **short-term orientation** is characterized by a demand for immediate results and a propensity not to save. Pacific Rim countries are noted for their long-term orientation. In contrast, the cultures of the United States and Canada are characterized more by short-term orientation.

6. *Formality versus informality.* A country that values **formality** attaches considerable importance to tradition, ceremony, social rules, and rank. At the other extreme, **informality** refers to a casual attitude toward tradition, ceremony, social rules, and rank. Workers in Latin American countries highly value formality, such as lavish public receptions and processions. Americans, Canadians, and Scandinavians are much more informal.

7. *Urgent time orientation versus casual time orientation.* Individuals and nations attach different importance to time. People with an **urgent time orientation** perceive time as a scarce resource and tend to be impatient. People with a **casual time orientation** view time as an unlimited and unending resource and tend to be patient. Americans are noted for their urgent time orientation. They frequently impose deadlines and are eager to get started doing business. Asians and Middle Easterners, in contrast, are patient negotiators.

8. *High-context versus low-context cultures.* Cultures differ in how much importance they attach to the surrounding circumstances, or context, of an event. **High-context cultures** make more extensive use of body language. Some cultures, such as the Asian, Hispanic, and African-American cultures, are high context. In contrast, northern European cultures are low context and make less use of body language. The Anglo-American culture is considered to be medium-low context. People in low-context cultures seldom take time in business dealings to build relationships and establish trust.

How might a person use information about cultural differences to improve his or her interpersonal relations on the job? A starting point would be to recognize that a person's national values might influence his or her behavior. Assume that you wanted to establish a good working relationship with a person from a high-context culture. An effective starting point would be to emphasize body language when communicating with the individual. Self-Assessment Quiz 6-2 will help you think about how values might be influencing your interpersonal relations in the workplace.

CULTURAL BLOOPERS

An effective way of being culturally sensitive is to minimize actions that are likely to offend people from another culture based on their values. Cultural bloopers are most likely to take place when you are visiting another country. The same bloopers, however, can also be committed with people from a different

Self-Assessment Quiz 6-2

CHARTING YOUR CULTURAL VALUE PROFILE

Directions: For each of the eight value dimensions, circle the number that most accurately fits your standing on the dimension. For example, if you perceive yourself to be "highly formal," circle 7 on the sixth dimension (item 6).

1. Individualism   Collectivism

    1   2   3   4   5   6   7

2. High power distance   Low power distance

    1   2   3   4   5   6   7

3. High uncertainty avoidance   Low uncertainty avoidance

    1   2   3   4   5   6   7

4. Materialism (masculinity)   Concern for others (femininity)

    1   2   3   4   5   6   7

5. Long-term orientation   Short-term orientation

    1   2   3   4   5   6   7

6. Informality   Formality

    1   2   3   4   5   6   7

7. Urgent time orientation   Casual time orientation

    1   2   3   4   5   6   7

8. High context   Low context

    1   2   3   4   5   6   7

Scoring and Interpretation: After circling one number for each dimension, use a felt-tipped pen to connect the circles, thereby giving yourself a *profile of cultural values*. Do not be concerned if your marker cuts through the names of the dimensions. Compare your profile to others in the class. Should time allow, develop a class profile by computing the class average for each of the eight points and then connecting the points.

culture within your own country. To avoid these bloopers, you must carefully observe persons from another culture. Studying another culture through reading is also helpful.

E-commerce and other forms of Internet communication have created new opportunities for creating cultural bloopers. The Web site developers and the workers responsible for adding content must have good cross-cultural literacy, including an awareness of how the information might be misinterpreted. Here is a sampling of potential problems:

➤ Numerical date formats can be readily misinterpreted. To an American, 4/9/01 would be interpreted as April 9, 2001 (or 1901!). However, many Europeans would interpret the same numerical expression as September 4, 2001.

➤ Colors on Web sites must be chosen carefully. For example, in some cultures purple is the color of royalty, whereas in Brazil purple is associated with death.

➤ Be careful of metaphors that may not make sense to a person for whom your language is a second language. Examples include "We've encountered an ethical meltdown" and "Our biggest competitor is over the hill."

International business specialist Rick Borelli recommends that being able to communicate your message directly in your customer's mother tongue provides a competitive advantage.[9] The translator, of course, must have good knowledge of the subtleties of the language to avoid a blooper. An English-to-French translator used the verb *baiser* instead of *baisser* to describe a program of lowering prices. *Baisser* is the French verb "to lower" whereas *baiser* is the verb "to kiss." Worse, in slang *baiser* is a verb that refers to having intimate physical relationships!

Keep two key facts in mind when attempting to avoid cultural mistakes. One is that members of any cultural group show individual differences. What one member of the group might regard as an insensitive act, another might welcome. Recognize also that one or two cultural mistakes will not peg you permanently as a boor. Skill-Building Exercise 6-2 will help you minimize certain cultural bloopers.

OVERCOMING CROSS-CULTURAL COMMUNICATION BARRIERS

We have already discussed the importance of overcoming communication barriers in Chapter 3. Cultural differences create additional barriers. Here are some guidelines for overcoming cross-cultural communication barriers.

1. *Be sensitive to the fact that cross-cultural communication barriers exist. If you are aware of these potential barriers, you will be ready to deal with them.* When you are dealing with a person in the workplace with a different cultural background than yours, solicit feedback in order to minimize cross-cultural barriers to communication. Being aware of these potential barriers will help you develop cultural sensitivity.

2. *Show respect for all workers.* The same behavior that promotes good cross-cultural relations in general helps overcome communication barriers. A widely-used comment that implies disrespect is to say to another person from another culture, "You have a funny accent." Should you be transposed to that person's culture, you, too, might have a "funny accent."

3. *Use straightforward language and speak slowly and clearly.* When working with people who do not speak your language fluently, speak in an easy-

Skill-Building Exercise 6-2

CULTURAL MISTAKES TO AVOID WITH SELECTED CULTURAL GROUPS

EUROPE

Great Britain
- Asking personal questions. The British protect their privacy.
- Thinking that a businessperson from England is unenthusiastic when he or she says, "Not bad at all." English people understate positive emotion.
- Gossiping about royalty.

France
- Expecting to complete work during the French two-hour lunch.
- Attempting to conduct significant business during August—*les vacances* (vacation time).
- Greeting a French person for the first time and not using a title such as "sir" or "madam" (or "monsieur," "madame," or "mademoiselle").

Italy
- Eating too much pasta, as it is not the main course.
- Handing out business cards freely. Italians use them infrequently.

Spain
- Expecting punctuality. Your appointments will usually arrive 20 to 30 minutes late.
- Making the American sign for "okay" with your thumb and forefinger. In Spain (and many other countries) this is vulgar.

Scandinavia (Denmark, Sweden, Norway)
- Being overly rank conscious. Scandinavians pay relatively little attention to a person's place in the hierarchy.

ASIA

All Asian countries
- Pressuring an Asian job applicant or employee to brag about his or her accomplishments. Asians feel self-conscious when boasting about individual accomplishments; they prefer to let the record speak for itself. In addition, they prefer to talk about group rather than individual accomplishment.

Japan
- Shaking hands or hugging Japanese (as well as other Asians) in public. Japanese consider these practices to be offensive.
- Not interpreting "We'll consider it" as a no when spoken by a Japanese businessperson. Japanese negotiators mean no when they say "We'll consider it."
- Not giving small gifts to Japanese when conducting business. Japanese are offended by not receiving these gifts.
- Giving your business card to a Japanese businessperson more than once. Japanese prefer to give and receive business cards only once.

China
- Using black borders on stationary and business cards, because black is associated with death.

(Continued)

- Giving small gifts to Chinese when conducting business. Chinese are offended by these gifts.
- Making cold calls on Chinese business executives. An appropriate introduction is required for a first-time meeting with a Chinese official.

Korea
- Saying no. Koreans feel it is important to have visitors leave with good feelings.

India
- Telling Indians you prefer not to eat with your hands. If the Indians are not using cutlery when eating they expect you to do likewise.

MEXICO AND LATIN AMERICA

Mexico
- Flying into a Mexican city in the morning and expecting to close a deal by lunch. Mexicans build business relationships slowly.

Brazil
- Attempting to impress Brazilians by speaking a few words of Spanish. Portuguese is the official language of Brazil.

Most Latin American countries
- Wearing elegant and expensive jewelry during a business meeting. Most Latin Americans think people should appear more conservative during a business meeting.

Note: A cultural mistake for Americans to avoid when conducting business in most countries outside the United States and Canada is to insist on getting down to business quickly. North Americans in small towns also like to build a relationship before getting down to business. The preceding suggestions will lead to cross-cultural skill development if practiced in the right setting. During the next 30 days, look for an opportunity to relate to a person from another culture in the way described in these suggestions. Observe the reaction of the other person for feedback on your cross-cultural effectiveness.

to-understand manner. Minimize the use of idioms and analogies specific to your language. A computer analyst from Greece left confused after a discussion about a software problem with her manager. The manager said, "Let's talk about this another time because *I can't seem to get to first base with you.*" (The manager was referring to the fact that the conversation was headed nowhere because he couldn't come to an agreement with the analyst.) The computer analyst did not ask for clarification because she did not want to appear uninformed.

4. *Observe cultural differences in etiquette.* Violating rules of etiquette without explanation can erect immediate communication barriers. A major rule of etiquette in many countries is that people address each other by last name unless they have worked together for a long time. Letitia Baldrige recommends that you explain the difference in custom to prevent misunderstanding. Imagine this scenario, in which you are working with a man from Germany and you are speaking:

Herr Schultz, in my country by now I would be calling you Heinrich and you would be calling me Charlie. Would you be comfortable with that? Because if you wouldn't, I would be glad to call you Herr Schultz until you tell me it is time to call you Heinrich.[10]

5. *Be sensitive to differences in nonverbal communication.* Stay alert to the possibility that your nonverbal signal may be misinterpreted by a person from another culture. An engineer for a New Jersey company was asked a question by a German coworker. He signaled OK by making a circle with his thumb and forefinger. The German worker stormed away, because in his country the same gesture is a personal insult and a vulgar gesture.

6. *Do not be diverted by style, accent, grammar, or personal appearance.* Although these superficial factors are all related to business success, they are difficult to interpret when judging a person from another culture. It is therefore better to judge the merits of the statement or behavior.[11] A brilliant individual from another culture may still be learning your language and thus make basic mistakes in speaking your language. Also, he or she might not yet have developed a sensitivity to dress style in your culture.

BUSINESS IMPLICATIONS OF UNDERSTANDING CULTURAL DIFFERENCES

Top-level management at many companies emphasizes cross-cultural understanding, including overcoming communication barriers, because such activities improve profits. If you establish rapport with people from other cultures—and avoid antagonizing them—they will most likely become and remain your customers. Similarly, if you establish good rapport with valuable employees from other cultures, they are more likely to stay with the company. Following are two examples of how cross-cultural understanding has improved profits or reduced costs:

➤ A marketing firm specializing in targeting cultural groups developed a concept for a JCPenney ad campaign based on an intimate knowledge of African-American culture. African-American women have a tradition of wearing white dresses to church on the fifth Sunday of the month. The marketing firm created an elegant photo layout of black churchgoers wearing white dresses from JCPenney. The ad led to brisk sales of white dresses at JCPenney in top markets.[12]

➤ Xerox Corp. has a longstanding reputation of reaching out to minorities and appreciating the contributions of people from diverse cultures. As a result, Xerox has been able to recruit and retain talented people from many cultural groups. One of many examples is Ursula Burns, the head of worldwide manufacturing, who is helping the company find ways to cut per-unit manufacturing costs by 15 to 20 percent. Burns is the highest placed black woman in American manufacturing.

➤ Several large automobile dealerships across the United States and Canada have deliberately cultivated a culturally diverse sales force. This type of cultural diversity often leads to much improved sales to the diverse cultural groups. A Cadillac dealer in New York City reported that sales to Asiatic Indians have quadrupled since he hired a sales representative raised in India. The same dealer reports that more cultural diversity in the service end of the business has also boosted sales to diverse ethnic and racial groups.

TECHNIQUES FOR IMPROVING CROSS-CULTURAL RELATIONS AND VALUING DIFFERENCES

Many training programs have been developed to improve cross-cultural relations and to help employees value diversity. All of the information presented so far in this chapter is likely to be included in such programs. In this section we describe programs for improving cross-cultural relations, language training, and valuing diversity. A skill-building exercise accompanies a description of each program. We will also describe some precautions regarding how valuing differences can sometimes backfire.

CULTURAL TRAINING

For many years companies and government agencies have prepared their workers for overseas assignments. The method most frequently chosen is **cultural training**, a set of learning experiences designed to help employees understand the customs, traditions, and beliefs of another culture. In today's diverse business environment and international marketplace, learning about individuals raised in different cultural backgrounds has become more important. Many industries therefore train employees in cross-cultural relations. Here we describe one such program geared to a particular industry—real estate sales.

Cross-cultural training is taken seriously in the home-building and real estate industries. Workers in these industries are learning the Asian cultural language.[13] Such training does not necessarily involve taking crash courses in Chinese or Japanese. Instead, it means the workers have been learning about subtle cultural differences between Eastern and Western people. (Some forms of cross-cultural training do emphasize learning another language, as described in the next section.)

One justification for this training is that Asians represent 3 percent of the population in the United States, totaling 7.3 million people. Also, because the fast-expanding Asian population is affluent, they are a target market for home builders and sellers. In California, for example, Asians and Asian-Americans account for 30 to 40 percent of the first-time buyers' market.

Builders and Realtors hire cultural diversity specialists to help them learn how to communicate with and accommodate their customers from China, Japan, Taiwan, Korea, Vietnam, and the Philippines. (*Realtor* is a trademark name for a certified real estate broker.) Home builders and Realtors receive cultural training in issues such as the following:

➤ Negotiating styles

➤ Money-matter discussions

➤ Use of body language such as eye contact

➤ Business etiquette

➤ Design preferences in a home, such as *feng shui* (term referring to the ancient Chinese philosophy of creating a harmonious home environment, leading to good luck and prosperity for the inhabitants)

One cultural training seminar teaches participants to examine the mind-set of Asian people in order to understand their actions. Real estate personnel are taught the dynamics of an Asian family who might look at model homes as a group. A home-buying decision involves the entire family. As a trainer notes, "So when a professional couple comes in with Grandma, Grandpa, and the kids, be very respectful to everyone. Probably the older couple will be making the down payment."

Participants are also taught that carefully observing body language will help the seller determine who is the boss in the family. The trainer explains as follows: "In the United States, we always can tell who's the decision maker. It's usually the one who talks the most. But in Asian cultures, very often the one who doesn't talk is the one who has the power."

Realtors are also taught how to sell to Asian customers. Asians frown on familiarity, so sales representatives are urged not to be aggressive. Patience is a virtue in selling to Asians. Chinese, in particular, prefer to develop a relationship gradually rather than close a deal quickly. A point established early in the seminar is that the worst error is to mistake a person of one Asian extraction for one of another (such as a Vietnamese for a Japanese). The Asian continent comprises 41 countries, with 19 in the Pacific Rim.

Dozens of other small, yet important, details are presented in the seminar to improve relationships with Asian clients. Participants learn different types of handshakes, how to bow the correct ways, and how to exchange business cards. Participants even learn about the significance of colors and certain numbers to Asians. For example, Asians consider white, blue, and yellow to be funeral colors and might reject a house lavishly decorated with these colors. Some Asians might choose a house based on whether the numbers in the address are thought to bring good or bad luck.

To practice improving your cross-cultural relations, do Skill-Building Exercise 6-3. Asian and Asian-American class members may have a natural advantage in playing the roles in the exercise.

LANGUAGE TRAINING

Learning a foreign language is often part of cultural training, yet it can also be a separate activity. Knowledge of a second language is important because it builds better connections with people from other cultures than does relying on a translator. Many workers, aside from international business specialists, also

Skill-Building Exercise 6-3

CROSS-CULTURAL RELATIONS ROLE PLAY

To get started applying cross-cultural sensitivity, a group of students engage in the following role play. One person plays the role of a Realtor who is showing a single-family dwelling to the Wong family (Chinese Americans). The Realtor recognizes that the family is a hot prospect, because they are affluent, headed by two business professionals. Six students play the role of the Wong family: two parents, two grandparents, and two elementary-school-age children. The Wong family would like to purchase this luxurious home at a fair price. The grandparents in particular think that they should buy only from a Realtor who respects their culture.

The Realtor and the Wong family engage in the selling transaction for about 10 minutes. The balance of the class will critically observe the interaction and then provide feedback.

choose to develop skills in a target language. Speaking another language can help build rapport with customers and employees who speak that language.

Almost all language training has elements similar to taking a course in another language or self-study. Companies invest heavily in helping employees learn a target language because it facilitates conducting business in other countries. Medical specialists, police workers, and fire fighters also find second language skills to be quite helpful because clients under stress, such as an injured person, are likely to revert to their native tongue. Here is a sampling of the range of activities and costs for language training used in business:[14]

$50—A language training CD-ROM and a microphone for speech recognition.

$275—One person participating in a group language-training course.

$475—A language-training CD-ROM, 12 interactive lessons with a teacher over the Internet and homework incorporating Web sites in foreign languages.

$4000—A one-time fee to set up video conferencing equipment ($1,500) and 50 hours of instruction from a language-training teacher ($50 per hour).

$10,000—A two-day cross-cultural program and eight days in a language immersion program for the employee and partner.

As with any other skill training, these investments can pay off only if the trainee is willing to work hard at developing the new skill outside the training sessions. Allowing even 10 days to pass without practicing your target language will result in a sharp decline in your ability to use that language.

Skill-Building Exercise 6-4 presents a low-cost, pleasant method of enhancing your foreign language and cross-cultural skills.

Skill-Building Exercise 6-4

USING THE INTERNET TO HELP DEVELOP FOREIGN LANGUAGE SKILLS

A useful way of developing skills in another language, and learning more about another culture, is to create a "bookmark" or "favorite" written in your target language. In this way, each time you go to the Internet on your own computer, your cover page will contain fresh information in the language you want to develop.

To get started, use a search engine such as Yahoo! or Excite that offers choices in several languages. Enter a search word such as "newspaper" or "current events" in the search probe. After you find a suitable choice, enter the edit function for "Favorites" or "Bookmarks" and insert that newspaper as your cover page. For example, imagine that French is your target language and culture. The Yahoo! France search engine might have brought you to www.france2.fr. This Web site keeps you abreast of French and international news, sports, and cultural events—written in French. Now every time you access the Internet, you can spend five minutes on your second language and becoming multicultural. You can save a lot of travel costs and time using the Internet to help you become multicultural, including developing proficiency in another language.

DIVERSITY TRAINING (TRAINING IN VALUING DIFFERENCES)

The general purpose of cultural training is to help workers understand people from other cultures. Understanding can lead to dealing more effectively with them as work associates or customers. **Diversity training** (or **valuing-differences training**) has a slightly different purpose. It attempts to bring about workplace harmony by teaching people how to get along better with diverse work associates. Quite often the program is aimed at minimizing open expressions of racism and sexism. Valuing-differences training takes a number of forms. Nevertheless, all center around increasing awareness of and empathy for people who are different in some noticeable way from oneself.

Training sessions in valuing differences focus on the ways that men and women or people of different races reflect different values, attitudes, and cultural backgrounds. These sessions can vary from several hours to several days. Training sessions can also be held over a long period of time. Sometimes the program is confrontational, sometimes not. As described by diversity consultant H. Roosevelt Thomas, Jr., the objectives of valuing-differences training include one or more of the following:[15]

➤ Fostering awareness and acceptance of individual differences.

➤ Helping participants understand their own feelings and attitudes about people who are "different."

➤ Exploring how differences might be tapped as assets in the workplace.

➤ Enhancing work relations between people who are different from each other.

An essential part of relating more effectively to diverse groups is to empathize with their points of view. To help training participants develop empathy, representatives of various groups explain their feelings related to workplace issues. A representative segment of a training program designed to enhance empathy took the following format. A minority group member was seated at the middle of a circle. First, the coworkers listened to a Vietnamese woman explain how she felt excluded from the in-group composed of whites and African-Americans in her department. "I feel like you just tolerate me. You do not make me feel that I am somebody important."

The next person to sit in the middle of the circle was a Muslim. He complained about people wishing him Merry Christmas. "I would much prefer that my coworkers stop to think that I do not celebrate Christian holidays. I respect your religion, but it is not my religion."

Skill-Building Exercise 6-5 provides you an opportunity to simulate an empathy-building experience in a valuing-differences training program.

Cautions About Diversity Training

Diversity (or valuing-differences) training has frequently improved cross-cultural relationships in the workplace. Yet such programs can also create ill will and waste time. One problem is that participants are sometimes encouraged to be too confrontational and express too much hostility. Companies have found that when employees are too blunt during these sessions, it may be difficult to patch up interpersonal relations in the work group later on.

Another problem is that revelations made during a diversity training session may backfire against the company. During one session, for example, a manager admitted that the company had intentionally denied a promotion to an African-American sales representative because he was perceived as a troublemaker. Several months later the sales representative initiated a lawsuit against the company.

A negative consequence of diversity training programs is that they sometimes result in perpetuating stereotypes about groups, such as people from Latin America not placing much value on promptness for meetings. A related problem is that a valuing-differences program might focus too much on differences instead of similarities.[16] For example, even if people are raised with different cultural values they must all work harmoniously together to accomplish work. Although a worker believes that relationships are more important than profits, he or she must still produce enough to be a good investment for the company.

SUMMARY

Today's workplace has become more culturally diverse, and business has become increasingly international. As a result, to succeed one must be able to relate effectively to people from different cultural groups from within and outside one's country. The true meaning of valuing diversity is to respect and enjoy a wide range of cultural and individual differences. The diversity umbrella con-

Skill-Building Exercise 6-5

DEVELOPING EMPATHY FOR DIFFERENCES

Class members come up to the front of the room one by one and give a brief presentation (perhaps even three minutes) of any way in which they have been perceived as different, and how they felt about this perception. The difference can be of any kind, relating to characteristics such as ethnicity, race, choice of major, physical appearance, height, weight, hair color, or body piercing. After each member of the class (perhaps even the instructor) has presented, class members discuss what they learned from the exercise. It is also important to discuss how this exercise can improve relationships on the job.

tinues to include more people as the workforce encompasses a greater variety of people.

The groundwork for developing effective cross-cultural relations is to understand cultural differences. Three important goals for understanding cultural differences are (1) cultural sensitivity, (2) respect for all workers and all cultures, and (3) cultural fluency—the ability to conduct business in a diverse, international environment.

Countries differ in their national values, leading to differences in how most people from a given country will react to situations. The values studied here are (a) individualism versus collectivism; (b) high power distance (accepting authority) versus low power distance; (c) low uncertainty avoidance versus high uncertainty avoidance; (d) materialism versus concern for others; (e) long-term orientation versus short-term orientation; (f) formality versus informality; (g) urgent time orientation versus casual time orientation; and (h) high context versus low-context cultures.

An effective way of being culturally sensitive is to minimize actions that are likely to offend people from another culture based on their values. These cultural bloopers can take place when working in another country or when dealing with foreigners in one's own country. Studying potential cultural bloopers is helpful, but recognize also that individual differences may be of significance.

Communication barriers created by cultural differences can often be overcome by the following: (a) Be sensitive to the fact that these barriers exist; (b) show respect for all workers; (c) use straightforward language and speak slowly and clearly; (d) observe cultural differences in etiquette; (e) be sensitive to differences in nonverbal communication; and (f) do not be diverted by style, accent, grammar, or personal appearance.

Improved cross-cultural understanding can improve profits through attracting and retaining diverse customers. Similarly, establishing good rapport with valuable employees from other cultures can improve employee retention.

Cultural training is a set of learning experiences designed to help employees understand the customs, traditions, and beliefs of another culture. In today's diverse business environment and international marketplace, learning about individuals raised in different cultural backgrounds has become more important. Learning a foreign language is often part of cultural training, yet it can also be a separate activity.

Diversity training (or valuing-differences training) attempts to bring about workplace harmony by teaching people how to get along better with diverse work associates. Most forms of valuing-differences training center around increasing awareness of and empathy for people who are different in some noticeable way from yourself.

QUESTIONS FOR DISCUSSION AND REVIEW

1. Several well-known companies conduct *awareness weeks* to celebrate certain diverse groups such as Hispanics or homosexuals. What is your opinion of the effectiveness of such activities for bringing about workplace harmony?

2. In recent years many middle-aged white males have emphasized that they want to be included under the diversity umbrella. What is your reaction to their demands?

3. Some companies, such as Singapore Airlines, make a deliberate effort for customer-contact personnel to all be of the same ethnic group (Singapore natives). How justified is this practice in an era of cultural diversity and valuing differences?

4. A major purpose of diversity programs is to help people celebrate differences. Why should people celebrate a difference such as an attention deficit disorder?

5. Provide an example of cultural insensitivity of any kind that you have seen, read about, or could imagine.

6. Classified ads for positions listed in the French newspaper *Le Figaro* often require the applicant to be fluent in two languages in addition to French. What implications might this information have for your career?

7. How could you use the information presented in Table 6-1, comparing U.S. values to those of other countries, to help you succeed in business?

8. If you were a supervisor, how would you deal with a group member who had a very low value for power distance?

9. The cultural bloopers presented in Skill-Building Exercise 6-2 all dealt with errors people make in regard to people who are not American. Give an example of a cultural blooper a person from another country might make in the United States.

10. Many people speak loudly to deaf people, blind people, and those who speak a different language. Based on the information presented in this chapter, what mistakes are these people making?

CONFUSED AND CONCERNED IN SOUTH KOREA

Annie Lee, an American business student with Korean heritage, was given the opportunity several summers ago to work for SKAC, the largest animation company in South Korea. SKAC is known for its advanced technology animation used in such projects as Disney's *The Little Mermaid* and *The Simpsons* television show. To help establish itself as a major player in the animation industry, SKAC launched *Animatoon*, the first animation magazine. The purpose of the magazine was to inform other animation companies about new technology, new faces, and events around the globe in the animation industry. Another division of the company produced animated cartoons.

Lee was hired by the founder, Nelson Shin, to work in the magazine department translating reports and interviews from English into Korean and vice versa. Shin warmly welcomed Lee. He, too, was Korean American, and he acknowledged the differences in working environments between the two countries. At the outset of employment Shin said, "Your day starts at eight and ends at five, Monday through Friday. Saturdays are optional since we don't work on weekends in the States."

The translation department consisted of 60 percent Korean Americans. All business was therefore supposed to be conducted in accordance with Western (non-Asian) business culture. Annie Lee enjoyed working with fellow Korean Americans in a prestigious company and receiving high pay.

SKAC worked with big U. S. entertainment companies such as Warner Brothers and Disney Corporation on a long-term basis. Annie Lee and her coworkers were held accountable to maintain the positive working relationships with the U.S. companies. A major reason for emphasizing the positive relationships is that SKAC could not stay in business if these customers were lost.

From Annie Lee's perspective, her job was going well and she was making a good contribution to the translation department. Then one day her manager, Kim Young, confronted her in these words: "Why don't you come in at six in the morning like the secretaries do? You could clean the office, make coffee, and run small errands."

Surprised by Young's comments, Annie said, "Why should I do those things? To my knowledge, my job title does not include the word 'secretary'."

Young replied, "You Americans have no sense of values and respect. How can you call yourself Korean? You are in Korea, and you must listen to your elders."

Upset and frustrated, Annie left without making further comment. During lunch hour, she expressed her concerns to her coworkers. Her close friend, Jen Sooko, who had been working at the company for six months, told Annie about a similar experience she had with Young. "I was ready to punch him out when he said he needed a pack of cigarettes," she said.

"So what did you do?" asked Annie.

Jen replied, "What was I supposed to do? I went across the street and bought him a pack of cigarettes."

Other employees had similar experiences, but no one had tried to resolve the problem. During a six-month period, six women employees quit, with no one explaining to top management why they quit.

Annie started to feel increasingly uncomfortable working under Young's supervision. She began to see the quality of her work diminish rapidly. She was no longer proud of the translations she was producing.

Jen took Annie aside one day and said, "You've been making a lot of mistakes lately. I'm worried about you."

Case Questions

1. What cross-cultural errors is Kim Young committing?

2. What cross-cultural errors are Annie Lee and her coworkers committing?

3. What can higher management do to restore harmony in the translation department?

Case researched by Annie Lee, Rochester Institute of Technology, 1999.

Chapter 7

Resolving Conflicts with Others

Learning Objectives

After reading and studying this chapter and doing the exercises you should be able to

➤ Specify why so much interpersonal conflict exists in organizations.

➤ Recognize your typical method of resolving conflict.

➤ Identify the five modes of handling conflict.

➤ Develop effective techniques for resolving conflict and negotiating.

➤ Understand how to combat sexual harassment in the workplace.

"Sorry, I can't let you take off three days to attend your friend's wedding in Indianapolis," said Gerry, the accounting supervisor, to Wendy, the accountant. "This is our busiest season, and I just can't spare you."

"What do you mean you can't spare me?" asked Wendy. "My best friend is getting married, and I'm the maid of honor. I have to go."

"You may think you have to attend the wedding," replied Gerry, "but we need you here to help us manage our peak workload. If you decide to take three unauthorized days from work, you will face company discipline."

The unfortunate incident between Gerry and Wendy illustrates several different meanings of **conflict**. A conflict is a situation in which two or more goals, values, or events are incompatible or mutually exclusive. Gerry wants Wendy to be present every day during the busy tax season, and Wendy wants to attend an out-of-town wedding. A conflict is also a strife, quarrel, or battle. Gerry and Wendy are in a quarrel. Finally, conflict is said to occur when one side interferes with, disrupts, or in some way makes the other side less effective. This aspect of conflict will occur only if Wendy is disciplined by a harsh measure such as suspension or termination.

This chapter will help you improve your ability to resolve conflicts with people at work. The same techniques are also useful in personal life. To improve your understanding of how to resolve conflict, we will present specific techniques and also explain why so much conflict exists. To get you started relating the topic of conflict to yourself, take Self-Assessment Quiz 7-1.

SOURCES OF INTERPERSONAL CONFLICT IN ORGANIZATIONS

Conflict between and among people has many sources, or causes. In this section we describe some of the leading sources. If you understand the cause of a conflict, it can help you resolve the conflict and help prevent a similar recurrence. For example, if you learn that much conflict on the job is caused by a series of little hurts *(pinches)*, you can apologize for these hurts. You can also be on guard to avoid such pinches in the future. Although specific sources of conflict can be identified, keep in mind an important fact. All conflict includes the underlying theme of incompatibility between your goals, values, or events and those of another person.

COMPETITION FOR LIMITED RESOURCES

An underlying source of job conflict is that few people can get all the resources they want. These resources include money, material, and human resources (or personnel). Conflicts arise when two or more people squabble over who should get the resources. Even in a prosperous organization, resources have to be divided in such a manner that not everybody gets what he or she wants.

Assume that you believe you need to have a desktop computer immediately accessible the full workday. Yet the company has decided that three people

STYLES OF CONFLICT MANAGEMENT

Directions: Check the alternative that best fits your typical reaction to the situation described.

Part I: The Quiz

1. When someone is overly hostile toward me, I usually:

    _____ A. respond in kind

    _____ B. persuade him or her to cool down

    _____ C. hear the person out

    _____ D. walk away

2. When I walk in on a heated argument, I'm likely to:

    _____ A. jump in and take sides

    _____ B. mediate

    _____ C. keep quiet and observe

    _____ D. leave the scene

3. When I suspect that another person is taking advantage of me, I:

    _____ A. try to get the person to stop

    _____ B. rely on persuasion and facts

    _____ C. change how I relate to the person

    _____ D. accept the situation

4. When I don't see eye to eye with someone, I typically:

    _____ A. try to get him or her to see things my way

    _____ B. consider the problem logically

    _____ C. search for a workable compromise

    _____ D. let the problem work itself out

5. After a run-in with someone I care about a great deal, I:

    _____ A. try to make him or her see it my way

    _____ B. try to work out our differences

    _____ C. wait before renewing contact

    _____ D. let it lie

(Continued)

6. When I see conflict developing between two people I care about, I usually:

_____ A. express disappointment

_____ B. try to mediate

_____ C. watch to see what develops

_____ D. leave the scene

7. When I see conflict developing between two people who are relatively unimportant to me, I usually:

_____ A. express disappointment

_____ B. try to mediate

_____ C. watch to see what develops

_____ D. leave the scene

8. The feedback people give me indicates that I:

_____ A. push hard to get what I want

_____ B. try to work out differences

_____ C. take a conciliatory stance

_____ D. sidestep conflict

9. When having serious disagreements, I:

_____ A. talk until I've made my point

_____ B. talk a little more than I listen

_____ C. listen and make sure I understand

_____ D. listen passively

10. When someone does something that angers me, I generally:

_____ A. use strong, direct language

_____ B. try to persuade him or her to stop

_____ C. go easy, explaining how I feel

_____ D. say and do nothing

(Continued)

Part II: Score Analysis

When you've completed the questions, add all the As, Bs, Cs, and Ds to find where you collected the most responses. Then consider these profiles:

A. *Competitive.* If you picked mostly *A* responses, you feel best when you're able to direct and control others. Taken to extremes, you can be intimidating and judgmental. You are generally contemptuous of people who don't stand up for themselves, and you feel frustrated when you can't get through to someone.

B. *Collaborative.* If you scored high in this category, you may be from the "use your head to win" school of conflict management-strong—willed and ambitious, but not overbearing. You'll use persuasion, not intimidation, and are willing to compromise to end long-running conflicts.

C. *Sharing.* People who score high here don't get fired up. They listen to the opponent's point of view, analyze situations, and make a factual pitch for their case. But in the end, they will defer to opponents in the interest of harmony.

D. *Accommodative.* A high score suggests that you avoid conflict and confrontation at all costs and suppress your feelings—strong as they may be—to keep peace.

Observation: No one style of conflict management is better than another. Most people use all four, depending on the situation. But if you rely too much on one, start shifting your approach.

Source: Adapted with permission from *Executive Strategies*, National Institute of Business Management, February 20, 1990, p. 6.

must share one computer. As a result, you are likely to enter into conflict with the two others sharing the computer. The conflict will be intense if your two coworkers also think they need full-time access to a desktop computer.

ROLE CONFLICT

A major source of conflict (and stress) on the job relates to being placed in a predicament. **Role conflict** is having to choose between two competing demands or expectations. If you comply with one aspect of a role, compliance with the other is difficult or impossible. An important example would be receiving contradictory orders from two people above you in your company. If you comply with the wishes of one person, you will antagonize the other.

A high-performing sales representative received a job offer from a manager in another division in her company. Her present manager told her she was not allowed to transfer and made her a counteroffer. The sales representative found herself in conflict with the two managers. Distraught over the conflict, she found employment with a competitive firm in a comparable position to the internal job offer she had received.

Role conflict can take various forms. You might be asked to accomplish two objectives that are in apparent conflict. If your boss asked you to hurry up and finish your work but also decrease your mistakes, you would experience this type of conflict (plus perhaps a headache!). Another problem is when two or more people give you incompatible directions. Your immediate supervisor may want you to complete a crash project on time, but company policy temporarily prohibits authorizing overtime payments to clerical help or hiring office temporaries.

Role conflict also results when two different roles that you play are in conflict. Your company may expect you to travel 50 percent of the time, whereas your spouse threatens a divorce if you travel over 25 percent of the time. To complete the picture, a form of role conflict takes place when the role(s) your organization expects you to occupy are in conflict with your basic values. Your company may ask you to fire substandard performers, but this could be in conflict with your humanistic values.

BUILDING STONE WALLS

The slow and steady growth of a conflict situation has been likened by Richard J. Mayer to the building of a stone wall. The seed of the conflict is a minor incident that is not dealt with openly, called a *pinch*. Next, the person pinched unconsciously gathers data to support his or her view of the situation because of a need to be right. Much of the data are subject to perceptual distortion (seeing things in a way that fits our needs). As a result, a wall of minor incidents is built. The incidents eventually become an insurmountable obstacle (or stone wall), preventing honest and candid interaction with the *pincher*.[1]

A typical pinch occurs when an employee fails to share credit for a good idea he or she received from a coworker. The coworker feels slighted and then looks for other incidents of the first person being dishonest. Communication breaks down between the two, and they are involved in frequent arguments. The employee who failed to share credit may be unaware of how or why the conflict began. If the pinched worker had confronted the issue early on, the conflict might not have festered. Have you ever been pinched psychologically and said nothing about it?

PERSONALITY CLASHES

Many workplace disagreements arise because people simply dislike each other. A **personality clash** is thus an antagonistic relationship between two people based on differences in personal attributes, preferences, interests, values, and styles. A personality clash reflects negative chemistry between two people, while personal differences are based more specifically on a value clash.

People involved in a personality clash often have difficulty specifying why they dislike each other. The end result, however, is that they cannot maintain an amiable work relationship. A peculiarity about personality clashes is that people who get along well may begin to clash after working together for a number of years. A contributing factor is that as both people change and as the situation changes, the two people may no longer be compatible.

AGGRESSIVE PERSONALITIES, INCLUDING BULLIES

Coworkers naturally disagree about topics, issues, and ideas. Yet some people convert disagreement into an attack that puts down other people and damages their self-esteem. As a result, conflict surfaces. **Aggressive personalities** are people who verbally, and sometimes physically, attack others frequently. Verbal aggression takes the form of insults, teasing, ridicule, and profanity. The aggression may also be expressed as attacks on the victim's character, competence, background, and physical appearance.[2]

Aggressive personalities are also referred to as *workplace bullies*. Among their typical behaviors are interrupting others, ranting in a loud voice, and making threats. One bullying manager would frequently ask people, "Are you going to be stupid the rest of your life?" Bullied workers complain of a range of psychological and physical ailments such as the following: anxiety, sleeplessness, headache, irritable bowel syndrome, skin problems, panic attacks, and low self-esteem.[3]

Aggressiveness can also take the extreme form of the shooting or knifing of a former boss or colleague by a mentally unstable worker recently dismissed from the company. Violence has become so widespread that homicide is a leading cause of workplace deaths. Most of these deaths result from a robbery or commercial crime. Many of these killings, however, are perpetrated by a disgruntled worker or former employee harboring an unresolved conflict. As companies have continued to reduce their workforce despite being profitable, these incidents have increased in frequency.[4]

CONFLICT-MANAGEMENT STYLES

The information presented so far is designed to help you understand the nature of conflict. Such background information is useful for resolving conflict because it helps you understand what is happening in a conflict situation. The next two sections offer more specific information about managing and resolving conflict. Before describing specific methods of resolving conflict, it is useful to present more details about five general styles, or modes, of handling conflict. You received preliminary information on four of these five styles when you completed Self-Assessment Quiz 7-1.

As shown in Figure 7-1, Kenneth Thomas identified five major styles of conflict management. Each style is based on a combination of satisfying one's own concerns (assertiveness) and satisfying the concerns of others (cooperativeness).[5]

Competitive Style

The competitive style is a desire to win one's own concerns at the expense of the other party, or to dominate. A person with a competitive orientation is likely to engage in power struggles in which one side wins and the other loses (an approach referred to as *win-lose*).

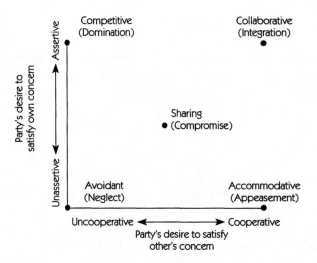

Figure 7-1 Conflict-Handling Styles According to Degree of Cooperation and Assertiveness

Source: Kenneth W. Thomas, "Organizational Conflict," in Steven Kerr, ed., *Organization Behavior* (Columbus, Ohio: Grid Publishing, 1979), p. 156.

Accommodative Style

The accommodative style favors appeasement, or satisfying the other's concerns without taking care of one's own. People with this orientation may be generous or self-sacrificing just to maintain a relationship. An irate customer might be accommodated with a full refund, just to calm down the person. The intent of such accommodation might also be to retain the customer's loyalty.

Accommodation sounds harmless, but, according to Sidney Simon, when it runs unchecked at the expense of what somebody really wants it can lead to debilitating resentment, sickness, or even violence.[6] The problem is that the suppressed feelings create inner conflict and stress.

Sharing Style

The sharing style is halfway between domination and appeasement. Sharers prefer moderate but incomplete satisfaction for both parties, which results in a compromise. The term *splitting the difference* reflects this orientation and is commonly used in such activities as purchasing a house or car.

Collaborative Style

In contrast to the other styles, the collaborative style reflects a desire to fully satisfy the desires of both parties. It is based on an underlying philosophy of **win-win**, the belief that after conflict has been resolved, both sides should gain something of value. The use of a win-win approach is genuinely aimed at arriving at a settlement that meets the needs of both parties, or at least does not badly damage the welfare of the other side. The option chosen results in a *mutual gain*. When collaborative approaches to resolving conflict are used, the relationships among the parties are built on and improved. The following example uses a win-win approach to resolve conflict.

Skill-Building Exercise 7-1

WIN-WIN CONFLICT RESOLUTION

The class organizes into small problem-solving groups. Each group spends about 10 minutes finding a win-win solution to one of the following conflict situations:

1. Two coworkers want you to go to lunch with them more regularly, but you believe that you are too busy to go out to lunch regularly.

2. Deborah, a computer operator, wants workmates to call her "Deborah." Yet several people in the office persist in calling her "Deb" or "Debbie."

3. You are offered a transfer within your company to an exciting job that you want strongly. Your manager says he cannot let you go because you are too valuable.

Bruce is an office assistant in a company that supplies food to restaurants, hospitals, and nursing homes. According to his budget analysis, Bruce needed a 5 percent salary increase to meet his monthly expenses. The company owner explained that there was no money in the budget for a salary increase. A cordial discussion about the issue led to an option for mutual gain. Bruce would receive the 5 percent salary increase as long as he increased his productivity enough to cover the increase. His target was to increase his productivity to the point that the company could decrease the hours worked by an office temporary. The amount of the decrease covered the 5 percent salary increase.

Finding win-win solutions to problems (or options for mutual gain) is one of the most important conflict-resolution skills. To obtain practice in this skill, do Skill-Building Exercise 7-1.

Avoidant Style
The avoider is a combination of uncooperative and unassertive. He or she is indifferent to the concerns of either party. The person may actually be withdrawing from the conflict to rely upon fate.

In the following description of specific techniques for resolving conflict, attempt to relate most of them to these five key styles. For example, you will observe that the confrontation and problem-solving technique reflects the collaborative style.

GUIDELINES AND TECHNIQUES FOR RESOLVING CONFLICTS

Interpersonal conflict in organizations is inevitable. A career-minded person must therefore learn effective ways of resolving conflict. In this section we describe methods of conflict resolution that you can use on your own. All are based somewhat on the underlying model of win-win, or integrating the interests of both parties. Integrating the interests focuses on resolving the underlying concerns of the parties in conflict. By dealing with these concerns, it is more worthwhile for both sides to resolve the conflict than it is to have no agreement.[7]

> Suppose a man named Bill Budweiser wanted to open a beer brewery and name his beer Budweiser. The company lawyers from Anheuser-Busch who own the rights to the brand name Budweiser would attempt to block him from using the same brand name—even if his family name is Budweiser. Bill Budweiser would hire his own lawyer to fight back. Two key concerns must be addressed. Mr. Budweiser's underlying concern is that he feels his civil liberties have been violated because he cannot name a business after himself. And Bill Budweiser must deal with Anheuser-Busch's concern about a smaller company capitalizing on its well-known name (brand equity).

Later in the chapter you will be asked to resolve the beer company conflict. For now, the five methods are as follows:

1. Confrontation and problem solving.

2. Constructive handling of criticism.

3. Image exchanging.

4. Cognitive restructuring.

5. Negotiating and bargaining.

CONFRONTATION AND PROBLEM SOLVING

The ideal approach to resolving any conflict is to confront the real issue and then solve the problem. Confrontation means taking a problem-solving approach to differences and identifying the underlying facts, logic, or emotions that account for them. When conflicts are resolved through confronting and understanding their causes, people feel responsible for finding the soundest answer.[8]

Confrontation can proceed gently, in a way that preserves a good working relationship, as shown by this example. Assume that Mary, the person working at the desk next to you, loudly cracks chewing gum while she works. You find the gum chewing both distracting and nauseating. If you don't bring the problem to Mary's attention, it will probably grow in proportion with time. Yet you are hesitant to enter into an argument about something that a person might regard as a civil liberty (the right to chew gum in public places).

A psychologically sound alternative is for you to approach her directly in this manner:

You: Mary, there is something bothering me that I would like to discuss with you.

She: Go ahead, I don't mind listening to other people's problems.

You: My problem concerns something you are doing that makes it difficult for me to concentrate on my work. When you chew gum you make loud cracking noises that grate on my nerves. It may be my problem, but the noise does bother me.

She: I guess I could stop chewing gum when you're working next to me. It's probably just a nervous habit.

CONSTRUCTIVE HANDLING OF CRITICISM

Learning to profit from criticism is an effective way of benefitting from conflict. People who benefit from criticism are able to stand outside themselves while being criticized. It is as if they are watching the criticism from a distance and looking for its possible merits. People who take criticism personally anguish when receiving negative feedback. Following are several specific suggestions for dealing with criticism, including two methods that will often get the other party on your side.[9]

1. *See yourself at a distance.* Place an imaginary Plexiglas shield between you and the person giving the criticism. Attempt to be a detached observer looking for useful information.

2. *Ask for clarification and specifics.* Ask politely for more details about the negative behavior in question so you can change if change is warranted. If your boss is criticizing you for being rude to customers, you might respond: "I certainly do not want to be rude. Can you give me a couple of examples of how I was rude? I need your help in working on this problem." After asking questions, you can better determine whether the criticism is valid.

3. *Decide on a response.* An important part of learning from criticism is to respond appropriately to the critic. Let the criticizer know what you agree with. Apologize for the undesirable behavior, such as saying, "I apologize for being rude to customers. I know what I can do differently now. I'll be more patient so as not to appear rude."

4. *Disarm the opposition.* As an extension of the point just made, you will often decide to agree with the criticizer because the person has a legitimate complaint about you. If you deny the reality of that person's complaint, he or she will continue to harp on that point and the issue will remain unresolved. By agreeing with the criticism of you, you may set the stage for a true resolution of the problem.

Agreeing with criticism made by a person with formal authority over you is effective, because by doing so you are then in a position to ask for his or her help in improving the situation. Rational managers realize that it is their responsibility to help subordinates overcome problems, not merely to criticize them. Imagine that you have been chronically late with reports during the last six months. It is time for a performance review, and you know that you will be reprimanded for your tardiness. You also hope that your manager will not

---

Skill-Building Exercise 7-2

DISARMING THE OPPOSITION

In each of these two scenarios, one person plays the role of the person with more power in the situation. The other person plays the role of the individual attempting to disarm the criticizer.

1. A representative from a credit organization telephones you at work to inform you that you are 60 days behind schedule on your car payment. The agent wants a settlement as soon as possible. Unfortunately, the credit agent is correct. Run this happy scenario for about five minutes.

2. Your manager calls you into the office to discuss the 10-page report you just submitted. The boss says in a harsh tone, "Your report is a piece of trash. I counted 25 word-use mistakes such as writing *whether* for *weather* and *seen* for *scene*. (Your spell checker couldn't catch these errors.) Besides that I can't follow many of your sentences, and you left out the table of statistics. I'm wondering if you are qualified for this job."

---

downgrade all other aspects of your performance because of your tardy reports. Here is how disarming the opposition would work in this situation:

Your manager: Have a seat. It's time for your performance review, and we have a lot to talk about. I'm concerned about some things.

You: So am I. It appears that I'm having a difficult time getting my reports in on time. I wonder if I'm being a perfectionist. Do you have any suggestions?

Your manager: Well, I like your attitude. Maybe you are trying to make your reports too perfect before you turn them in. I think you can improve in getting your reports in on time. Try not to figure everything out to five decimal places. We need thoroughness around here, but we can't overdo it.

Disarming is effective because it takes the wind out of the other person's sails and has a calming effect. The other person is often waiting to clobber you if you deny guilt. If you admit guilt, you are more difficult to clobber. Skill-Building Exercise 7-2 gives you an opportunity to practice disarming the opposition.

IMAGE EXCHANGING

The essential point of **image exchanging** is that you and your antagonist make it clear that you understand each other's point of view. Empathy of this kind may then lead to a useful and productive compromise. A convenient application of this method is for you to list on a sheet of paper (a) your side of the argument and (b) what you think is the other person's side of the argument. Next, the other person does the same for you. Figure 7-2 is an example of how images might be exchanged. Each person makes up an image sheet without

You: My side of the story	What I think is your side of the story
1. I'm usually on time for work. 2. I live on the other side of town. 3. Public transportation is unreliable in this city.	1. I'm not very dependable. 2. I live too far from the office. 3. I take the last possible bus.
Your boss: My side of the story	What I think is your side of the story
1. You are late too often. 2. If you cared more about your job you would consider moving closer to the office. 3. If you got out of bed earlier, you could take an earlier bus.	1. I'm as punctual as most people in the office. 2. I think you don't take my transportation problems seriously. 3. I try hard to get here on time. It's not my fault that I'm late sometimes.

Figure 7-2 An Image-Exchanging List Between You and Your Team Leader, Based on a Conflict About Punctuality

consulting the other person. After the images are exchanged, discussion (and sometimes fireworks) begins.

COGNITIVE RESTRUCTURING

An indirect way of resolving interpersonal conflict is to lessen the conflicting elements in a situation by viewing them more positively. According to the technique of **cognitive restructuring**, you mentally convert negative aspects into positive ones by looking for the positive elements in a situation.[10] How you frame or choose your thoughts can determine the outcome of a conflict situation. Your thoughts influence your actions. If you search for the beneficial elements in the situation, there will be less area for dispute. Although this technique might sound like a *mind game* to you, it can work effectively.

Imagine that a coworker of yours, Jeff, has been asking you repeated questions about how to carry out a work procedure. You are about ready to tell Jeff, "Go bother somebody else; I'm not paid to be a trainer." Instead, you look for the positive elements in the situation. You say to yourself, "Jeff has been asking me a lot of questions. This does take time, but answering these questions is valuable experience. If I want to become a manager, I will have to help group members with problems."

After having completed this cognitive restructuring, you can then deal with the conflict situation more positively. You might say to Jeff, "I welcome the opportunity to help you, but we need to find a mutually convenient time. In that way, I can better concentrate on my own work." To get started with cognitive restructuring, do Skill-Building Exercise 7-3.

NEGOTIATING AND BARGAINING

Conflicts can be considered situations calling for **negotiating**, or conferring, with another person to resolve a problem. When you are negotiating a fair salary for yourself, you are trying to resolve a conflict. At first the demands of

Skill-Building Exercise 7-3

COGNITIVE RESTRUCTURING

The following are examples of negative statements about coworkers. In the space provided, cognitively restructure (reframe) each comment in a positive way.

Negative: Nancy is getting on my nerves. It takes her two weeks longer than anyone else on the team to complete her input.

Positive: _____

_____

_____

_____

Negative: My boss is driving me crazy. He is forever telling me what I did wrong and making suggestions for improvement. He makes me feel like I'm in elementary school.

Positive: _____

_____

_____

_____

_____

the two parties may seem incompatible, but through negotiation, a salary figure may emerge that satisfies both.

Managers and staff specialists must negotiate both internally (e.g., with subordinates, managers, and team leaders) and externally (e.g., with suppliers and government agencies). Considerable negotiation also takes place among coworkers. Team members, for example, sometimes negotiate among themselves about work assignments. One might say to the other, "I'm willing to be notetaker this year if there is some way I can cut back on the amount of plant visits I make this year." Five leading negotiating tactics are presented here. Before studying them, do Self-Assessment Quiz 7-2.

Focus on Interests, Not Positions

Rather than clinging to specific negotiating points, keep your overall interests in mind and try to satisfy them. Remember that the true object of negotiation is to satisfy the underlying interests on both sides, as in the case of Bill Budweiser. Here is how this strategy works:

You are considering accepting a job offer that will enable you to work on the type of problems you prefer and also develop your professional skills. You have a starting salary in mind that would make you very happy—15

Self-Assessment Quiz 7-2

THE NEGOTIATOR QUIZ

Directions: The following quiz is designed to give you tentative insight into your tendencies toward being an effective negotiator. Answer each statement "Mostly true" or "Mostly false" as it applies to you.

	Mostly true	Mostly false
1. Settling differences of opinion is a lot of fun.	_____	_____
2. I try to avoid conflict and confrontation with others as much as possible.	_____	_____
3. I am self-conscious asking people for favors they have not offered me spontaneously.	_____	_____
4. I am generally unwilling to compromise.	_____	_____
5. How the other side feels about the results of our negotiation is of little consequence to me.	_____	_____
6. I think very well under pressure.	_____	_____
7. People say that I am tactful and diplomatic.	_____	_____
8. I'm known for my ability to express my viewpoint clearly.	_____	_____
9. Very few things in life are not negotiable.	_____	_____
10. I always (or would always) accept whatever salary increase is offered to me.	_____	_____
11. A person's facial expression often reveals as much as what the person actually says.	_____	_____
12. I wouldn't mind taking a few short-range losses to win a long-range battle.	_____	_____
13. I'm willing to work long and hard to win a small advantage.	_____	_____
14. I'm usually too busy talking to do much listening.	_____	_____
15. It's fun to haggle over price when buying a car.	_____	_____
16. I almost always prepare in advance for a negotiating session.	_____	_____
17. When there is something I need from another person I usually get it.	_____	_____
18. It would make me feel cheap if I offered somebody only two-thirds of his or her asking price.	_____	_____
19. People are usually paid what they are worth, so there's no use haggling over starting salaries.	_____	_____
20. I rarely take what people say at face value.	_____	_____

(Continued)

142 ➤ CHAP. 7   RESOLVING CONFLICTS WITH OTHERS

	Mostly true	Mostly false
21. It's easy for me to smile when involved in a serious discussion.	___	___
22. For one side to win in negotiation, the other side has to lose.	___	___
23. Once you start making concessions, the other side is bound to get more than you.	___	___
24. A good negotiating session gets my competitive urges flowing.	___	___
25. When negotiations are completed, both sides should walk away with something valuable.	___	___

Total Score _____

Scoring and Interpretation: Score yourself +1 for each of your answers that agrees with the scoring key. The higher your score, the more likely it is that you currently have good negotiating skills, *providing your self-assessment is accurate.* It might prove useful to also have somebody who has observed you negotiate on several occasions to answer the Negotiator Quiz for you. Scores of 7 or lower and 20 or higher are probably the most indicative of weak or strong negotiating potential. Here is the scoring key:

1. Mostly true	8. Mostly true	15. Mostly true	22. Mostly false
2. Mostly false	9. Mostly true	16. Mostly true	23. Mostly false
3. Mostly false	10. Mostly false	17. Mostly true	24. Mostly true
4. Mostly false	11. Mostly true	18. Mostly false	25. Mostly true
5. Mostly false	12. Mostly true	19. Mostly false	
6. Mostly true	13. Mostly true	20. Mostly true	
7. Mostly true	14. Mostly false	21. Mostly true	

percent higher than you are currently making. Your negotiating position is thus your present salary plus 15 percent. However, your true interests are probably to have more discretionary income than at present. (You want to make more purchases and invest more.) You will therefore be better off negotiating for a work situation that spreads your money further. You can now accept the offer by negotiating other points in addition to a 15 percent higher salary, including (a) working in a geographic area with a lower cost of living, (b) a better opportunity for earning a bonus, or (c) a generous expense account.

Compromise
The most widely used negotiating tactic is **compromise**, settlement of differences by mutual concessions. One party agrees to do something if the other party agrees to do something else. Compromise is a realistic approach to resolving conflict. Most labor-management disputes are settled by compromise. For instance, labor may agree to accept a smaller salary increase if management will subcontract less work to other countries.

Some people argue that compromise is not a win-win tactic. The problem is that the two parties may wind up with a solution that pacifies both but does not solve the problem. One example would be purchasing for two department heads half the new equipment each one needs. As a result, neither department really shows a productivity gain. Nevertheless, compromise is both inevitable and useful.

Begin with a Plausible Demand or Offer, Yet Allow Room for Negotiation

The commonsense approach to negotiation suggests that you begin with an extreme, almost fanciful demand or offer. The final compromise will therefore be closer to your true demand or offer than if you opened the negotiations more realistically. However, a plausible demand is useful because it shows you are bargaining in good faith. Also, if a third party has to resolve a conflict, a plausible demand or offer will receive more sympathy than an implausible one will.

> A judge listened to the cases of two people who claimed they were the victims of age discrimination by the same employer. The lawyer for the first alleged victim asked for $10 million in damages; the lawyer for the second victim asked for $200,000. The first person was awarded $50,000 in damages, and the second person $150,000. An inside source reported that the judge was so incensed by the first lawyer's demands that she decided to teach him a lesson.

Although it is advisable to begin with a plausible demand, one must still allow room for negotiation. A basic strategy of negotiation is to begin with a demand that allows room for compromise and concession. If you think you need $5,000 in new software for your department, you might begin negotiations by asking for a $7,000 package. Your boss offers you $4,000 as a starting point. After negotiation, you may wind up with the $5,000 you need.

Make Small Concessions Gradually

Making steady concessions leads to more mutually satisfactory agreements in most situations. Gradually, you concede little things to the other side. The hard-line approach to bargaining is to make your concession early in the negotiation and then grant no further concession. The tactic of making small concessions is well suited to purchasing a new car. In order to reach a price you consider acceptable, you might grant concessions such as agreeing to finance the car through the dealer or purchasing a service contract.

Know Your Best Alternative to a Negotiated Agreement (BATNA)

The reason you would probably negotiate would be to produce something better than the result obtainable without negotiating. The goal of negotiating is thus not just to agree, but to obtain more valuable results than would otherwise have occurred. When you are aware of your best alternative to a negotiated agreement (BATNA), it sets a floor to the agreement you are willing to accept. Your BATNA becomes the standard that can protect both parties from accepting terms that are too unfavorable. It also keeps you from walking away from terms that would be beneficial for you to accept.

What might a BATNA look like in practice? Suppose you are negotiating a starting salary for a full-time, professional position. The figure you have in mind is $35,000 per year. Your BATNA is $29,500 because this is the salary your future in-laws will pay you to enter the family business. You will therefore walk away from any offer of less than $30,000—just taking salary into account.

Knowing the other side's BATNA is also important because it helps define the other participant's bargaining zone. Understanding each other's bargaining zones makes it possible to arrive at mutually profitable trade-offs. In the preceding salary negotiations, the company's BATNA might be to hire a less well educated job candidate at $25,000 and then upgrade his or her knowledge on the job.

Effective negotiation, as with any other form of conflict resolution, requires extensive practice and knowledge of basic principles and techniques. As a starting point you might take one of the negotiating tactics just described and practice it where the stakes are not so high. You might attempt to negotiate the price of a consumer electronics device, or negotiate for getting a particular Friday afternoon off from work.

COMBATTING SEXUAL HARASSMENT: A SPECIAL TYPE OF CONFLICT

Many employees face conflict because they are sexually harassed by a supervisor, coworker, or customer. **Sexual harassment** is generally defined as unwanted sexually oriented behavior in the workplace that results in discomfort and/or interference with the job. It can include an action as violent as rape or as subtle as a sexually oriented comment about a person's body or appearance. Here we will focus on the types and frequency of sexual harassment, recent legal rulings on the nature of harassment, the effects of harassment, and guidelines for dealing with the problem.

TYPES AND FREQUENCY OF HARASSMENT

Two types of sexual harassment are recognized by the courts. In quid pro quo sexual harassment, the individual suffers job loss, or threatened loss of a job benefit, as a result of his or her responses to a request for sexual favors. The demands of a harasser can be explicit or implied. An example of quid pro quo harassment would be a manager promising an employee a promotion in exchange for sexual favors and then not promoting the employee because the employee refused.

The other form of sexual harassment is hostile environment harassment. It occurs when someone in the workplace creates an intimidating, hostile, or offensive working environment. No tangible loss has to be suffered in this form of sexual harassment. An employee who is subjected to sexually suggestive comments, lewd jokes, or advances is a victim of hostile environment harassment.

Sexual harassment through creating an intimidating environment received worldwide attention starting in 1991. The occasion was Congressional hearings to determine whether Judge Clarence Thomas, a Supreme Court justice nominee, had sexually harassed a former employee, Professor Anita F. Hill. Although Congress subsequently approved Thomas as a Supreme Court justice, employers became more sensitive to the problem of sexual harassment. A long series of sexual harassment charges against U.S. Senator Robert Packwood two years later brought further attention to the problem. Still later, President Bill Clinton was charged with sexual harassment for an incident that allegedly took place when he was governor of Arkansas. A higher court judge later ruled the complaint did not merit a trial, and the woman making the complaint received an out-of-court settlement.

Sexual harassment is also regarded as an expression of power by one individual over another, because the harasser has more formal power than the harassed. The harasser, following this logic, is a power abuser as well as a legal offender.

Sexual harassment is widespread in the U. S. workplace and in other countries as well. According to one compilation of figures, at least one-half of all women have been harassed at some point in their career. Furthermore, at least 10 percent have quit a job because of sexual harassment. Women in nontraditional jobs (such as welder or pressroom supervisor) are especially likely to be harassed. In a study of women business firm employees, 68 percent indicated that they had experienced at least one sexually harassing behavior on the job during the previous 24 months. Also, the number of sexual harassment claims reported to the Equal Employment Opportunity Commission keeps rising.[11]

RECENT SUPREME COURT RULINGS ON SEXUAL HARASSMENT

An important fact to understand about sexual harassment is that the definition of what constitutes harassment continues to evolve. Many courts at all levels continue to create new rules about liability for sexual harassment and what specific act can be considered a form of sexual harassment. To illustrate the complexity of the problem, we will look at the essence of three U. S. Supreme Court rulings made in 1998.[12]

1. *Can the behavior be considered sexual harassment when the misconduct is between members of the same sex?* In *Oncale vs. Sundowner Offshore Services Inc.,* the Supreme Court ruled unanimously that sexual harassment is actionable even when the people involved are of the same sex. The case involved a male deckhand whose supervisors and coworkers forcibly subjected him on numerous occasions to humiliating, sex-related actions in front of the rest of the crew. What matters is the conduct at issue, not the sex of the people involved. Also of importance, the presence or absence of sexual desire, same sex or opposite sex, is not a determining factor for behavior to be considered sexual harassment.

2. *Can the behavior be considered sexual harassment where there is no tangible adverse effect to the job?* In *Burlington Industries Inc. vs. Ellerth,* the Court ruled 7 to 2 that an employer can be liable for sexual harassment whether or not a supervisor's threats to job status are carried out. However, the employer can be relieved of liability if it exercised reasonable care to prohibit and remedy harassment. An equally important factor is whether the employee took advantage of the corrective opportunities offered by the employer. The case involved a marketing assistant whose manager, a regional vice president, made repeated passes at her. Despite rebuffing his advances, the woman did not suffer any job detriment. Also, the woman never informed the company about the manager's misconduct.

3. *Is an organization liable for sexual harassment when the organization is unaware of a supervisor's misconduct?* In *Farager vs. City of Boca Raton, Florida,* the Court ruled 7 to 2 that an employer is liable for a pervasive, hostile atmosphere of harassment. At the same time, an employer is potentially liable for its supervisors' misconduct, whether the company was aware of the harassment or not. The case involved a woman lifeguard who claimed she endured repeated sexual harassment from two male supervisors during the five years she worked on the Boca Raton beaches. The city had failed to disseminate its anti-sexual-harassment policy to its lifeguard employees and supervisors.

THE ADVERSE EFFECTS OF SEXUAL HARASSMENT

Aside from being unethical, immoral, and illegal, sexual harassment is widely thought to have adverse consequences. The harassed person may experience job stress, lowered morale, severe conflict, and lowered productivity. A study with business and university workers documents some of the problems associated with sexual harassment. It was found that even at low levels of frequency, harassment exerts a significant impact on women's psychological well-being, job attitudes, and work behaviors. For both business and university workers, women who had experienced high levels of harassment reported the worst job-related and psychological effects. The study also found that women who had experienced only a moderate level of harassment suffered from negative outcomes.[13]

A related study of the long-term effects of sexual harassment indicated that the negative effects remained two years after the incident. For example, 24 months after an incident of sexual harassment many women still experienced stress, a decrease in job satisfaction, and lowered productivity.[14]

GUIDELINES FOR PREVENTING AND DEALING WITH SEXUAL HARASSMENT

A starting point in dealing with sexual harassment is to develop an awareness of the types of behaviors that are considered sexual harassment. Often the difference is subtle. Suppose, for example, you placed copies of two nudes painted by Renoir, the French painter, on a coworker's desk. Your coworker might call that harassment. Yet if you took that coworker to a museum to see the originals of the same nude prints, your behavior usually would not be classified as harassment. Following is a sampling of behaviors that will often be interpreted as environmental harassment:[15] If people refrain from doing them, many instances of sexual harassment will be avoided.

➤ *Inappropriate remarks and sexual implications.* Coworkers, subordinates, customers, and suppliers should not be referred to as sexual beings, and their appearance should not be referred to in a sexual manner. Telling a coworker she has gorgeous feet, or he has fabulous biceps, is out of place at work.

➤ *Terms of endearment.* Refrain from calling others in the workplace by names such as "cutie," "sweetie pie," "honey," "dear," or "hunk." One might argue that these terms are simply *sexist* (different roles for men and women) and not sexual harassment. However, this argument is losing ground, because any behavior that puts people down based on their gender can be interpreted as harassment from a legal perspective. Keep in mind also that some people find terms of endearment to have a sexual connotation. If you felt no physical attraction toward another adult would you call that person "cutie" or "hunk"?

➤ *Suggestive compliments.* It is acceptable to tell another person he or she looks nice, but avoid sexually tinged comments such as mentioning that the person's clothing shows off his or her body to advantage.

➤ *Physical touching.* To avoid any appearance of sexual harassment it is best to restrict physical touching to handshakes and an occasional sideways hug. Hugging a long-term work associate is much more acceptable than hugging a new hire. Minimize such behaviors as adjusting a coworker's earring, touching hair, and tweaking a person's chin.

➤ *Work-related kissing.* It is best to avoid all kissing in a work context—except, perhaps, a light kiss at an office party. It is much more professional to greet a work associate with a warm, sincere handshake.

Company management also plays a major role in preventing and dealing with sexual harassment. Based on the observations of dozens of human resource specialists and employment law attorneys, several actions by management are critical.[16] The cornerstone of control of sexual harassment is creating and widely disseminating a policy about harassment. Dissemination includes stuffing copies of the sexual harassment policy in pay envelopes, distributing the policy to all employees by e-mail, and discussing the policy in department meetings.

The policy should carefully define harassment and state that the company has zero tolerance for such behavior. Company officials designated for hearing complaints should be specified. In addition, the company should have an *open door policy* about harassment. Such a policy means that any employee with a con-

The potential or actual victim of sexual harassment is advised to use the following methods and tactics to deal with the problem.

Formal Complaint Procedure. Whenever an employee believes that he or she has encountered sexual harassment, or if an employee is suspected to be the perpetrator of sexual harassment, the complainant should report the incident to his or her immediate supervisor (if that person is not the harasser) or to the next higher level of management if the supervisor *is* the harasser. The supervisor contacted is responsible for contacting a designated company official immediately regarding each complaint. The officer will explain the investigative procedures to the complainant and any supervisor involved. All matters will be kept strictly confidential, including private conversations with all parties.

Dealing with the Problem on Your Own. The easiest way to deal with sexual harassment is to speak up before it becomes serious. The first time it happens, respond with a statement such as: "I won't tolerate this kind of talk." "I dislike sexually oriented jokes." "Keep your hands off me."

Write the harasser a stern letter shortly after the first incident. Being confronted in writing dramatizes your seriousness of purpose in not wanting to be sexually harassed. Tell the actual or potential harasser: "You're practicing sexual harassment. If you don't stop, I'm going to exercise my right to report you to management." Or: "I think I heard you right. Would you like to accompany me to the boss's office and repeat what you said to me?"

Figure 7-3 How to Deal with Sexual Harassment

cern about being harassed is able to go directly to a senior manager without worrying about his or her supervisor's taking revenge.

Brief company training programs covering the type of information presented in this chapter are also part of a serious program to prevent and deal with sexual harassment. However, a one-time presentation of a 15-minute videotape about sexual harassment is not sufficient. Periodic discussion about the topic is recommended.

After sexual harassment has taken place, the victim will usually want to resolve the conflict. Two key strategies are either to use a formal complaint procedure or to resolve the conflict on your own. If you choose the latter course you will save yourself the time of going through a lengthy investigation procedure. Figure 7-3 presents details about the two key strategies for dealing with sexual harassment. Skill-Building Exercise 7-4 offers you an opportunity to simulate the control of sexual harassment.

SUMMARY

A conflict is a situation in which two or more goals, values, or events are incompatible or mutually exclusive. Interpersonal conflicts have many sources or causes. An underlying source of job conflict is that people compete for limited resources. Another leading cause of incompatibility is role conflict,

Skill-Building Exercise 7-4

COMBATTING SEXUAL HARASSMENT

The two role plays in this exercise provide practice in applying the recommended techniques for combatting sexual harassment. The activities have an implied sexual content, and they are for educational purposes only. Any students offended by these role plays should exclude themselves from participating.

Scenario 1: The Offensive Jester. One student plays the role of Max, a man who delights in telling sexually oriented jokes and anecdotes in the office. He often brings a tabloid newspaper to the office to read sexually oriented passages to coworkers, both male and female. Another student assumes the role of Maxine, a woman in the office who takes offense to Max's humor. She wants to convince Max that he is committing sexual harassment with his sexually oriented humor. Max does not see himself as committing sexual harassment.

Scenario 2: The Flirtatious Office Manager. One student assumes the role of Bertha, an office manager who is single. Another student plays the role of Bert, a married man who recently joined the company as an office assistant. Bert reports to Bertha, and she finds him physically attractive. Bertha visits Bert at his desk and makes such comments as "It looks like you have great quadriceps. I wonder what you look like in running shorts?" Bert wants to be on good terms with Bertha, but he feels uncomfortable with her advances. He also wants to behave professionally in the office.

Run both role plays in front of the class for about eight minutes. Other students in the class will observe the role plays and then provide feedback about how well Maxine and Bert were able to prevent or stop sexual harassment.

having to choose between two competing demands or expectations. Other key sources of conflict are as follows: building of stone walls (the accumulation of minor hurtful incidents); personality clashes; and aggressive personalities, including bullies.

Five major styles of conflict management have been identified: competitive, accommodative, sharing, collaborative (win-win), and avoidant. Each style is based on a combination of satisfying one's own concerns (assertiveness) and satisfying the concerns of others (cooperativeness).

Confrontation and problem solving is the ideal method for resolving conflict. Learning to benefit from criticism is an effective way of benefitting from conflict. People who benefit from criticism are able to stand outside themselves while being criticized. Another way to deal with criticism is to disarm the opposition by agreeing with his or her criticism. Image exchanging deals with conflict by enabling each party to understand the other's viewpoint. Cognitive restructuring lessens conflict by the person looking for the positive elements in a situation.

An Interpersonal Relations Case Problem

SMOKERS' RIGHTS

Child-Decor, a manufacturer of children's furniture, recently placed a total smoking ban on employees. The official policy stated that company employees were not allowed to smoke on company premises, but they were allowed to smoke outside the building. If caught smoking inside the factory or office they would be subject to discipline, such as written documentation in their personnel files, suspension, or demotion. Repeated violators would be subject to dismissal.

Company president Bill Garrison, himself a former two-pack-a-day smoker, was proud of Child-Decor's new policy. In a speech to employees, he stated: "Our company has taken a giant step forward in creating a safe work environment. We are helping hundreds of our employees avoid the biggest job hazard they will ever face—passive smoking. It is much more dangerous than anything else you will inhale in a furniture factory. Every Child-Decor employee has a right to breathe air unpolluted with carcinogens. I am certain that the few remaining smokers among you will agree that the health and safety of the majority must take precedence over the addictions of the minority.

"My door is always open to discuss our new policy. And please keep your supervisors informed of any difficulties encountered in creating a smoke-free environment."

Thirty days after the new policy began, Garrison asked his administrative assistant, Kathy Chang, to investigate how well the policy was working. While wandering around the office and the factory, Chang spoke to a number of Child-Decor employees to obtain a clear perspective on how well the smoking ban was being received.

"To be truthful," commented Bruce Garcia, a production scheduler, "this new policy is making me physically sick. And I intend to fight back. These smokers are revolting. They gather outside every doorway to smoke throughout the day. When you walk in on a still day you hit this wall of putrid smoke. It's as bad as the rest rooms used to be when smoking was only allowed there. Smokers should not be allowed to smoke within 50 feet of a building entrance."

Inge Goldfarb, an office assistant, offered these observations with anger in her voice: "Never in my 15 years of working for this company have I been treated so shabbily. Forcing me to go outside my building to engage in a perfectly legal activity smacks of totalitarianism. What right do nonsmokers have to make smoking a crime? Show me the scientific evidence that smoking in a ventilated area is harming people who do not smoke. If you ask me, Mr. Garrison has gone overboard."

Terry McWorth, an industrial engineer, said to Chang: "It's too early to provide hard data, but I think the smoking ban is lowering productivity. I've heard a lot of complaints that the smokers are spending too much time outside the building smoking. They are missing time from work, and people have to be shifted around to cover for them. It's a tough sell to convince a nonsmoking worker to cover for a smoker who is outside the building puffing away.

"Another problem the smoking ban has created is that I see evidence of hard feelings between some smokers and nonsmokers. The smoking ban has been divisive. It shows up in little ways, like a smoker not cooperating with a nonsmoker. The reason seems to be that the smoker now feels like a second-class citizen."

Melody Lewis, a purchasing assistant, informed Chang: "I and a few other smokers are willing to put up with this policy for now. So far the weather has been cooperating. But can you imagine being forced to smoke outside the building when it's snowing, raining, sleeting, or freezing cold? Smoking outside in 100-degree weather wouldn't be too comfortable either. It's ludicrous. Give us back our smoking lounge,

(Continued)

and treat us like human beings. This is a furniture factory, not a prison. I'm getting ticked off at these smug nonsmokers who have made life so uncomfortable for us."

Gil McAlister, a customer service representative, told Chang: "I like the policy. I was smoking a pack a day on the job. I'm now down to 10 cigarettes, and I enjoy the breaks outside. Since it's company policy to smoke outside, I don't have to feel guilty. I wish those other smokers would stop complaining. They may be killing off a good thing."

Chang reported back to Garrison that the ban on smoking inside the building was creating problems, and she wondered whether something should be done about the situation. "There are more animosities being created than is good for the company," said Chang.

Case Questions

1. What actions, if any, should the company take to resolve conflict between smokers and nonsmokers?

2. What methods of conflict resolution should smokers and nonsmokers use to resolve conflict among themselves?

3. What is your opinion about whether the rights of smokers are being violated?

Negotiating is a major approach to resolving conflict. It includes focusing on interests rather than positions, compromise, beginning with a plausible demand or offer yet allowing room for negotiation, and making small concessions gradually. It is also important to know your BATNA (best alternative to a negotiated agreement).

Sexual harassment is a form of interpersonal conflict with legal implications. The two forms of sexual harassment are (1) demanding sex in exchange for favors and (2) creating a hostile environment. Sexual harassment is widespread in the workplace, and the U. S. Supreme Court has reached three recent decisions to help interpret the meaning of sexual harassment. Research has pinpointed adverse mental and physical consequences of sexual harassment.

A starting point in dealing with sexual harassment is to develop an awareness of the types of behaviors it encompasses. Company policies and complaint procedures about harassment are a major part of dealing with the problem. To deal directly with harassment, the harassed person can file a formal complaint or confront the harasser when the behavior first begins.

QUESTIONS FOR DISCUSSION AND REVIEW

1. How might conflict among students to obtain high grades be seen as competition for limited resources?

2. What good does it do for you to know a work associate's conflict style?

3. What are the disadvantages of having an accommodative style of handling conflict?

4. Remember the hypothetical conflict between Bill Budweiser and the Anheuser-Busch Company? What solution do you propose to satisfy the underlying interests of both parties?

An Interpersonal Relations Role Play

IMAGE EXCHANGING

Assume that the company decides to resolve some of the conflict between smokers and non-smokers using image exchanging. Several students play the role of representatives of the smokers, and another group plays the role of representatives of the nonsmokers. Play out the image exchange, going through the steps outlined in Figure 7-2. The four key elements are as follows: (1) the nonsmokers' side of the story, (2) the nonsmokers' perception of the smokers' side of the story, (3) the smokers' side of the story, and (4) the smokers' perception of the nonsmokers' side of the story.

5. Experts have observed that it is difficult for most people to confront others. Why is confrontation so difficult for so many people?

6. Have you ever attempted to disarm the opposition? How effective was the tactic?

7. How might a student use cognitive restructuring to get over the anger of having received a low grade in a course?

8. Visualize yourself buying a new car of your choice. Which negotiating technique (or techniques) would you be the most likely to use?

9. What would be an appropriate punishment or reprimand for a company president or CEO who was found guilty of quid pro quo sexual harassment with 10 different women during one year?

10. Is inviting a coworker to dinner a second time a form of sexual harassment if the coworker refused the first invitation?

Chapter 13

Enhancing Ethical Behavior

Learning Objectives

After reading and studying this chapter and doing the exercises you should be able to

➤ Recognize the importance of ethical behavior for establishing good interpersonal relationships in organizations.

➤ Identify several character traits associated with being an ethical person.

➤ Identify job situations that often present ethical dilemmas.

➤ Use a systematic method for making ethical decisions and behaving ethically.

"I like this sedan quite a lot," said Malcolm to the new-car sales representative. "We agree on the price, and I'm ready to buy today, with one exception. I would like a sunroof. How much extra would that cost?" Paula, the sales representative, said she would return shortly with the information.

After checking in the office, Paula said that the sunroof would cost $525. She told Malcolm, "We are adding the sunroof at cost as a service to you. Auto Works will install it. They do a great job."

Later that day Malcolm was speaking to a friend about his new purchase. His friend said, "You'll love a sunroof. My neighbor just had one installed at Auto Works. I remember it cost him $425." Puzzled by this price discrepancy, Malcolm telephoned Auto Works to inquire about the price of his sunroof. The company representative said, "We charged $425. I can show you the invoice."

Infuriated by the price markup, Malcolm went back to the dealer and confronted Paula. She explained that the dealership typically charges a handling fee when an outside shop installs an option. The fee is part of the cost. Enraged, Malcolm spoke to the manager of the dealership. The manager agreed to refund the handling fee. Malcolm was satisfied with the refund but felt mistreated by Paula and the dealership.

The situation at the auto dealership illustrates ethical issues in the workplace. By being deceptive about the cost of the sunroof, Paula added to the deal a little profit for the firm and a small commission for herself. Some would say Paula was using a clever business tactic, while others might question her ethics. **Ethics** refers to what is good and bad, right and wrong, just and unjust, and what people should do.

We study ethics here because a person's ethical code has a significant impact on his or her interpersonal relationships. Our approach will emphasize the importance of ethics, common ethical problems, and guidelines for behaving ethically. Self-Assessment Quiz 13-1 gives you the opportunity to examine your ethical beliefs and attitudes.

WHY BE CONCERNED ABOUT BUSINESS ETHICS?

When asked why ethics is important, most people would respond something to the effect that, "ethics is important because it's the right thing to do. You behave decently in the workplace because your family and religious values have taught you what is right and wrong." All true so far, but the justification for behaving ethically is more complex, as described next.[1]

A major justification for behaving ethically on the job is to recognize that people are motivated by both self-interest and moral commitments. Most people want to maximize gain for themselves (remember the expectancy theory of motivation?). At the same time, most people are motivated to do something morally right. As one of many examples, vast numbers of people donate money to charity, although keeping that amount of money for themselves would provide more personal gain.

THE ETHICAL REASONING INVENTORY

Directions: Describe how well you agree with each of the following statements. Use the following scale: Disagree strongly (DS); Disagree (D); Neutral (N); Agree (A); Agree strongly (AS).

	DS	D	N	A	AS
1. When applying for a job, I would cover up the fact that I had been fired from my most recent job.	5	4	3	2	1
2. Cheating just a few dollars in one's favor on an expense account is OK if a person needs the money.	5	4	3	2	1
3. Employees should inform on each other for wrongdoing.	1	2	3	4	5
4. It is acceptable to give approximate figures for expense account items when one does not have all the receipts.	5	4	3	2	1
5. I see no problem with conducting a little personal business on company time.	5	4	3	2	1
6. Just to make a sale, I would stretch the truth about a delivery date.	5	4	3	2	1
7. I would fix up a purchasing agent with a date just to close a sale.	5	4	3	2	1
8. I would flirt with my boss just to get a bigger salary increase.	5	4	3	2	1
9. If I received $200 for doing some odd jobs, I would report it on my income tax return.	1	2	3	4	5
10. I see no harm in taking home a few office supplies.	5	4	3	2	1
11. It is acceptable to read the e-mail messages and faxes of other workers, even when not invited to do so.	5	4	3	2	1
12. It is unacceptable to call in sick in order to take a day off, even if only done once or twice a year.	1	2	3	4	5
13. I would accept a permanent, full-time job even if I knew I wanted the job for only six months.	5	4	3	2	1
14. I would first check company policy before accepting an expensive gift from a supplier.	1	2	3	4	5
15. To be successful in business, a person usually has to ignore ethics.	5	4	3	2	1
16. If I felt physically attracted toward a job candidate I would hire that person over a more qualified candidate.	5	4	3	2	1
17. On the job, I tell the truth all the time.	1	2	3	4	5
18. If a student were very pressed for time, it would be acceptable to either have a friend write the paper or purchase one.	5	4	3	2	1
19. I would authorize accepting an office machine on a 30-day trial period, even if I knew we had no intention of buying it.	5	4	3	2	1
20. I would never accept credit for a coworker's ideas.	1	2	3	4	5

(Continued)

Scoring and Interpretation: Add the numbers you have circled to obtain your total score.

90–100 You are a strongly ethical person who may take a little ribbing from coworkers for being too strait-laced.

60–89 You show an average degree of ethical awareness, and therefore should become more sensitive to ethical issues.

41–59 Your ethics are underdeveloped, but you at least have some awareness of ethical issues. You need to raise your level of awareness of ethical issues.

20–40 Your ethical values are far below contemporary standards in business. Begin a serious study of business ethics.

Many business executives want employees to behave ethically because a good reputation can enhance business. A favorable corporate reputation may enable firms to charge premium prices and attract better job applicants. A favorable reputation also helps attract investors, such as mutual fund managers who purchase stock in companies. Certain mutual funds, for example, invest only in companies that are environmentally friendly. Managers want employees to behave ethically because unethical behavior is costly—for example, employee theft, lost production time, lawsuits.

Behaving ethically is also important because many unethical acts are also illegal, which can lead to financial loss and imprisonment. A company that knowingly allows workers to engage in unsafe practices might be fined and the executives held personally liable. Furthermore, unsafe practices can kill people. In recent history, two employees burned to death in a fire they could not escape in a chicken processing plant. Management had blocked the back doors to prevent employees from sneaking chicken parts out of the plant.

A subtle reason for behaving ethically is that high ethics increases the quality of work life. Ethics provides a set of guidelines that specify what makes for acceptable behavior. Being ethical will point you toward actions that make life more satisfying for work associates. A company code of ethics specifies what constitutes ethical versus unethical behavior. When employees follow this code, the quality of work life improves. Several sample clauses from ethical codes are as follows:

➤ Demonstrate courtesy, respect, honesty, and fairness.

➤ Do not use abusive language.

➤ Do not bring firearms or knives to work.

➤ Do not offer bribes.

➤ Maintain confidentiality of records.

➤ Do not harass (sexually, racially, ethnically, or physically) subordinates, superiors, coworkers, customers, or suppliers.

To the extent that all members of the organization abide by this ethical code, the quality of work life will improve. At the same time, interpersonal relations in organizations will be strengthened.

COMMON ETHICAL PROBLEMS

To become more skilled at behaving ethically, it is important to familiarize yourself with common ethical problems in organizations. Whether or not a given situation presents an ethical problem for a person depends to some extent on its **moral intensity**, or how deeply others might be affected.[2] A worker might face a strong ethical conflict about dumping mercury into a water supply but would be less concerned about dumping cleaning fluid. Yet both acts would be considered unethical and illegal. Here we look at some data about the frequency of ethical problems and an analysis of predictable ethical temptations. We also examine the subtle ethical dilemma of choosing between rights.

A SURVEY OF THE EXTENT OF ETHICAL PROBLEMS

A substantial number of managers and employees engage in unethical behavior, often because they feel pressured into making a quick profit. Feeling under pressure, in general, or not taking the time to think through the ethics of an issue, can lead to unethical behavior in order to save time. A study of 1,324 workers conducted by the American Society of Chartered Life Underwriters & Chartered Financial Consultants and the Ethics Officer Association provides some illuminating facts. Highlights of the study are that:[3]

➤ 60 percent of workers feel a substantial amount of pressure on the job.

➤ 56 percent of workers feel some pressure to act unethically or illegally on the job.

➤ 48 percent of workers admitted they had engaged in one or more unethical and/or illegal actions during the last year, such as: cutting corners on quality; abusing or lying about sick days; lying to or deceiving customers; lying to or deceiving a manager about a serious matter; and taking credit for a coworker's ideas.

➤ 52 percent of workers feel more pressure from balancing work and family.

➤ 60 percent of workers believe that ethics and business practices can indeed mix.

The 60 percent of respondents just mentioned believed that ethical dilemmas could be reduced if more communication about ethical problems took place. Also, top-level managers must show a stronger commitment to ethical behavior.

FREQUENT ETHICAL DILEMMAS

According to Linda K. Treviño and Katherine A. Nelson, mishandling an ethical issue can severely damage your career. Although this observation may be disturbing, there is also comforting news. Many ethical dilemmas in business are predictable. Here we list a number of common ethical problems faced by business executives as well as workers at lower job levels.[4]

The Temptation to Illegally Copy Software

A rampant ethical problem is whether or not to illegally copy software. Figure 13-1 offers details about and insight into this widespread ethical dilemma.

Treating People Unfairly

Being fair to people means equity, reciprocity, and impartiality. Fairness revolves around the issue of giving people equal rewards for accomplishing equal amounts of work. The goal of human resource legislation is to make decisions about people based on their qualifications and performance—not on the basis of demographic factors such as sex, race, or age. A fair working environment is where performance is the only factor that counts (*equity*). Employer–employee expectations must be understood and met (*reciprocity*). Prejudice and bias must be eliminated (*impartiality*).

To treat people fairly—and therefore ethically—an overemphasis on political factors would be unethical. Yet this ethical doctrine is not always easy to implement. It is human nature to want to give bigger rewards (such as fatter raises or bigger orders) to people we like.

Job Discrimination

A major aspect of unfairness is **job discrimination**, or an unfavorable action brought against a person because of a characteristic unrelated to job performance. Discriminating against others is illegal as well as unethical. Many federal, state, and local laws prohibit discrimination in all phases of employment. A case in point is the Americans with Disabilities Act (ADA) of 1991. The act is designed to protect people with disabilities from discrimination in employment, public accommodations, transportation, and telecommunications. The ADA defines **disability** as a physical or mental condition that substantially limits an individual's major life activities. In recent years many workers have made unethical interpretations of the ADA to protect themselves from job loss. An example is an employee who physically attacked another employee and was therefore dismissed. He claimed he was suffering from job stress and should not have been fired because job stress is a disability! At first he won his case, but a higher court overruled.

The obvious situations in which to guard against discrimination are in hiring and promoting people. It is also important to guard against discrimination when choosing coworkers as team members and luncheon companions. A highly ethical person reaches out to diverse people, including young and old, able-bodied and disabled, white and people of color.

A flagrant unethical *and illegal* job behavior is unauthorized copying of software. When confronted with software pirating, people are quick to rationalize their actions. Here are the top ten defenses of software pirates. (None of them are likely to hold up if you are caught.)

1. *I'm allowed to make a backup disk in case something happens to the original, so it must be okay to use it on another machine.* A backup is strictly a backup to be used on the same computer. The original should be safely locked away, and the copy should be stored away only.

2. *I didn't copy it—a friend gave it to me.* Technically you are right. You would not be guilty of illegally copying software in this case, although your friend would. However, since illegally copied software is regarded as stolen property, you are just as guilty as you would be for stealing it in the first place.

3. *My boss (or department head, or instructor) told me to. It's that person's problem.* The defense "I was just following orders" is a weak one. Complying with your boss's demands to commit an illegal act does not get you off the hook. You could be fired for obeying an order to commit a crime.

4. *I bought the software; shouldn't I be able to do what I want with it?* Software is seldom ever sold to individuals. What is sold is a license to use the software, not full rights to do what you want. When you break open the package, the law assumes that you have agreed to abide by those terms.

5. *It's not like I'm robbing somebody.* Software is intellectual property just like a song, a book, an article, or a trademark. You are taking bread from the table of software engineers when you copy their work.

6. *It's OK if you're using the software for educational purposes.* If education were a justification for theft, driving instructors would be able to steal cars with impunity. There is a doctrine of *fair use* that allows some limited use of written materials in classrooms without permission from the copyright holder.

7. *I needed it, but the price was unreasonably high. If I had to actually pay for it, there is no way I could ever afford it.* Software prices are high for the same reason the price of houses is high: both require a lot of highly skilled labor to create. You cannot steal a VCR just because you cannot afford one.

8. *I didn't know it was illegal.* Unauthorized duplication of software is a felony in many states and provinces. State and federal laws provide for civil and criminal penalties if you are convicted. It would be difficult to convince a judge or jury that you had no idea that unauthorized copying was illegal.

9. *It's only illegal if you get caught.* Criminal behavior is illegal whether or not you are caught. If you do get caught illegally copying software, you could face fines, imprisonment, and/or civil penalties. Some educational institutions take disciplinary action against software pirates, including suspension.

10. *Oh, come on, everyone is doing it.* This excuse has been used to justify everything from speeding to lynching. The popularity of a criminal act does not make it legal.

Figure 13-1 The Top Ten Reasons for Illegally Copying Software (and Why None of Them Are Good Enough)

Source: Adapted with permission from Vince Incardona, "The Top Ten Reasons for Illegally Copying Software (and Why None of Them Are Good Enough)," *ITS News* (Rochester Institute of Technology), October 1998, p. 3.

Sexual Harassment

In Chapter 7 we looked at sexual harassment as a source of conflict and an illegal act. Sexual harassment is also an ethical issue, because it is morally wrong and unfair. All acts of sexual harassment flunk an ethics test. Before sexually harassing another person, the potential harasser should ask, "Would I want a loved one to be treated this way?"

Conflict of Interest

Part of being ethical is making business judgments only on the basis of the merits or facts in a situation. Imagine that you are a supervisor who is romantically involved with a worker within the group. When it comes time to assign raises, it will be difficult for you to be objective. A **conflict of interest** occurs when your judgment or objectivity is compromised. Conflicts of interest often take place in the sales end of business. If a company representative accepts a large gift from a sales representative, it may be difficult to make objective judgments about buying from the representative. Yet being taken to dinner by a vendor would not ordinarily cloud one's judgment. Another common example of a conflict of interest is making a hiring decision about a friend who badly needs a job, but is not well qualified for the position.

Dealing with Confidential Information

An ethical person can be trusted by others not to divulge confidential information unless the welfare of others is at stake. Suppose a coworker tells you in confidence that she is upset with the company and is therefore looking for another job. Behaving ethically, you do not pass this information along to your supervisor even though it would help your supervisor plan for a replacement. Now suppose the scenario changes slightly. Your coworker tells you she is looking for another job because she is upset. She tells you she is so upset that she plans to destroy company computer files on her last day. If your friend does find another job, you might warn the company about her contemplated activities.

The challenge of dealing with confidential information arises in many areas of business, many of which affect interpersonal relations. If you learned that a coworker was indicted for a crime, charged with sexual harassment, or facing bankruptcy, there would be a temptation to gossip about the person. A highly ethical person would not pass along information about the personal difficulties of another person.

Use of Corporate Resources

A corporate resource is anything the company owns, including its name and reputation. If Jake Petro worked for Ford Motor Company, for example, it would be unethical for him to establish a body shop and put on his letterhead "Jake Petro, Manufacturing Technician, Ford Motor Company." Other uses of corporate resources fall more into the gray area. It might be quite ethical to borrow a laptop computer for the weekend from your employer to conduct work at home. But it would be less ethical to borrow the laptop computer to prepare income taxes. In the latter case you might be accused of using corporate resources for personal purposes.

1. Do not use a computer to harm other people. (This includes not taking precautions against others' developing repetitive motion disorders.)
2. Do not interfere with other people's computer work. (This includes intentionally spreading computer viruses.)
3. Do not snoop around in other people's files.
4. Do not use a computer to steal.
5. Do not use a computer to bear false witness.
6. Do not use or copy software for which you have not paid (see Figure 13-1).
7. Do not use other people's resources without authorization.
8. Do not appropriate other people's intellectual output.
9. Do think about the social consequences of the program you write.
10. Do use a computer in ways that show consideration and respect.

Figure 13-2 The Ten Commandants for Computer Ethics

Source: Adapted and updated from Arlene H. Rinaldi and Florida Atlantic University, rinaldi @acc.fau.edu.

Possible Ethical Violations with Computers and Information Technology

As computers dominate the workplace, many ethical issues have arisen in addition to pirating software. One ethical dilemma that surfaces frequently is the fairness of tracking the Web sites a person visits and those he or she buys from. Should this information be sold, like a mailing list? Another issue is the fairness of having an employee work at a keyboard for 60 hours in one week when such behavior frequently leads to repetitive motion disorder. Figure 13-2 lists some major ethical issues involved in computer use.

You may have observed that these common ethical problems are not always clear cut. Aside from obvious matters such as prohibitions against stealing, lying, cheating, and intimidating, subjectivity enters into ethical decision making. Skill-Building Exercise 13-1 provides an opportunity to try out your ethical reasoning.

CHOOSING BETWEEN TWO RIGHTS: DEALING WITH DEFINING MOMENTS

Ethical decision making usually involves choosing between two options: one we perceive to be right and one we perceive to be wrong. A challenging twist to ethical decision making is to sort through your values when you have to choose between two *rights,* or two morally sound choices. Joseph L. Badaracco, Jr., uses the term **defining moment** to describe choosing between two or more ideals in which we deeply believe.[6] If you can learn to work through defining moments, your ethical skills will be enhanced. Let's first take a nonwork example to illustrate a defining moment.

Imagine yourself as a basketball referee in a league for boys 10 years old and younger. Luis, the smallest boy on the team has a self-confidence problem in general, and he has not scored a goal yet this season. This is the final game of the season. The other team is ahead by 10 points with one

Skill-Building Exercise 13-1

THE ETHICS GAME

Citicorp (now part of Citigroup) has developed an ethics game, *The Work Ethic*.[5] The game teaches ethics by asking small teams of employees to confront difficult scenarios such as those that follow. Discuss these ethical problems in teams. As you discuss the scenarios, identify the ethical issues involved.

Scenario 1: One of your assignments is to find a contractor to conduct building maintenance for your company headquarters. You invite bids for the job. High-Performance Cleaners, a firm staffed largely by teenagers from troubled families who have criminal records, bids on the job. Many of these teenagers also have severe learning disabilities and cannot readily find employment. High-Performance Cleaners proves to be the second-highest bidder. You:

   a. Advise High-Performance Cleaners that its bid is too high for consideration and that your company is not a social agency.

   b. Award the bid to High-Performance Cleaners and justify your actions with a letter to top management talking about social responsibility.

   c. Falsify the other bids in your report to management, making High-Performance Cleaners the low bidder—and thus the contract winner.

   d. Explain to High-Performance Cleaners that it lost the bid, but you will award the company a piece of the contract because of its sterling work with needy teenagers.

Scenario 2: You live in Texas and your company sends you on a three-day trip to New York City. Your business dealings in the Big Apple will keep you there Wednesday, Thursday, and Friday morning. You have several friends and relatives in New York, so you decide to stay there until Sunday afternoon. Besides, you want to engage in tourist activities such as taking a boat tour around Manhattan and visiting Radio City Music Hall. When preparing your expense report for your trip, you request payment for all your business-related costs up through Friday afternoon, *plus*

   a. Your return trip on Sunday.

   b. The return trip and the room cost for Friday and Saturday nights.

   c. The return trip and one-half of your weekend food expenses and two extra nights in the hotel.

   d. The return trip and your food costs for the weekend (which you justify because you ate at fast-food restaurants on Wednesday, Thursday, and Friday).

Scenario 3: You are the leader of a self-managing work team in a financial services company. The work of your team has expanded to the point where you are authorized to hire another team member. The team busily interviews a number of candidates from inside and outside the company. The other team members agree that one of the candidates (Pat) has truly outstanding credentials. You agree that Pat is a strong candidate. Yet you don't want Pat on the team because you and Pat were emotionally involved with each other for about one year in the past. You think that working with Pat would disrupt your concentration and bring back hurtful memories. You decide to

(Continued)

a. Tell the group that you have some negative information about Pat's past that would disqualify Pat for the job.

b. Telephone Pat and beg that Pat find employment elsewhere.

c. Tell the group that you agree Pat is qualified, but explain your concerns about the disruption in concentration and emotional hurt.

d. Tell the group that you agree Pat is right for the position, and mention nothing about the past relationship.

Scoring and Observation:

Scenario 1, about High-Performance Cleaners, raises dozens of ethical questions, including whether humanitarian considerations can outweigh profit concerns. Teams that chose *a* receive 0 points; *b,* 20 points; *c,* –10 points; *d,* 10 points.

Scenario 2 raises ethical issues about using company resources. Teams that chose *a* receive 20 points; *b,* –10 points; *c,* –15 points; *d,* 0 points.

Scenario 3 raises issues about fairness in making selection decisions. Teams that choose *a* receive –20 points; *b,* –10 points; *c,* 15 points; *d,* 0 points.

minute to go. Luis lets fly with a shot that goes into the basket, but his right heel is on the line. If the goal is allowed, Luis will experience one of the happiest moments in his life, and his self-confidence might increase. You strongly believe in helping people grow and develop. Yet you also strongly believe in following the rules of sports. What to do?

You may have recognized that a defining moment is a role conflict in which you have to choose between competing values. A CEO might deeply believe that she has an obligation to the stockholders to make a profit, and also believe in being generous and fair toward employees. However, to make a profit this year she will be forced to lay off several good employees with long seniority. The CEO now faces a moment of truth. Badaracco suggests that the individual can work through a defining moment by discovering "Who am I?" You discover who you are by soul searching answers to three questions:

1. What feelings and intuitions are coming into conflict in this situation?

2. Which of the values that are in conflict are the most deeply rooted in my life?

3. What combinations of expediency and shrewdness, coupled with imagination and boldness, will help me implement my personal understanding of what is right?

Skill-Building Exercise 13-2 gives you an opportunity to deal with defining moments. The three questions just asked could help you find answers, but do not be constrained by these questions.

Skill-Building Exercise 13-2

DEALING WITH DEFINING MOMENTS

The toughest ethical choices for many people occur when they have to choose between two *rights*. The result is a defining moment, because we are challenged to think in a deeper way by choosing between two or more ideals. Working individually or in teams, deal with the two following defining moments. Explain why these scenarios could require choosing between two rights, and explain the reasoning behind your decisions.

Scenario 1: You are the manager of a department in a business firm that assigns each department a fixed amount of money for salary increases each year. An average-performing member of the department asks you in advance for an above-average increase. He explains that his mother has developed multiple sclerosis and requires the services of a paid helper from time to time. You are concerned that if you give this man an above-average increase, somebody else in the department will have to receive a below-average increase.

Scenario 2: You are the team leader of an e-tailing (retail selling over the Internet) group. In recent months each team member has been working about 60 hours per week, with little prospect of the workload decreasing in the future. Since the e-tailing project is still losing money, higher management insists that one person be dropped from the team. One member of the team, Mildred, is willing to work only about 45 hours per week because she spends considerable time volunteering her time to work with autistic children. Mildred's work is satisfactory, but her output is the lowest in the group because of her shorter number of working hours. You must make a decision about whether to recommend that Mildred be dismissed.

GUIDELINES FOR BEHAVING ETHICALLY

Following guidelines for ethical behavior is the heart of being ethical. Although many people behave ethically without studying ethical guidelines, they are usually following guidelines programmed into their minds early in life. The Golden Rule exemplifies a guideline taught by parents, grandparents, and kindergarten teachers. In this section we approach ethical guidelines from four perspectives: (1) developing the right character traits, (2) using corporate programs for ethics, (3) following a guide for ethical decision making, and (4) developing close relationships with work associates.

DEVELOPING THE RIGHT CHARACTER TRAITS

Character traits develop early in life, yet with determination and self-discipline many people can modify old traits or develop new ones. A **character trait** is an enduring characteristic of a person that is related to moral and ethical behavior that shows up consistently. For example, if a person has the character trait of untruthfulness, he or she will lie in many situations. Conversely, the character trait of honesty leads to behaving honestly in most situations.

The Character Counts Coalition is an organization formed to encourage young people to develop fairness, respect, trustworthiness, responsibility, caring, and good citizenship. The Coalition has developed a list of 10 key guidelines as a foundation for character development.[7] If you develop, or already have, these traits, it will be easy for you to behave ethically in business. As you read the following list, evaluate your own standing on each character trait. Remember, however, that extra effort is required to evaluate one's character traits, because most people have an inflated view of their honesty and integrity.

1. *Be honest.* Tell the truth; be sincere; do not mislead or withhold information in relationships of trust; do not steal.

2. *Demonstrate integrity.* Stand up for your beliefs about right and wrong; be your best self; resist social pressure to do wrong.

3. *Keep promises.* Keep your word and honor your commitments; pay your debts and return what you borrow.

4. *Be loyal.* Stand by family, friends, employers, community, and country; do not talk about people behind their backs.

5. *Be responsible.* Think before you act; consider consequences; be accountable and "take your medicine."

6. *Pursue excellence.* Do your best with what you have; do not give up easily.

7. *Be kind and caring.* Show you care through generosity and compassion; do not be selfish or mean.

8. *Treat all people with respect.* Be courteous and polite; judge all people on their merits; be tolerant, appreciative, and accepting of individual differences.

9. *Be fair.* Treat all people fairly; be open-minded; listen to others and try to understand what they are saying and feeling.

10. *Be a good citizen.* Obey the law and respect authority; vote; volunteer your efforts; protect the environment.

If you score high on all of the preceding character traits and behaviors, you are an outstanding member of your company, community, and school. Your ethical behavior is superior.

USING CORPORATE ETHICS PROGRAMS

Many organizations have various programs and procedures for promoting ethical behavior. Among them are committees that monitor ethical behavior, training programs in ethics, and vehicles for reporting ethical violations. The presence of these programs is designed to create an atmosphere in which unethical behavior is discouraged and reporting on unethical behavior is encouraged.

Ethics hot lines are one of the best-established programs to help individuals avoid unethical behavior. Should a person be faced with an ethical dilemma, the person calls a toll-free line to speak to a counselor about the dilemma. Sometimes employees ask questions to help interpret a policy, such as "Is it okay to ask my boss for a date?" or "Are we supposed to give senior citizen discounts to customers who qualify but do not ask for one?" At other times, a more pressing ethical issue might be addressed, such as "Is it ethical to lay off a worker just five months short of his qualifying for a full pension?"

Sears, Roebuck and Co., has an ethics hot line the company refers to as an "Assist Line" because very few of the 15,000 calls it receives per year represent crises. Often the ethics specialists who handle the calls just listen; at other times they intervene to help resolve the problem. The Ethics Assist Line is designed to help with these kinds of calls: guidance about company policy; company Code of Conduct issues; workplace harassment/discrimination; selling practices; theft; and human resource issues. At times an ethical problem of such high moral intensity is presented that employee confidentiality cannot be maintained. However, the Ethics Office handles the inquiries in as confidential a manner as practical and assigns them case identification numbers for follow up.[8]

Despite the help of the Ethics Office, Sears has faced well-publicized ethical problems in its auto service centers, such as being accused of charging customers for tire balancing that was not performed. Quite often the individual must resist pressures from managers to carry out acts of questionable ethics.

FOLLOWING A GUIDE TO ETHICAL DECISION MAKING

A powerful strategy for behaving ethically is to follow a guide for ethical decision making. Such a guide for making contemplated decisions includes testing their ethics. **Ethical screening** refers to running a contemplated decision or action through an ethics test. Such screening makes the most sense when the contemplated action or decision is not clearly ethical or unethical. If a sales representative were to take a favorite customer to McDonald's for lunch, an ethical screen would not be necessary. Nobody would interpret a Big Mac to be a serious bribe. Assume, instead, that the sales rep offered to give the customer an under-the-table gift of $400 for placing a large offer with the rep's firm. The sales representative's behavior would be so blatantly unethical that conducting an ethical screen would be unnecessary.

Several useful ethical screens, or guides to ethical decision making, have been developed. A guide developed by Treviño and Nelson is presented here because it is current and incorporates the basic ideas in other ethical tests.[9] After studying this guide, you will be asked to ethically screen two different scenarios. The eight steps to sound ethical decision making follow.

1. *Gather the facts.* When making an important decision in business it is necessary to gather relevant facts. Ask yourself the following questions: "Are there any legal issues involved here?" "Is there precedent in our firm with respect to this type of decision?" "Do I have the authority to make this decision?" "Are there company rules and regulations governing such a decisions?"

The manager of a child-care center needed to hire an additional child-care specialist. One of the applicants was a 55-year-old male with experience as a father and grandfather. The manager judged him to be qualified, yet she knew that many parents would not want their preschool children to be cared for by a middle-aged male. Many people perceive that a younger woman is better qualified for child care than an older man. The manager therefore had to gather considerable facts about the situation, including facts about job discrimination and precedents in hiring males as child-care specialists.

2. *Define the ethical issues.* The ethical issues in a given decision are often more complicated than a first glance suggests. When faced with a complex decision, it may be helpful to talk over the ethical issues with another person. The ethical issues might involve character traits such as being kind and caring and treating others with respect. Or the ethical issues might relate to some of the common ethical problems described earlier in the chapter. Among them are conflict of interest, dealing with confidential information, and use of corporate resources.

The manager of the child-care center is facing such ethical issues as fairness, job discrimination, and meeting the demands of customers at the expense of job applicants. The manager is also facing a diversity issue: Should the workforce in a child-care center be culturally diverse, or do we hire only young women?

3. *Identify the affected parties.* When faced with a complex ethical decision it is important to identify all the affected parties. Major corporate decisions can affect thousands of people. If a company decides to shut down a plant and move the manufacturing to a low-wage country, thousands of individuals and many different parties are affected. Workers lose their jobs, suppliers lose their customers, the local governments loses out on tax revenues, and local merchants lose many of their customers. You may need to brainstorm with a few others to think of all the parties affected by a given decision.

The parties affected by the decision about hiring or not hiring the 55-year-old male include the applicant himself, the children, the parents, and the board of directors of the child-care center. The government might also be involved if the man were rejected and filed charges of age and sex discrimination.

4. *Identify the consequences.* After you have identified the parties affected by a decision, the next step is to predict the consequences for each party. It may not be necessary to identify every consequence, yet it is important to identify the consequences with the highest probability of occurring and those with the most negative outcomes. The problem is that many people can be harmed by an unethical decision, such as not fully describing the possible side effects of a diet program.

Both short-term and long-term consequences should be specified. The company's closing a plant might create considerable short-term turmoil, but in the long term the company might be healthier. People participating in a diet program might achieve their short-term objective of losing weight. Yet in the long term, their health might be adversely affected because the diet is not nutritionally balanced.

The *symbolic* consequences of an action are important. Every action and decision sends a message (the decision is a symbol of something). If a company moves manufacturing out of a community to save on labor costs, it means that the short-term welfare of domestic employees is less important than profit.

Let's return to the day-care manager and the job applicant. If the applicant does not get the job, his welfare will be adversely affected. He has been laid off by a large employer and cannot find work in his regular field. His family will also suffer because he will not be able to make a financial contribution to the family. Yet if the man is hired, the day-care center may suffer. Many traditionally minded parents will say, "Absolutely not. I do not want my child cared for by a middle-aged man. He could be a child molester." (It may be unethical for people to have vicious stereotypes, yet they still exist.) If the child-care center does hire the man, the act will symbolize the fact that the owners of the center value diversity.

5. *Identify the obligations.* Identify the obligations and the reasons for each obligation when making a complex decision. The manufacturer of automotive brakes has an obligation to produce and sell only brakes that meet high safety standards. The obligation is to the auto manufacturer who purchases the brakes and, more important, to the ultimate consumer whose safety depends on effective brakes. The reason for the obligation to make safe brakes is that lives are at stake.

The child-care owner has an obligation to provide for the safety and health of the children at the center. She must also provide for the peace of mind of the parents and be a good citizen of the community in which the center is located. The decision about hiring the candidate in question must be balanced against all these obligations.

6. *Consider your character and integrity.* A core consideration when faced with an ethical dilemma is to consider how relevant people would judge your character and integrity. What would your family, friends, significant others, teachers, and coworkers think of your actions? To refine this thinking even further, how would you feel if your actions were publicly disclosed in the local newspaper or over e-mail? Would you want the world to know that you gave an under-the-table kickback or that you sexually harassed a frightened teenager working for you? If you would be proud for others to know what decision you made when you faced an ethical dilemma, you are probably making the right decision.

The child-care center manager might ponder how she would feel if the following information were released in the local newspaper:

> The manager of Good Times Child Care recently rejected the application of a 55-year-old man for a child-care specialist position. She said that although Mr. _____ was well qualified from an experience and personality standpoint, she couldn't hire him. She said that Good Times would lose too much business because many parents would fear that Mr. _____ was a child molester.

7. *Think creatively about potential actions.* When faced with an ethical dilemma, put yourself in a creative-thinking mode. Stretch your imagination to invent several options rather than thinking you have only two choices—to do or not to do something. Creative thinking may point toward a third, and even fourth, alternative. Imagine this ethical dilemma: A purchasing agent is told that if her firm awards a contract to the sales representative's firm, she will find a leather jacket of her choice delivered to her door. The purchasing agent says to herself, "I think we should award the contract to the firm, but I cannot accept the gift. Yet if I turn down the gift, I will be forfeiting a valuable possession that the company simply regards as a cost of doing business."

The purchasing agent can search for another alternative. She can say to the sales rep, "We will give the contract to your firm because your product fits our requirements. I thank you for the offer of the leather jacket. But instead, I would like you to give that jacket to the Salvation Army instead of to me."

A creative alternative for the child-care manager might be to offer the applicant the next position that opened for an office manager or maintenance person in the center. In this way she would be offering a qualified applicant a job, but placing him in a position more acceptable to parents. Or do you feel this is a cop-out?

8. *Check your intuition.* So far we have emphasized the rational side of ethical decision making. Another effective way of conducting an ethical screen is to rely on your intuition. How does the contemplated decision feel? Would you be proud of yourself or would you hate yourself if you made the decision? Imagine how you would feel if you took money from the handbag of a woman sleeping in the park. Would you feel the same way if you went ahead and took a kickback, sold somebody a defective product, or sold an 80-year-old man an insurance policy he didn't need? How will the manager of the child-care center feel if she turns down the man for the child-care specialist position?

You are encouraged to use the guide for ethical decision making when you next face an ethical dilemma of consequence. Skill-Building Exercise 13-3 gives you an opportunity to practice using the eight steps for ethical decision making.

Skill-Building Exercise 13-3

ETHICAL DECISION MAKING

Working in small groups, take one or more of the following ethical dilemmas through the eight steps for screening contemplated decisions. If more than one group chooses the same scenario, compare your answers for the various steps.

Scenario 1: To Recycle or Not. Your group is the top management team at a large insurance company. Despite the movement toward computerization, your firm still generates tons of paper each month. Customer payments alone account for truckloads of envelopes each year. The paper recyclers in your area claim they can hardly find a market any longer for used paper, so they will be charging you just to accept your paper for recycling. Your group is wondering whether to recycle.

Scenario 2: The Job Applicants with a Past. A state (or provincial) government official approaches your bank asking you to hire three people who are soon to be released from prison. All were found guilty of fraudulently altering computer records in a bank for personal gain. The official says the men have paid their debt to society, and they need jobs. Your company has three openings for computer specialists; all three men obviously have good computer skills. Your group is wondering whether to hire these people.

Scenario 3: The High-Profit Toys. You are a toy company executive starting to plan your holiday season line. You anticipate that the season's hottest item will be Robo-Woman, a battery-operated crime fighter and superheroine. Robo-Woman should wholesale for $18.50 and retail for $38.00. Your company figures to earn $10 per unit. You receive a sales call from a manufacturing broker who says he can produce any toy you want for one-third of your present manufacturing cost. He admits that the manufacturer he represents uses prison labor in China, but insists that his business arrangement violates no law. You estimate you can earn $14 per unit if you do business with the manufacturing broker. Your decision is whether to do business with him.

DEVELOPING CLOSER RELATIONSHIPS WITH WORK ASSOCIATES

A recent explanation of the causes of unethical behavior emphasizes the strength of relationships among people.[10] Assume that two people have close ties to each other, such as having worked together for a long time or knowing each other both on and off the job. As a consequence they are likely to behave ethically toward one another on the job. In contrast, if a weak relationship exists between two people, either party is more likely to engage in an unethical relationship. The owner of an auto service center is more likely to behave unethically toward a stranger passing through town than toward a long-time customer. The opportunity for unethical behavior between strangers is often minimized because individuals typically do not trust strangers with sensitive information or valuables.

The ethical skill-building consequences of information about personal relationships is that building closer relationships with people is likely to enhance ethical behavior. If you build close relationships with work associates, you are likely to behave more ethically toward them. Similarly, your work associates are likely to behave more ethically toward you. The work associates we refer to are all your contacts, or internal and external customers.

SUMMARY

Ethics refers to what is good and bad, right and wrong, just and unjust, and what people should do. A person's ethical code has a significant impact on his or her interpersonal relationships.

Understanding ethics is important for a variety of reasons. First, people are motivated by self-interest and a desire to be morally right. Second, good ethics can enhance business and avoid illegal acts. Third, high ethics improves the quality of work life.

A substantial number of managers and employees engage in unethical behavior, often because they feel pressured into making a quick profit. Commonly faced ethical problems include the following: the temptation to illegally copy software; treating people unfairly; job discrimination; sexual harassment; conflict of interest; mistreating confidential information; misuse of corporate resources; and misuse of computers and information technology.

A challenging twist to ethical decision making is to sort through your values when you have to choose between two morally sound choices. A defining moment is when you have to choose between two or more ideals in which you deeply believe.

One strategy for behaving ethically is to develop the right character traits, as specified by the Character Counts Coalition. Among these traits are honesty, integrity, promise keeping, loyalty, responsibility, kindness, respect for others, fairness, and good citizenship. At times using a corporate program such as an ethics hot line can help a person resolve ethical dilemmas.

Another strategy for behaving ethically is to follow eight steps in making a contemplated decision:

1. Gather the facts.

2. Define the ethical issues.

3. Identify the affected parties.

4. Identify the consequences.

5. Identify the obligations (such as to customers and society).

6. Consider your character and integrity.

7. Think creatively about potential actions.

8. Check your intuition.

Another way to raise the level of ethical behavior is to form close relationships with work associates. This is true because people tend to behave more ethically toward people who are close to them.

QUESTIONS FOR DISCUSSION AND REVIEW

1. How can behaving ethically improve a person's interpersonal relationships on the job?

2. What would most likely be some of the specific behaviors of a manager who scored 20 points on the ethical reasoning inventory?

3. Professions such as medicine, law, accounting, and psychology have their own ethical codes. Why do professional people need an ethical code?

4. Give an example from your own experiences or the media in which a business executive did something of significance that was morally right.

5. Provide an example of an action in business that might be unethical but not illegal.

6. If pirating software is illegal and unethical, why is it practiced so frequently?

7. What "commandment" about computer use would you like to add to the list in Figure 13-2?

8. Is it unethical for a company owner to buy products for the company from a relative even if the products are not the best buy in terms of price and quality?

9. What decision of ethical consequence have you made in the last year that you would not mind having publicly disclosed?

10. Why is using your intuition an effective guide to ethical decision making?

THE OFFICE CHAMELEON

Tom Chatworth joined Ace Industrial Products four years ago as a trainee in the sales order department. His job was to process repeat business from established customers. The inside sales position fit into Tom's career plan. He wanted to become an outside sales representative and also learn the business thoroughly. He aspired to someday become a sales manager in an industrial company.

After three years of good performance as an order specialist, Tom was promoted to outside sales representative. He now had a territory of his own, selling various small pumps and motors to other manufacturers. Tom thought to himself that he was on the right path toward reaching his goals. Tom was achieving his sales quota, yet his sales manager had some concerns about his sales tactics.

During one coaching session, Karen Deauville, his manager, explained to Tom, "I get the impression that you are not telling our customers a consistent story. I can tell from some of the comments they have made to our customer service department. Here's a specific example: You told Albany Machine Works that the reason our pump cost a little more than average is that it meets incredibly high quality standards.

"The next week you told Three Rivers Machining that the reason you could offer the pump to them at such a low price is that it was not built to last 50 years." With a puzzled look on his face, Tom responded: "Hold on, Karen, that's just good salesmanship. If a customer is concerned about quality, you emphasize quality. If the customer is concerned about price, you tell him the price is low. But you need a sensible explanation as to why the price is low."

"I disagree," said Karen. "A professional sales representative sticks with a consistent story about a product. If you tell the truth, you don't have to switch stories."

Tom said, "OK, I get the message. But I don't agree 100 percent. You sometimes have to manipulate the facts just a little to keep a customer happy."

Karen received no further feedback on inconsistencies in Tom's sales presentations, so she dropped her concern that Tom was not creating the best image for the company. Several months later, Karen and Tom were attending the company sales meeting. As she approached the bar for a drink, she heard Tom talking to the vice president of marketing, Grant Edgewood. He commented to Edgewood, "Grant, I can't help admiring that bow tie. It adds a little class to the meeting." Edgewood thanked him for the compliment and went on to explain how he had mastered tying a bow tie.

Later that evening, Karen encountered Tom at the buffet table for desserts. Tom stood right behind Karen as they shuffled along among the choice of desserts. With a smile on his face, Tom said, "Did you see Grant tonight? He's actually wearing a bow tie. The guy thinks he's a Harvard Business School professor or a senator. He makes me laugh."

"Tom, I think you and I must have a little chat again next week," said Karen. "I'll be in touch."

Tom thought to himself, "I wonder what I said to upset Karen? What's wrong with not liking bow ties?"

Case Questions

1. What ethical problems, if any, does Tom display?

2. Does Karen have a right to be concerned about Tom's behavior? Or is she being naive?

3. Should Karen be using information she gathered at a sales meeting as a basis for coaching?

4. Assuming Tom does need help, how should Karen help him?

5. How would you rate Tom on the personality trait of self-monitoring?

Chapter 14

Personal Productivity and Stress Management

Learning Objectives

After reading and studying this chapter and doing the exercises you should be able to

➤ Reduce any tendencies you might have toward procrastination.

➤ Identify attitudes and values that will enhance your productivity.

➤ Identify skills and techniques that will enhance your productivity.

➤ Pinpoint potential time wasters that drain your productivity.

➤ Explain many of the symptoms and consequences of stress, including burnout.

➤ Describe personality factors and job factors that contribute to stress.

➤ Be prepared to manage your own stress effectively.

Forty-one year-old Randolph Blatt of Raleigh, North Carolina, decided to operate a recruiting firm for computer professionals out of his home. Part of his reasoning was that his productivity would increase if he saved commuting time and had fewer distractions than in a conventional office. Saving on office rent was also an attraction to setting up shop in his house. After four years of his home-based business, Blatt knew he would have to modify his work life. As he explains his problem, "I would get phone calls and I had screaming babies in the background. I would duck into my laundry room to hide. It never worked."

The solution to his problem was to affiliate with Your Office, a self-described superstore for the home-based entrepreneur. Your Office functions like a home away from home for home-based offices that lack certain equipment and for the owners who are lonely. Among the services offered are temporary office space for meeting with clients and customers, temporary meeting rooms, secretarial help, mailboxes, and videoconference equipment. Clients can rent office space by the hour, day, week, or month.

Blatt says, "At Your Office I regularly run into people, and I feel like I'm part of the world." He likes the opportunity to chit-chat with people that is lacking in his office at home.[1]

The story just presented about the man with a home-based business finding a solution to his job stress illustrates two major workplace themes. Workers strive to be more productive (for example, by working out of the home), and at the same time they must find ways to manage stress and avoid burnout (for example, by dropping by Your Office for some social interaction). Although this book is primarily about interpersonal skills, information about enhancing personal productivity and managing stress is relevant. Being more productive and having stress under control enhances relationships with others. Having your work under control and not being stressed out enables you to focus better on interpersonal relationships.

The first half of this chapter describes various approaches to improving personal productivity, whereas the second half deals with the nature of stress and how it can be managed. The two topics are as closely related as nutrition and health. When your work is under control, you avoid the heavy stress of feeling overwhelmed. And when you effectively manage stress, you can be more productive.

IMPROVING PERSONAL PRODUCTIVITY

Achieving personal productivity is more in vogue than ever. Companies strive to operate with smaller staffs than in the past by pushing workers to achieve higher productivity. At the same time, there is a movement toward simplifying personal life by reducing clutter and cutting back on tasks that do not add much to the quality of work life. **Personal productivity** refers to the amount of resources, including time, you consume to achieve a certain level of output. Assuming that two paralegals receive the same compensation and require the same amount of supervision. The paralegal who provides the finishing touches on 100 house closings in one month is more productive than the one who completes 50 comparable closings per month.

We approach productivity improvement from four perspectives: (1) dealing with procrastination, (2) attitudes and values that enhance personal productivity, (3) work habits and skills that enhance personal productivity, and (4) overcoming time wasters.

DEALING WITH PROCRASTINATION

The person who **procrastinates** delays action for no good reason. Procrastination lowers productivity because it wastes time and many important tasks never get done. Even productive people sometimes procrastinate. If these people did not procrastinate, they would be even more productive.

Many people regard procrastination as a laughable weakness, particularly because procrastinators themselves joke about the problem. Yet procrastination has been evaluated as a profound, debilitating problem.[2] The enormity of the problem makes it worthwhile to examine methods for bringing it under control. What will work for overcoming procrastination depends somewhat on a person's reason for procrastination. In the extreme case, a person might be procrastinating because he or wants to mess up as a form of self-punishment. Straightforward cognitive suggestions such as "Do it now" may not work for that individual. Do Self-Assessment Quiz 14-1 to think through your own tendencies toward procrastination—and don't wait until tomorrow.

Choose from among the following suggestions for controlling procrastination, based on those that appear to best fit your type of procrastination. A combination of techniques is likely to be the most effective.

1. *Calculate the cost of procrastination.* You can reduce procrastination by calculating its cost. You might lose out on obtaining a high-paying job you really want by not having your résumé and cover letter ready on time. Your cost of procrastination would include the difference in compensation between the job you do find and the one you really wanted. Another cost would be the loss of potential job satisfaction.

2. *Follow the WIFO principle, which stands for "worst in, first out."*[3] If you tackle the worst task on your list first, doing the other tasks may function like a small reward. You get to do what you dislike the least by doing first what you dislike the most. WIFO is particularly effective when faced with a number of tasks simultaneously.

3. *Break the task into manageable chunks.* To reduce procrastination, cut down a task that seems overwhelming into smaller projects that seem less formidable. If your job calls for preparing an enormous database, begin by assembling some readily available information. Then take the next step by assembling another small segment of the database—perhaps all customers whose last names begin with Z. Think of your task as pulling together a series of small databases that will fit into a master database.

Self-Assessment Quiz 14-1

PROCRASTINATION TENDENCIES

Directions: Circle yes or no for each item:

1. I usually do my best work under the pressure of deadlines.	**(Yes)**	No
2. Before starting a project I go through such rituals as sharpening every pencil, straightening up my desk more than once, and discarding bent paper clips.	Yes	**(No)**
3. I crave the excitement of the "last-minute rush."	Yes	**(No)**
4. I often think that if I delay something, it will go away, or the person who asked for it will forget about it.	Yes	**(No)**
5. I extensively research something before taking action, such as obtaining three different estimates before getting the brakes repaired on my car.	Yes	**(No)**
6. I have a great deal of difficulty getting started on most projects, even those I enjoy.	Yes	**(No)**
7. I keep waiting for the right time to do something, such as getting started on an important report.	Yes	**(No)**
8. I often underestimate the time needed to do a project, and say to myself, "I can do this quickly, so I'll wait until next week."	Yes	**(No)**
9. It is difficult for me to finish most projects or activities.	Yes	**(No)**
10. I have several favorite diversions or distractions that I use to keep me from doing something unpleasant.	**(Yes)**	No

Total Yes Responses   2

Scoring and Interpretation: The greater the number of yes responses, the more likely it is that you have a serious procrastination problem. A score of 8, 9, or 10 strongly suggests that your procrastination is lowering your productivity.

4. *Make a commitment to other people.* Try to make it imperative that you get something done on time by making it a commitment to one or more other people. You might announce to coworkers that you are going to get something accomplished by a certain date. If you fail to meet this date, you are likely to feel embarrassed.

5. *Remove some clutter from your mind.* Procrastination escalates when people have many unfinished projects in the back of their mind, draining their concentration. Too much to do can freeze us into inaction. Just eliminating a few trivial items from your to-do list can give you enough mental energy to overcome procrastination on a few major tasks.

Notice carefully that this approach to overcoming procrastination requires that you apply enough self-discipline to take the first step.

6. *Satisfy your stimulation quota in constructive ways.* If you procrastinate because you enjoy the rush of scrambling to make deadlines, find a more constructive way of using busyness to keep you humming. If you need a high level of stimulation, enrich your life with extra projects and learning new skills. The fullness of your schedule will provide you the stimulation you had been receiving from squeezing yourself to make deadlines and reach appointments on time.[4]

ATTITUDES AND VALUES THAT ENHANCE PERSONAL PRODUCTIVITY

Developing good work habits and time-management practices is often a matter of developing the right attitudes toward your work and toward time. If, for example, you think that your schoolwork or job is important and that time is a precious resource, you will be on your way toward developing good work habits. In this section, we describe a group of attitudes, values, and beliefs that can help a person become more productive through better use of time and improved work habits.

Begin with a Mission and Goals

A mission, or general purpose, propels you toward being productive. Assume that a person says, "My mission is to be an outstanding professional in my field and a loving, constructive spouse and parent." The mission serves as a compass to direct your activities, such as being well organized in order to accomplish more work and be highly valued by your employer. Goals are more specific than mission statements; they support the mission statement, but the effect is the same. Being committed to a goal also propels you toward good use of time. If you know that you can obtain the position in international business that you really want by mastering a second language, you are likely to work diligently on learning that language. Skill-Building Exercise 14-1 gives you the opportunity to establish a mission statement and supporting goals.

Work Smarter, Not Harder

People caught up in trying to accomplish a job often wind up working hard, but not in an imaginative way that leads to good results. Much time and energy are therefore wasted. A working-smart approach also requires that you spend a few minutes carefully planning how to implement your task. Searching information on the Internet provides many examples of the importance of working smarter rather than harder. One example will place you on the right mental track.

Suppose you are searching for information about a mutual fund that invests in Internet-related stocks. A *working hard* approach would be to load your search engine with general phrases that would take you to hundreds of Web sites that do not provide the information you are seeking. Among

Skill-Building Exercise 14-1

USING A MISSION STATEMENT AND GOALS TO POWER WORK HABITS

People with a well-defined mission statement and supporting goals tend to have better work habits and time management than those who do not. The following exercise is designed to help you establish a mission statement and goals so you will be energized to be more productive.

A. Mission Statement: To help develop your mission statement, or general purpose in life, ask yourself, "What are my five biggest wishes in life?" These wishes give you a hint to your purpose because they point toward an ideal purpose in life. Feel free to think big, because mission statements tend toward being idealistic.

B. Long-Range Goals to Support Mission Statement: Now write down what long-range goals would support your mission statement. Suppose your mission statement related to "creating a better life for disadvantaged people." Your long-range goals might include establishing a foundation that would fund your efforts. You would also need to be successful enough in your career to get the foundation started.

C. Intermediate-Range Goals to Support Long-Range Goals: Write down the intermediate-range goals needed to support the long-range goals. You will probably need to complete your education, obtain broad experience, and identify a lucrative form of self-employment.

D. Weekly Goals to Support Intermediate-Range Goals: Write down what you have to do this week to help you complete your education, such as researching and writing a paper for a particular course, registering for courses for next term, and inquiring about career opportunities in your field.

E. Today's Goals to Support Weekly Goals (My To-Do List): Here's where your lofty purpose in life gets translated into reality. What do you have to do today to get that paper written? Do you need to get your car battery replaced so you can get to the library so you can write your paper, so you can graduate, so you can become rich, so you can ultimately help all those disadvantaged people? Get going.

these general phrases would be "mutual funds," "Internet investments," and "Internet mutual funds." You might spend hours surfing these sites. The working-smart approach would be to start your search in a highly focused manner, and then branch out if you did not find the information you sought. Why not work very smart and attempt to skip the search engines all together? Take a chance finding your information directly by prefacing your key word with www and following the word with .com. The designation www.Internetfund.com provides exactly the information you were seeking, with a total search time of about three minutes.

Value Orderliness and Cleanliness

An orderly desk, work area, attaché case, or hard drive does not inevitably indicate an orderly mind. Yet it does help most people become more productive because they can better focus their mind. Also, less time is wasted and less energy is expended if you do not have to hunt for information that you thought you had on hand. Knowing where information is and what information you have available is a way of being in control of your job. When your job gets out of control, you are probably working at less than peak efficiency. Valuing cleanliness improves productivity in several ways. According to the Japanese system, cleanliness is the bedrock of quality. Also, after you have thoroughly cleaned your work area, you will usually attain a fresh outlook.

The core attitude here is to perceive clutter negatively. One reason that clutter is counterproductive is that managers spend an estimated five weeks per year hunting for things they have lost. Other workers spend about 10 weeks per year searching for information and things (Internet searches not included). Having less clutter reduces the time spent searching for misplaced items.[5]

Value Good Attendance and Punctuality

Good attendance and punctuality are expected of both experienced and inexperienced employees. You cannot be productive if you are not physically present in your work area. The same principle applies whether you work on company premises or at home. One exception is that some people can work through solutions to job problems while engaged in recreation. Keep in mind, too, that being late for or absent from meetings sends the silent message that you do not regard the meeting as being important.

The relationship of lateness to absenteeism and work performance has been researched. Based on 30 studies and over 9,000 workers it was found that employees who were late also tended to have high absenteeism records. In addition, employees who were late tended to have poorer work performance than workers who were prompt, but the relationship was not strong.[6] Despite this weak association, being late must still be regarded as a productivity drain.

Attain a Balance in Life and Avoid Being a Workaholic

A productive attitude to maintain is that overwork can lead to negative stress and burnout. Proper physical rest and relaxation can contribute to mental alertness and improved ability to cope with frustration. A strategy for preventing overwork is to strive for a balance in which you derive satisfaction from various spheres of life. Major spheres in addition to work include family life, romance, sports, the arts and music, faith, and intellectual growth.

Neglecting the normal need for rest and relaxation can lead to **workaholism**, an addiction to work in which not working is an uncomfortable experience. Some types of workaholics are perfectionists who are never satisfied with their work and therefore find it difficult to leave work behind. In addition, the perfectionist-type workaholic may become heavily focused on control, leading to rigid behavior and strained interpersonal relationships. However, some people who work long and hard are classified as achievement-oriented workaholics who thrive on hard work and are usually highly productive.[7]

WORK HABITS AND SKILLS THAT ENHANCE PERSONAL PRODUCTIVITY

Overcoming procrastination and developing the right attitudes contribute to personal productivity. Effective work habits and skills are also essential for high productivity. Five key work habits and skills are described next. They represent a mixture of traditional productivity boosters and those geared toward information technology.

Prepare a To-Do List and Set Priorities

At the heart of every time-management system is list making, whether the list is placed on an index card, in a leather-bound planner, or in a palm-size computer. As already described, the to-do list is the basic tool for achieving your daily goals, which in turn helps you achieve bigger goals and your mission. Almost every successful person in any field composes a list of important and less important tasks that need to be done. Before you compose a useful list, you need to set aside a few minutes of quiet time every day to sort out the tasks at hand. This is the most basic aspect of planning.

As is well known, it is helpful to set priorities for items on the to-do list. A typical system is to use A to signify critical or essential items, B to signify important items, and C for the least important ones. Although an item might be regarded as a C (for example, emptying the wood shavings from the electronic pencil sharpener), it still makes a contribution to your management of time and sense of well-being. Accomplishing anything reduces some stress. Also, many people obtain satisfaction from crossing off an item on their list, however trivial. If you are at all conscientious, small, unaccomplished items will come back to interfere with your concentration.

Streamline Your Work and Emphasize Important Tasks

As companies continue to operate with fewer workers than in the past despite prosperity, more unproductive work must be eliminated. Getting rid of unproductive work is part of *reengineering*, in which work processes are radically redesigned and simplified. Every employee is expected to get rid of work that does not contribute to productivity or help customers.

In general, to streamline or reengineer your work, look for duplication of effort and waste. An example of duplication of effort would be to routinely send people e-mail and fax messages covering the same topic. An example of waste would be to call a meeting for disseminating information that could easily be communicated by e-mail.

Emphasizing important tasks means that you make sure to take care of A items on your to-do list. It also implies that you search to accomplish a few work activities that, if done well, would make a big difference in your job performance. Although important tasks may take less time to accomplish than many routine tasks, they can represent the difference between success and failure. Five minutes of telephone conversation with a major customer might do more good for your company than three hours of arranging obsolete inventory in the warehouse.

Stay in Control of Paperwork and Electronic Work

Although it is fashionable to complain about paperwork in responsible jobs, the effective career person does not neglect paperwork. (Paperwork includes electronic work such as electronic mail and voice mail.) Paperwork involves taking care of administrative details such as correspondence, invoices, human resource reports, and inventory forms. Unless paperwork and electronic work are attended to, a person's job may get out of control. A small amount of time should be invested in paperwork every day. Nonprime time (when you are at less than your peak of efficiency but not overfatigued) is the best time to take care of paperwork.

Time management specialist Odette Pollar recommends that you sort and handle the papers in your in-basket twice a day. Decide what you will do with every piece of paper and put it in its proper location, not back in the basket.[8] A similar process can be used for e-mail. Respond quickly to high-priority messages, and permanently delete those you will mostly not need to refer to again. Avoid the hazard of making a hard copy of every message and filing it in your in-basket.

Work Productively from Your Home Office or Virtual Office

A growing segment of the workforce spends full or part time working either from home or from a **virtual office**. Such an office is a place of work without a fixed physical location from which the worker or workers communicate their output electronically. A virtual office might be in a car, train, airplane, or hotel room; on a park bench; or wherever the worker happens to be at the time. Many people adapt well to working at home and from virtual offices because they are self-starters and self-disciplined. Many other workers lack the self-discipline and effective work habits necessary to be productive outside a traditional office. Following is a list of representative suggestions for being productive while working independently:[9]

➤ Act as if you work in a traditional office. Set specific working hours, get dressed, go outside the house for a few minutes, then return and get to work. Also, close your office at home or virtual office at some regular time. Otherwise, you are open for business all the time. If you work at home, establish a clear workspace and let your family and friends know when you cannot be disturbed.

➤ Stay in touch with teammates to enhance your team player skills and not lose out on important information that could lower your effectiveness (such as missing an appointment at the traditional office).

➤ Minimize conducting your personal life at the same time as working (for example, such as watching television, talking to neighbors, or shopping over the Internet).

➤ Schedule regular times for meals and snacks, otherwise you will lose many minutes and gain many pounds taking food and beverage breaks.

➤ Use whatever information technology your employer offers to send and receive output. For example, software like *Hot-Office* acts as a command center for a virtual team. Members can place objects such as documents, images, and spreadsheets into a common location for review; retrieve files; and share ideas.

The practice of working at home or from virtual offices is increasing, so these suggestions merit careful consideration. Several of the productivity ideas also fit the conventional office.

Enhance Your Internet Search Skills

For many workers, an important job skill is searching the Internet for various information. It follows that if you develop your Internet search skills you will be more productive by obtaining the results you need within a reasonable time. The example given earlier about finding the Internet mutual fund illustrates the value of having effective Internet search skills. A few more suggestions follow.

First, it is important to rely on several search engines to seek needed information. Several metasearch engines claim to be so comprehensive that no other engine is required. Such claims are exaggerated, because the same search word entered into several different comprehensive engines will reveal a different list of sources. Second, give careful thought to the search word or phrase you use. The more specific the better. Assume that you wanted to find software to enhance your productivity, and that you enter the word "software" into a search engine. You will probably receive a message indicating that 3,500,000 entries have been located in response to your personal inquiry. You are better advised to use the search phrase "Software for increasing personal productivity."

Third, for many searches, framing the query as a phrase by enclosing it in quotation marks refines the number of hits (or sites) returned.[10] Simply place quotation marks before and after the search word, such as "Software for improving work habits." Fourth, if you don't find what you want in your initial search, reframe your question in another way or change the terms. How about, "Software for time management" or "Computer programs for increasing personal efficiency"?

Skill-Building Exercise 14-2 will help you make better use of the Internet to enhance your personal productivity.

OVERCOMING TIME WASTERS

Another basic thrust to improve personal productivity is to minimize wasting time. Many of the techniques already described in this chapter help save time, such as eliminating nonessential work. Whether or not an activity is a time waster depends on the purpose of the activity. Suppose you play computer solitaire for 10 minutes to reduce stress and then return to work refreshed. In contrast, another worker who spends 10 minutes playing solitaire just for fun is wasting time. Figure 14-1 presents a list of common time wasters. Being aware of time wasters will help sensitize you to the importance of minimizing them.

Internet Skill-Building Exercise 14-2

PRODUCTIVITY BOOSTING ON THE INTERNET

The number of people online continues to grow rapidly, with thousands of people around the world getting started every day. Gather into small teams or work individually to identify 10 ways in which the Internet can increase personal productivity, either on the job or at home. To supplement your own thinking, you might search the Internet for ideas on how the Internet is supposed to boost productivity. I look forward to being informed of your most creative ideas.

Happy surfing.
ajdubrin@frontiernet.net

Even if you saved just 10 minutes per work day, the productivity gain over a year could be enormous.

UNDERSTANDING AND MANAGING STRESS

A major challenge facing any worker who wants to stay healthy and have good interpersonal relationships is to manage stress effectively. Although *stress* is an everyday term, a scientific definition helps clarify its meaning. **Stress** is an adaptive response that is the consequence of any action, situation, or event that places special demands on a person. Note that stress refers to a *reaction* to the situation, not the situation or force itself. A **stressor** is the external or internal force that brings about the stress.

Individual differences play a key role in determining what events are stressful. Giving a presentation to management, for example, is stressful for some people but not for others. The term *special demands* is also critical, because minor adjustments, such as a pencil point that breaks, are usually not perceived as stressful.[11] Yet a piling on of minor adjustments, such as having 10 small things go wrong in one day, is stressful. This is true because stress is additive: A series of small doses of stress can create a major stress problem.

Our approach to understanding stress centers around its symptoms and consequences, personality and job factors that contribute to stress, and methods and techniques for stress management. Managing stress receives more emphasis because the same techniques can be used to combat a variety of stressors.

SYMPTOMS AND CONSEQUENCES OF STRESS

The physiological changes that take place within the body in response to stress are responsible for most stress symptoms. These physiological changes are almost identical for both positive and negative stressors. Ski racing, romantic attraction, and being downsized can make you feel about the same physically.

Wasted time is a major productivity drain, so it pays to search for time wasters in your work activities. The following list includes ways to minimize some of the major time wasters in the workplace. Most people can add a personal list of time leaks to this list.

1. Use a time log for two weeks to track time wasters.

2. Minimize daydreaming on the job by forcing yourself to concentrate.

3. Avoid the computer as a diversion from work, such as sending jokes back and forth to network members, playing video games, and checking out recreational Web sites during working hours.

4. Batch together tasks such as returning phone calls or responding to e-mail messages. For example, in most jobs it is possible to be polite and productive by reserving two or three 15-minute periods per day for taking care of e-mail correspondence.

5. Socialize on the job just enough to build your network. Chatting with coworkers is a major productivity drain and one of the reasons so many managers work at home part of the time when they have analytical work to get done.

6. Be prepared for meetings by, for example, having a clear agenda and sorting through the documents you will be referring to. Make sure electronic equipment is in working order before attempting to use it during the meeting.

7. Keep track of important names, places, and things to avoid wasting time searching for them.

8. Set a time limit for tasks after you have done them once or twice.

9. Prepare a computer template for letters and computer documents that you send frequently. (The template is essentially a form letter, especially with respect to the salutation and return address.)

10. When you only have to provide routine information by voice mail, telephone people before and after normal working hours, leaving a message on their voice mail. (This saves conversation time.)

11. Avoid perfectionism, which leads you to keep redoing a project. Let go and move on to another project.

12. Make use of bits of time—for instance, 5 minutes between appointments. Invest those 5 minutes in sending a business e-mail or revising your to-do list. (Note the exception to the batch principle.)

13. Minimize procrastination, the number one time waster for most people.

14. Avoid spreading yourself too thin by doing too many things at once, such as having one project too many to handle. When you are overloaded, time can be wasted because of too many errors.

Figure 14-1   Ways to Prevent and Overcome Time Wasting

Source: Suggestions 4, 5, and 6 are based on Stephen R. Covey with Hyrum Smith, "What If You Could Chop an Hour from Your Day for Things That Matter Most?" *USA Weekend,* January 22–24, 1999, pp. 4–5.

The experience of stress helps activate hormones that prepare the body to run or fight when faced with a challenge. This battle against the stressor is referred to as the **fight-or-flight response**. It helps you deal with emergencies.

An updating of the fight-or-flight response theory explains that, when faced with stress, the brain acts much like a thermostat. When outside conditions deviate from an ideal point, the thermostat sends a signal to the furnace to increase heat or air conditioning. The brain senses stress as damage to well-being and therefore sends out a signal to the body to cope. The purpose of coping is to modify the discrepancy between the ideal (low-stress) and actual (high-stress) conditions.[12] The brain is thus a self-regulating system that helps us cope with stressors.

Physiological Reactions

The activation of hormones when the body has to cope with a stressor produces a short-term physiological reaction. Among the most familiar reactions are an increase in heart rate, blood pressure, blood glucose, and blood clotting. To help you recognize these symptoms, try to recall your internal bodily sensations the last time you were almost in an automobile accident or heard some wonderful news. Less familiar changes are a redirection of the blood flow toward the brain and large muscle groups and a release of stored fluids from places throughout the body into the bloodstream.

If stress is continuous and accompanied by these short-term physiological changes, annoying and life-threatening conditions can occur. Damage occurs when stress levels rarely subside. A stressful life event usually leads to a high cholesterol level (of the unhealthy type) and high blood pressure. Other conditions associated with stress are cardiac disease, migraine headaches, ulcers, allergies, skin disorders, and cancer. To make matters worse, stress can hamper the immune system, thereby increasing the severity of many diseases and disorders. For example, people whose stress level is high recover more slowly from colds and injuries, and they are more susceptible to sexually transmitted diseases. Stress symptoms vary considerably from one person to another. A general behavioral symptom of intense stress is for people to exaggerate their weakest tendencies. For instance, a person with a strong temper who usually keeps cool under pressure may throw a tantrum under pressure. Some common stress symptoms are listed in Figure 14-2.

Job Performance Consequences

Despite all the problems just mentioned, stress also plays a positive role in our lives. The right amount of stress prepares us for meeting difficult challenges and spurs us on to peak intellectual and physical performance. An optimum level of stress exists for most people and most tasks.

In general, performance tends to be best under moderate amounts of stress. If the stress is too great, people become temporarily ineffective; they may freeze or choke. Under too little stress, people may become lethargic and inattentive. Figure 14-3 depicts the relationship between stress and performance. An exception to this relationship is that certain negative forms of stress are likely to lower performance even if the stress is moderate. For example, the stress created by an intimidating supervisor or worrying about radiation poisoning—even in moderate amounts—will not improve performance.

The optimum amount of stress is a positive force that is the equivalent of finding excitement and challenge. Your ability to solve problems and deal with challenge is enhanced when the right amount of adrenaline flows in your

Mostly Physical and Physiological

Shaking or trembling
Dizziness
Heart palpitations
Difficulty breathing
Chronic fatigue
Unexplained chest pains
Frequent teeth grinding
Frequent nausea

Mouth dryness
Upper and lower back pain
Frequent headaches
Low energy and stamina
Stomach problems
Constant craving for sweets
Increased alcohol or cigarette consumption
Frequent need to eliminate

Mostly Emotional and Behavioral

Difficulty concentrating
Nervousness
Crying
Anorexia
Declining interest in sex
Frequent nail biting or hair tugging

Anxiety or depression
Forgetfulness
Restlessness
Frequent arguments with others
Feeling high strung much of the time

Figure 4-2   A Variety of Stress Symptoms

blood to guide you toward peak performance. In fact, highly productive people are sometimes said to be hooked on adrenaline.

Burnout and Stress

One of the major problems of prolonged stress is that it may lead to **burnout**, a condition of emotional, mental, and physical exhaustion in response to long-term stressors. Burned-out people are often cynical. Burnout is a complex phenomenon, but it often occurs when people feel out of control. Other critical

Figure 14-3   Relationship Between Stress and Job Performance

factors that contribute to burnout are insufficient recognition and reward, a lack of emotional support in the workplace, or an absence of fairness. Christina Maslach observes that "When the workplace does not recognize the human side of work, then the risk of burnout grows, carrying with it a high price and hurting all the parties involved."[13]

The key feature of burnout is the distancing that occurs in response to work overload. Burnout sufferers shift into a mode of doing the minimum as a way of protecting themselves. They start leaving work early and dehumanizing their clients, patients, or customers. People experiencing burnout may do their jobs, but their heart is not in it any more.[14]

PERSONALITY AND JOB FACTORS CONTRIBUTING TO STRESS

Workers experience stress for many different reasons, including personal predispositions, factors stemming from the job, or the combined influence of both. If a person with an extreme negative predisposition has to deal with irate customers, he or she is most likely to experience substantial stress. Here we describe a sampling of important individual and organizational factors that contribute to job stress.

Personality Factors Predisposing People Toward Stress

Individuals vary considerably in their susceptibility to job stress based on their personality traits and characteristics. Four such factors are described next.

Low Perceived Control.   A key factor in determining whether workers experience stress is how much they believe they can control a given adverse circumstance. **Perceived control** is the belief that an individual has at his or her disposal a response that can control the negative aspects of an event. A survey of over 100 studies indicated that people with a high level of perceived control had low levels of physical and psychological symptoms of stress. Conversely, people with low perceived control are more likely to experience work stress.[15]

Low Self-Efficacy.   Related to the idea of low perceived control, workers with low self-efficacy tend to experience more emotional strain and physical strain than do workers with high self-efficacy. In short, people who are confident they can perform a particular task are more likely to either avoid stress of have much milder symptoms. The finding about self-efficacy was based on a study of 2,273 soldiers whose stressors were long work hours and work overload. The average age of the soldiers was 24.[16]

Type A Behavior.   A person with **Type A behavior** is demanding, impatient, and overstriving and is therefore prone to negative stress. Type A behavior has two main components. One is the tendency to try to accomplish too many things in too little time. This leads the Type A individual to be impatient and demanding. The other component is free-floating hostility. Because of this sense of urgency and hostility, these people are irritated by trivial things. People with Type A behavior are aggressive and hard working.

Type A personalities frequently have cardiac diseases, such as heart attacks and strokes, at an early age, but only certain features of the Type A personality

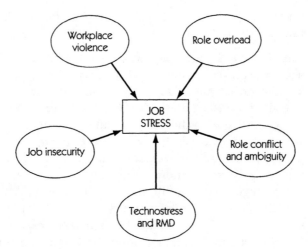

Figure 14-4   Five Major Sources of Job Stress

pattern may be related to coronary heart disease. The heart attack triggers are hostility, anger, cynicism, and suspiciousness, as contrasted to impatience, ambition, and being work driven.[17] Note that the heart attack triggers also make for strained interpersonal relationships.

Negative Affectivity.   A major contributor to being stress prone is **negative affectivity**, a tendency to experience aversive emotional states. In more detail, negative affectivity is a pervasive disposition to experience emotional stress that includes feelings of nervousness, tension, and worry. The same disposition also includes such emotional states as anger, scorn, revulsion, guilt, self-dissatisfaction, and sadness.[18] Such negative personalities seem to search for important discrepancies between what they would like and what exists. Poor interpersonal relationships often result from the frequent complaining of people with negative affectivity.

Job Sources of Stress

Almost any job situation can act as a stressor for some employees, but not necessarily for others. As just described, certain personality factors make it more likely that a person will experience job stress. Furthermore, other personal life stressors may spill over into the workplace, making it more likely that a person will experience job stress. Here we describe five frequently encountered job stressors, as outlined in Figure 14-4.

Role Overload.   Having too much work to do, **role overload**, can create negative stress in two ways. First, the person may become fatigued and thus be less able to tolerate annoyances and irritations. Second, a person subject to unreasonable work demands may feel perpetually behind schedule, a situation that is itself a powerful stressor. Downsizing often creates overload because fewer people are left to handle the same workload as previously. (If work is carefully streamlined, role overload is minimized.) The widespread problem of role overload was suggested by a Harris Research study of 5,300 adults in 16 countries. Fifty-four percent of the respondents indicated that the leading cause of stress was overwork.[19]

Role Conflict and Role Ambiguity. Role conflict, described in Chapter 7 as an important workplace conflict, is also a major workplace stressor. People experience stress when they have to choose between two sets of expectations. Suppose an accountant is asked by her manager to state company earnings in a way that conflicts with the professional norms of accountants. If she complies with her manager, she will feel that she is betraying her profession. If she does not comply with her manager, she will enter into dispute with the manager. The woman is likely to experience job stress.

Role ambiguity is a condition in which the job holder receives confusing or poorly defined expectations. Workers in many organizations are placed in situations in which they are unsure of their true responsibilities. Some workers who are placed on a self-managing work team experience role ambiguity because they are asked to solve many problems by themselves. It is less ambiguous to have the manager tell you what to do. Many people experience stress symptoms when faced with role ambiguity.

Technostress and Repetitive Motion Disorder. The computerization of the workplace, especially in information technology, has created a significant stressor labeled **technostress**. This condition refers to stress caused by an inability to cope with computer technologies in a constructive manner.[20] One contributor to technostress is the demand for continuous learning as software changes so rapidly. At the same time, software problems surface at unpredictable times, often leaving the computer operator feeling incompetent and helpless. Another contributor to technostress is that computer work can become so consuming that the person loses interest in human interaction. As a result, interpersonal relationships suffer.

Technostress also comes in the form of a repetitive motion disorder as a consequence of prolonged keyboarding. The repetitive motion disorder most frequently associated with keyboarding is **carpal tunnel syndrome**. The syndrome occurs when repetitive flexing and extension of the wrist causes the tendons to swell, thus trapping and pinching the median nerve. Carpal tunnel syndrome creates stress because of the pain and misery, and it sometimes makes it necessary to change jobs. Repetitive motion disorders are a major cause of worker compensation claims.

Job Insecurity. Worrying about losing your job is a major stressor. Even when jobs are plentiful, having to search for another job and facing the prospect of geographic relocation are stressors for many people. Downsizing and corporate mergers (which usually result in downsizing) have contributed to job insecurity. The anticipation of layoffs among employees can increase negative stress and lower job performance. In addition, the survivors of a downsizing often experience pressure from fear of future cuts, loss of friends, and worry about a sudden increase in workload.[21]

Workplace Violence. As DeFrank and Ivancevich observe, the issue of violence and stress is complex because violence may be both the cause and the result of stress. Workplace violence alarms many workers, with an average of 20 people murdered at work each week in the United States. Seventy-five percent or more of these murders occur during a robbery or other crime. Furthermore, 1 million workers are assaulted annually.[22] Workers who are victims of workplace assaults, or who watch a coworker being assaulted, experience intense negative stress. Worrying about being assaulted is also a stressor.

METHODS AND TECHNIQUES FOR STRESS MANAGEMENT

Unless stress is managed properly, it may lead to harmful long-term consequences, including disabling physical illness and career retardation. Managing stress refers to controlling stress by making it a constructive force in your life. Managing thus refers to both preventing and reducing stress. However, the distinction between methods of preventing and reducing stress is not clear cut. For example, physical exercise not only reduces stress, it also contributes to a relaxed lifestyle that helps you prevent stress.

Coping with, or managing, stress includes hundreds of activities, with substantial individual differences in which technique is effective. Running is a case in point. For many people running or jogging is an excellent method of stress reduction. Others find running creates new stressors, such as aching knees, shin splints, dizziness from breathing in vehicle exhausts, and worry about being hit by vehicles. In general, coping efforts involve cognitions and behaviors aimed at managing the stressor and its associated emotions. For example, you might have to decrease the troublesome elements in your job (such as role overload) and also deal with the tension generated by overwork. Here we describe six representative methods for managing stress, including a list of everyday stress busters.

Eliminate or Modify the Stressor. The most potent method of managing stress is to eliminate or modify the stressor giving you trouble. One value of relaxation techniques and tranquilizing medication is that they calm down a person enough so that he or she can deal constructively with the stressor. A helpful way to attack the cause of stress is to follow the steps in problem solving and decision making. You clarify the problem, identify the alternatives, weight the alternatives, and select one alternative. One difficulty, however, is that your evaluation of the real problem may be inaccurate. There is always a limit to self-analysis. For example, a person might think that work overload is the stressor when the true stressor is low self-efficacy.

Get Appropriate Physical Exercise. A moderate amount of physical exercise is a cornerstone of managing stress and achieving wellness. To manage stress it is important to select an exercise program that is physically challenging but does not lead to overexertion and muscle and bone injury. Competitive sports, if taken too seriously, can actually increase stress. Aerobic exercises are most beneficial because they make you breathe faster and raise your heart rate. A major mental and emotional benefit of physical exercise stems from endorphins produced in the thalamus portion of the brain. The endorphins are associated with a state of euphoria referred to as a "runner's high." Endorphins also work like painkillers, adding to their stress-reduction value.

Rest Sufficiently.   Rest offers benefits similar to those of exercise, such as stress reduction, improved concentration, improved energy, and better tolerance for frustration. Achieving proper rest is closely linked to getting proper exercise. The current interest in adult napping reflects the awareness that proper rest makes a person less stress prone and enhances productivity. A growing number of firms have napping facilities for workers, and many workers nap at their desks or in their parked vehicles during lunch breaks. *Power naps,* those of about 15 minutes duration taken during the work day, are used both as energizers and as stress reducers.[23] To keep the effectiveness of power napping in perspective, workers who achieve sufficient rest during normal sleeping hours have less need for a nap during working hours.

Build a Support Network.   A **support network** is a group of people who can listen to your problems and provide emotional support. These people, or even one person, can help you through your difficult episodes. Members of your network can provide you with a sense of closeness, warmth, and acceptance that will reduce your stress. Also, the simple expedient of putting your feelings into words can be a healing experience. The way to develop this support network is to become a good listener yourself so that the other person will reciprocate. A support network is therefore a method of stress management based squarely on effective interpersonal skills.

Practice Visualization.   Perhaps the most effortless and enjoyable relaxation technique for managing stress is to visualize a pleasant experience, as explained in Skill-Building Exercise 14-3. Visualization, like so many stress-reduction techniques, including meditation, requires concentration. Concentrating helps slow down basic physiological processes such as the heart beat and dissipates stress. Forcing yourself to concentrate is also valuable because a key stress symptom is difficulty in concentration.

Practice Everyday Methods of Stress Reduction.   The simple expedient of learning how to relax is an important method of reducing the tension and anxiety brought about by both positive and negative stress. Visualization of a pleasant experience is one such method. A sample of everyday suggestions for relaxation and other methods of stress reduction are presented in Figure 14-5. If you can accomplish these you are less likely to need tranquilizing medication to keep you calm and in control. Your stress symptoms will ordinarily return, however, if you do not eliminate and modify the stressor. If the stress is an emotional conflict you do not see or understand, assistance from a mental health professional is recommended.

SUMMARY

Achieving high personal productivity on the job is more in demand than ever. A starting point in improving productivity is to minimize procrastination, an

Skill-Building Exercise 14-3

VISUALIZATION FOR STRESS REDUCTION

A standard, easy-to-use method for reducing stress symptoms is to visualize a pleasant and calm experience. If you are experiencing stress right now, try the technique. Otherwise, wait until the next time you perceive your body to be experiencing stress. In this context, visualization means to picture yourself doing something that you would like to do. Whatever fantasy suits your fancy will work, according to the advocates of this relaxation technique. Visualizations that work for some people include smiling at a loved one, floating on a cloud, caressing a baby, petting a kitten or puppy, and walking in the woods. Notice that all of these scenes are relaxing rather than exciting. What visualization would work for you?

To implement the technique, close your eyes and bring the pleasant image into focus in your mind. Think of nothing else at the moment. Imagine that a videotape of the pleasant experience is playing on the television screen in your brain. Breathe softly and savor the experience. Slowly return to reality, refreshed, relaxed, and ready to tackle the challenges of the day.

➤ Give in to your emotions. If you are angry, disgusted, or confused admit your feelings. Suppressing your emotions adds to stress.

➤ Take a brief break from the stressful situation and do something small and constructive, such as washing your car, emptying a wastebasket, or getting a haircut.

➤ Get a massage, because it can loosen tight muscles, improve your blood circulation, and calm you down.

➤ Get help with your stressful task from a coworker, supervisor, or friend.

➤ Concentrate intensely on reading, surfing the Internet, a sport, or a hobby. Contrary to common sense, concentration is at the heart of stress reduction.

➤ Have a quiet place at home and have a brief idle period there every day.

➤ Take a leisurely day off from your routine.

➤ Finish something you have started, however small. Accomplishing almost anything reduces some stress.

➤ Stop to smell the flowers, make friends with a young child or elderly person, or play with a kitten or puppy.

➤ Strive to do a good job, but not a perfect job.

➤ Work with your hands, doing a pleasant task.

➤ Find somebody or something that makes you laugh, and have a good laugh.

➤ Minimize drinking caffeinated or alcoholic beverages, and drink fruit juice or water instead. Grab a piece of fruit rather than a can of beer.

➤ Help somebody less fortunate than yourself. The flood of good feelings will act like endorphins.

Figure 14-5   Stress Busters

enormous problem for many people that can be approached as follows: Calculate the cost of procrastination; use the worst in, first out (WIFO) principle; break the task into manageable chunks; make a commitment to other people; remove some clutter from your mind; and satisfy your stimulation quota in constructive ways.

Developing good work habits and time-management practices is often a matter of developing the right attitudes toward your work and toward time, as follows: (a) Begin with a mission statement and goals; (b) work smarter, not harder; (c) value orderliness and cleanliness; (d) value good attendance and punctuality; and (e) attain a balance in life and avoid being a workaholic.

Effective work habits and skills are essential for high productivity, including the following: (a) Prepare a to-do list and set priorities; (b) streamline your work and emphasize important tasks; (c) stay in control of paperwork and electronic work; (d) work productively from your home office or virtual office; and (e) enhance your Internet search skills.

Another basic thrust to improved personal productivity is to minimize time wasting. Whether or not an activity is a time waster depends on its purpose. Being aware of time wasters such as those presented in Figure 14-1 will sensitize you to the importance of minimizing them.

A major challenge facing any worker who wants to stay healthy and have good interpersonal relationships is to manage stress effectively. Individual differences play a big role in determining whether an event will lead to stress. The physiological changes that take place within the body in response to stress are responsible for most of the stress symptoms. The fight-or-flight response is the battle against the stressor.

The activation of hormones when the body has to cope with a stressor produces short-term physiological reactions, including an increase in heart rate and blood pressure. When stress levels rarely subside, the physiological changes create damage. However, the right amount of stress prepares us for meeting difficult challenges and improves performance. An optimum level of stress exists for most people and most tasks. In general, performance tends to be best under moderate amounts of stress.

One of the major problems of prolonged stress is that it may lead to burnout, a condition of emotional, mental, and physical exhaustion in response to long-term stressors. Burnout also creates cynicism and a distancing from tasks and people.

Four personality factors predisposing people toward stress are low perceived control, low self-efficacy, Type A behavior, and negative affectivity. The heart attack triggers associated with Type A behavior are hostility, anger, cynicism, and suspiciousness. Five frequently encountered job stressors are role overload, role conflict and ambiguity, technostress and repetitive motion disorder, job insecurity, and workplace violence.

Managing stress refers to controlling stress by making it become a constructive force in your life. Coping with, or managing, stress includes hundreds of activities, with substantial individual differences in which technique is effective. Six representative stress-management methods are to eliminate or modify the stressor, get appropriate physical exercise, rest sufficiently, build a support network, practice visualization, and use everyday methods of stress reduction.

QUESTIONS FOR DISCUSSION AND REVIEW

1. Provide an example from your own or somebody else's life of how having a major goal in life can help a person be better organized.

2. Describe any way in which you have used information technology to make you more productive.

3. Use information in this chapter to explain how a person might be well organized yet still not get very far in his or her career.

4. If you wanted to streamline your work as a student, what low-value activities could you eliminate?

5. Ask an experienced high-level worker to identify his or her most effective method of time management.

6. Some researchers have suggested that the term *challenge* be substituted for the term *stressor*. What do you think of the merit of their suggestion?

7. A student told his instructor, "You have to give me a deadline for my paper. Otherwise, I can't handle it." What does this statement tell you about (a) the stressor he was facing and (b) how pressure influences his work performance?

8. Why might having your stress under control improve your interpersonal relationships?

9. What are you going to do to prevent burning out in the next five years?

10. Interview a person in a high-pressure job in any field. Find out whether the person experiences significant stress and what method he or she uses to cope with it.

An Interpersonal Relations Case Problem

NOT GETTING IT DONE

Carol Winchester sat nervously outside the office of Daniel Delvin, a time-management consultant and personal coach. She kept thinking about how self-conscious she felt about seeking professional help just because she had a little trouble getting started on projects or finishing projects she had started. Carol said to herself, "This counselor is going to think there's something really wrong with me just because I have a small procrastination problem."

Winchester's thought pattern was interrupted by a warm welcome from Daniel Delvin, a neatly dressed, middle-age counselor. With a smile and an extended hand, Delvin said, "Hi. You must be Carol Winchester. I'm Dan Delvin. Come in and have a seat near the coffee table. That's where we'll be talking. Delvin sat in a chair a few feet away from Winchester.

"What kind of help do you want from me?" asked Delvin.

"The reason I'm here," answered Winchester, "is that both my boss and my boyfriend think I'm a procrastinator. Big Time. I don't disagree entirely, but I don't think I'm quite the basket case they do."

Delvin replied, "I doubt you're a basket case, but I don't think you would be here if you weren't experiencing a little pain. Hurting a little bit and admitting that you have a problem are the beginning points for overcoming your problem. Let's get started, Carol, by telling me about some of the ways in which you procrastinate."

"I've got a few horror stories to tell you," said Winchester with a nervous laugh. "A recent example is that it took me four months to make this appointment with you. [They both laugh.] I kept looking at my calendar and saying to myself that I was too busy to get help. I would pick up the phone to make an appointment. Then I would think of all the other things I needed to do. I finally set April 1 as an absolute firm date to call you. Then I realized I only had two more weeks to prepare my income tax forms for last

year. I guess you could say that I even procrastinated on my income tax. But I finally did get it in April 30, and the penalty only amounted to about $45. Those are two examples for you."

"Yes, they are two good examples. But I need more examples of your procrastination so I can better understand your problem."

"Okay, you asked for it," responded Winchester. "Lance, my boyfriend, whom I love very much, proposed to me one year ago. We were in a beautiful Greek restaurant called Acropolis. He pulled a ring out of the box. The group at the table across from us were watching intently. They were ready to clap when I said yes. Lance just assumed I would say yes. I didn't say yes, but I didn't say no. I just said I wasn't ready to make a decision that night.

"Two months later, when the engagement came up for about the tenth time in conversation, I did say yes. I know that by delaying my decision I took some of the romance out of Lance's proposal. His feelings are still a little hurt, but it didn't change his mind about wanting to marry me."

"Hold on a second," said Delvin. "Have you two agreed upon a wedding date yet?"

"Lance has been pressing me a little, but I'm just not ready to be that specific about getting married."

"Let's switch channels now," said Delvin. "What about on the job? What has prompted your boss to think you have a major procrastination problem?"

"It would be fair to say that I need more time than most people to get my projects done. I'm the assistant sales promotion manager. I have to do things like make some of the arrangements for trade shows and work with printers to have brochures ready. My boss says that I wait so long to make arrangements for booking hotels that we often have to pay premium rates. I think he exaggerates that problem. I'm very thorough, and that can be a big asset.

(Continued)

"A few times I have been late in getting computer disks ready for the printer so they can do their job on time. Yet since we're supposed to be the customer, I think they should be adapting to our schedule. I can think of another recent example. We were going to hire a new assistant for the office. We all agreed she was the right person to do the job. My boss had to go out of town for an important sales meeting. So he told me to contact this woman and tell her about the job offer.

"I got so busy with other stuff that I didn't call her for a week. By that time she had accepted another job. My boss was upset and blamed losing her on my procrastination. My take on it is a little different. If that woman really wanted to work for us, she could have waited for the job offer instead of taking another position."

Delvin asked, "Carol, why do you think you procrastinate so much?"

Carol replied, "You're a little bit like my boss and my boyfriend. You assume that every time I delay doing something, it's procrastination. Sometimes something else very important comes up that prevents me from going down a particular path. At other times I might be just a little forgetful, like filing the taxes on time."

Case Questions

1. What do you see as some of the reason behind Winchester's procrastination?

2. What evidence do you find that Winchester might be defensive about her problem (or denying its reality)?

3. What advice can you offer Carol Winchester for overcoming her procrastination problem?

Chapter 15

Job Search and Career Management Skills

Learning Objectives

After reading and studying this chapter and doing the exercises you should be able to

➤ Acquire new insights into conducting a job search, including writing an impressive cover letter, preparing a résumé, and being interviewed.

➤ Describe the difference between a vertical and a horizontal career path.

➤ Identify a handful of career-enhancing skills you intend to use.

➤ Explain how to overcome several different career barriers.

John Cirello is chief executive of MP Water Resources Group, the largest private water-supply utility company in Florida. His company has used adversity training extensively. For example, his company irrigates lawns for golf courses, hotels, and other businesses. A big problem occurs when it rains five times as much as average and demand for irrigation dries up.

Adversity training helped MP employees cope by focusing on the things over which they have control. Cirello said that after the training, "My people knew they couldn't control the weather, but they could control the cost." The employees cut power costs and other extras. The company has been using adversity training seminars for close to three years, and Cirello says he has seen a major change. The employees are more able to come up with innovative ways to solve problems.[1]

As the experience of the company just described suggests, leaning to cope with adversity is an important behavioral skill for performing well in your career. This final chapter of the book focuses on career success, including a description of strategies and tactics that will help you gain advantage. Learning to cope with adversity is but one such tactic.

Our approach to achieving career success is divided into four major segments: conducting a job campaign, understanding two major types of career paths, using career advancement strategies and tactics, and overcoming career barriers. The previous 14 chapters also deal with topics and skills that facilitate success. However, the information presented in this chapter is more specifically about managing your career.

CONDUCTING A JOB SEARCH

A relatively small number of people are sought out by employers because they possess skills in short supply, or they are invited by family members or friends to join an existing firm. However, the vast majority of workers have to conduct a job search at various times in their career. Job searches are conducted to find employment in a firm the job hunter is not already working for, or sometimes to find a new position within one's own firm. Even during the most prosperous of times, when jobs are in ample supply, learning more about conducting a job search is useful. It can help you land an excellent position. Included in the job search are job-hunting tactics and preparing a résumé and cover letter.

JOB-HUNTING TACTICS

Most people already have usable knowledge about how to find a job. Some of the ideas discussed next will therefore be familiar; some will be unfamiliar. We recommend using this list of tactics as a checklist to ensure that you have not neglected something important. It is easy to overlook the obvious when job hunting, because your emotions may cloud your sense of logic.

Identify Your Job Objectives

An effective job search begins with a clear perception of what kind of position (or positions) you want. If you express indecision about the type of work you seek, the prospective employer will typically ask in a critical tone, "What kind of work are you looking for?" Your chances of finding suitable employment increase when several different types of positions will satisfy your job objectives. Assume that one person who majored in business administration is only willing to accept a position as an office manager in a corporation. Another person with the same major is seeking a position as (a) an office manager; (b) a management trainee in a corporation; (c) an assistant manager in a retail store, restaurant, or hotel; (d) a sales representative; (e) an assistant purchasing agent; or (f) a management analyst. The second person has a much better chance of finding a suitable position.

Be Aware of Qualifications Sought by Employers

What you are looking for in an employer must be matched against what an employer is looking for in an employee. If you are aware of what employers are seeking, you can emphasize those aspects of yourself when applying for a position. For example, applicants for almost any type of position should emphasize their computer skills. Job interviewers and hiring managers do not all agree on the qualifications they seek in employees. Nevertheless, a number of traits, characteristics, skills, and accomplishments are important to many employers.[2] Self-Assessment Quiz 15-1 summarizes these qualifications in a way that you can apply to yourself as you think about your job hunt.

Identify Your Skills and Potential Contribution

Today's job market is skill based. Employers typically seek out job candidates with tangible skills (including interpersonal skills) that can be put to immediate use in accomplishing work. Job-relevant skills you might identify include computer skills, written communication skills, oral communication skills, math skills, and listening skills. A successful candidate for a help-desk position at a telecommunications company told the interviewer, "I know I can help your customers with their software and hardware problems. I worked on the help desk at college, and my friends and family members are forever coming to me with their computer problems. I even get long-distance calls for help. Give me a chance to help your customers." (Notice that this candidate implied good listening skills.)

Develop a Comprehensive Marketing Strategy

A vital job-finding strategy is to use multiple approaches to reach the right prospective employer. This is particularly true when the position you seek is in short supply. Among the many approaches employers use to recruit candidates are employee referrals, newspaper ads, online recruiting, college and professional school recruitment, job fairs, temporary help firms, walk-ins, unsolicited résumés and phone calls, and government employment services. Some people looking for a highly specialized job place a position-wanted ad in a newspaper or on the Internet. Such ads receive many inquiries from career agents who offer to help you find a suitable position.

Self-Assessment Quiz 15-1

QUALIFICATIONS SOUGHT BY EMPLOYERS

Following is a list of qualifications widely sought by prospective employers. After reading each qualification, rate yourself on a 1 to 5 scale on the particular dimension. 1 = very low; 2 = low; 3 = average; 4 = high; 5 = very high.

1. Appropriate education for the position under consideration and satisfactory grades	1	2	3	4	5
2. Relevant work experience	1	2	3	4	5
3. Communication and other interpersonal skills	1	2	3	4	5
4. Motivation and energy	1	2	3	4	5
5. Problem-solving ability (intelligence) and creativity	1	2	3	4	5
6. Judgment and common sense	1	2	3	4	5
7. Adaptability to change	1	2	3	4	5
8. Emotional maturity (acting professionally and responsibly)	1	2	3	4	5
9. Teamwork (ability and interest in working in a team effort)	1	2	3	4	5
10. Positive attitude (enthusiasm about work and initiative)	1	2	3	4	5
11. Emotional intelligence (ability to deal with own feelings and those of others)	1	2	3	4	5
12. Customer service orientation (wanting to meet customer needs)	1	2	3	4	5
13. Computer skills	1	2	3	4	5
14. Willingness to continue to study and learn about job, company, and industry	1	2	3	4	5
15. Likableness and sense of humor	1	2	3	4	5
16. Dependability, responsibility, and conscientiousness (including good work habits and time management)	1	2	3	4	5
17. Willing and able to work well with coworkers and customers from different cultures.	1	2	3	4	5

Interpretation: Consider engaging in some serious self-development, training, and education for items on which you rated yourself low or very low. If you accurately rated yourself as 4 or 5 on all the dimensions, you are an exceptional job candidate.

Use Networking to Reach Company Insiders

An estimated 80 percent of successful job campaigns stem from personal contacts. Employers rely heavily on referrals from employees to fill positions. Positions that have not been filled by word of mouth are then publicly announced, for example, through Internet listings. In regard to job hunting, **networking** is contacting friends and acquaintances and building systematical-

➤ Coworkers and previous employers

➤ Friends and neighbors

➤ Faculty and staff

➤ Graduates of any schools you have attended

➤ Former employers

➤ Present employers (assuming you hold a temporary position)

➤ Professional workers such as bankers, brokers, and clergy

➤ Political leaders at the local level

➤ Members of your club or athletic team

➤ Community groups, churches, temples, and mosques

➤ Trade and professional associations

➤ Student professional associations

➤ Career fairs

➤ People met in airports and on airplanes

➤ People met in aerobic classes and health clubs

➤ People you get to know through Internet chat rooms

Figure 15-1   Potential Sources of Network Contacts

ly on these relationships to create a still wider set of contacts who might lead to employment. Figure 15-1 presents a list of potential network contacts. In addition, a skill-building exercise about networking as a method of career enhancement, including a job search, is presented toward the end of this chapter.

The networking technique is so well known today that it suffers from overuse. It is therefore important to use a tactful, low-key approach with a contact. For example, instead of asking a person in your network to furnish you a job lead, ask that person how a person with qualifications similar to yours might find a job. And guard against taking up a large portion of a busy person's work day, for instance, by insisting on a luncheon meeting.

Another way of reaching company insiders is to write dozens of letters to potential employers. A surprisingly large number of people find jobs by contacting employers directly. Many company Web sites have a section allocated to inviting job inquiries as part of the employee recruitment program. Prepare a prospective employer list, including the names of executives to contact in each firm. The people who receive your letters and e-mail messages become part of your network. A variation of this approach is to develop a 30-second telephone presentation of your background. After you have researched firms that may have opportunities for you, call them and make your pitch.

Use the Internet and Résumé Database Services

The Internet is a standard avenue for job hunting, even for middle-management and executive positions. For little or no cost, the job seeker can post a résumé or scroll through hundreds of job opportunities. The Career Mosaic

TABLE 15-1 Popular Job Search Web Sites

100 Hot Most Popular Job Sites	www.100hot.com/directory/business/jobs.html
Career Magazine	www.careermag.com
Career Mosaic	www.careermosaic.com
Career Path	www.careerpath.com
Hot Jobs	www.hotjobs.com
JOBTRAK	www.jobtrak.com
Monster Board	www.monster.com
PeopleSoft	www.peoplesoft.com
Recruiting on the Web	www.recruitersnetwork.com
Yahoo!	www.jobs.yahoo.com
America's JobBank	www.ajb.dni.us
CareerWeb	www.cweb.com
NationJob Network	www.nationjob.com
JOB HUNT: ONLINE JOB META-LIST	www.job-hunt.org
EuroJobs	www.eurojobs.com
The Career Crossroads	www.careerxroads.com (job seekers can scan as many as 50 databases with one search engine)

Web site alone receives about 35 million hits per month, from both job seekers and recruiters. Web sites such as Career Mosaic and E-Span are résumé database services because they give employers access to résumés submitted by job hunters. The organizers of E-Span explain to employers that the service provides access to millions of qualified candidates through the World Wide Web, the Internet, and more than 10 online networks and bulletin boards.

Many position announcements on the Internet require the job seeker to send a résumé by attached file, or an electronic résumé (described later in this chapter). Others request that the résumé by sent by fax or paper mail. Technical positions such as computer programmer, engineering technician, or accountant are more likely to be found on the Internet than general positions. The Internet is also a source of job openings for working on the Internet, including jobs such as *cybersmith* (creates and edits information in cyberspace) and *cybernaut* (navigates through cyberspace to locate data and information). Thousands of nontechnical positions are also listed on the Internet, even some at very high income levels. Job hunting on the Internet is menu driven, as you will discover if you visit the Web sites listed in Table 15-1.

Job hunting on the Internet can lead to a false sense of security. Using the Internet, a résumé is cast over a wide net, and hundreds of job postings can be explored. As a consequence, the job seeker may think that he or she can sit back and wait for a job offer to come through e-mail. In reality, the Internet is just one source of leads that should be used in conjunction with other job-finding methods. Remember also that thousands of other job seekers can access the same job opening, and many of the positions listed have already been filled.

An important danger in placing your résumé on the Internet is that is will be accessed by a third party and passed along to thousands of other prospective employers. Your résumé may wind up on the computer of your present employer, much to your embarrassment. Pam Dixon, an Internet job search

Skill-Building Exercise 15-1

JOB HUNTING ON THE WEB

Job hunting on the Web can be a rewarding or frustrating experience, depending on your skill in navigating job search Web sites and the availability of positions for a person with your qualifications. Use several job search Web sites to locate a position opening for the following three persons:

Position 1: You. Find a position listed on the Web that would appear to be an excellent fit for you at this time in your career.

Position 2: Sales representative, fluent in English and Japanese. Attempt to find an opening for an industrial sales representative or retail sales position that requires the applicant to be fluent in English and Japanese.

Position 3: Sports administrator. Attempt to find an opening for a sports administrator, typically a person who does administrative work for a professional sports team.

Set a time limit for your surfing, perhaps 60 minutes. If you are working in a team, each team member can search for one position. Share with each other your approaches and Web sites that appear to achieve the best results.

specialist, says "I get a minimum of two messages a week from readers saying they've lost their job from posting on the Net."[3] Yet Dixon also notes that some companies appoint a human resource specialist to search the Internet looking for résumés posted by present employees. The specialist then brings in the job seeker to attempt to *salvage,* or find ways to prevent the employee from leaving.[4] (Perhaps you will be offered more money and a nicer cubicle!)

Skill-Building Exercise 15-1 will give you an opportunity to learn first hand about job hunting on the Web.

Smile at Network Members and Interviewers

Assuming that you have the right qualifications, the simple act of smiling can be an effective job-hunting technique. According to career specialist James Challenger, "People would rather work with people who have pleasant dispositions. If you have been looking for a job for three months with no success, it may be hard to smile, but make yourself do it. It works."[5]

Smooth Out Rough Spots in Your Background

About 95 percent of employers routinely conduct background investigations of prospective employees. A background investigation by a firm hired for the purpose could include speaking to neighbors and coworkers about your reputation. In addition, the investigator may delve into your driving record, check for criminal charges or convictions, survey your credit record, and find out whether you have had disputes with the government about taxes. The information just mentioned is used to supplement reference checks because so many employers are hesitant to say anything negative about past employees.

Any job seeker who has severe negative factors in his or her background cannot readily change the past. Yet the job seeker can receive copies of a credit bureau report to make sure it is fair and accurate. If inaccuracies exist, or certain credit problems have been resolved, the credit report might be changed in the applicant's favor. It might also be possible to obtain a more favorable reference from an employer by making a polite request. A third step can be to request a copy of the *consumer report,* which is a report of your reputation based on interviews with coworkers, neighbors, and others. A person might be able to negotiate a deletion of damaging information that is incorrect or exaggerated.[6]

THE JOB RÉSUMÉ AND COVER LETTER

No matter what method of job hunting you choose, inevitably somebody will ask you for a résumé. Sometimes you will be asked to complete a job application form instead of, or in addition to, a résumé. Résumés are also important for job hunting within your own firm. You may need one to be considered for a transfer with a large firm, or to be assigned to a team or project.

Résumé Purpose
Regard your résumé as a marketing tool for selling your skills and potential to handle new responsibilities. The most specific purpose of a résumé is to help you obtain an interview that can lead to a job. Your résumé must therefore attract enough attention for an employer to invite you for an interview. Recognize that you are competing against many carefully prepared résumés, some of which have been prepared with assistance from others. If the demand for your skills is high enough, it is conceivable that you will be hired without an interview.

Résumé Length and Format
Opinions vary about the desirable length for a résumé. For a recent graduate with limited work experience, a one-page résumé may be acceptable. For more experienced people, it would seem too short. Employers today demand considerable detail in résumés, particularly about the candidate's skills, accomplishments, and teamwork and leadership experience. Nevertheless, a four-page or longer résumé may irritate an impatient reader. Two pages is therefore recommended for early stages in your career.

A general-purpose hard-copy résumé is presented in Figure 15-2. Recognize that hiring managers and human resource professionals have widely different perceptions of what constitutes an effective résumé. Check at least two résumé guides before preparing a final version of your résumé.

A current development in résumé construction is to prepare one primarily for electronic databases. Many companies store résumés electronically, making it important to prepare one that is suitable for an electronic database. Should you prepare an electronic résumé, remember to create a file for your hard drive and a disk. If a job search Web site calls for an electronic résumé, it

Scott Wayland
170 Glenview Drive
Dallas, Texas 75243
Phone/Fax (312) 555-3986
swayland@frontiernet.net

Qualification Summary	Experience in selling industrial machinery. Education in business administration, combined with apprenticeship in tool and die making. In one year sold $375,000 worth of excess machine inventory. Received letter of commendation from company president.
Job Objective	Industrial sales, handling large, complex machinery. Willing to work largely on commission basis. Want to help my employer earn more profit.
Job Experience 2000–present	Industrial account representative, Bainbridge Corporation, Dallas. Sell line of tool and die equipment to companies in Southwest. Responsibilities include servicing established accounts and canvassing new ones. Served on team establishing E-commerce capability.
1998–2000	Inside sales representative, Bainbridge Corporation. Answered customer inquiries. Filled orders for replacement parts. Trained for outside sales position. Served as sales team representative on company quality-improvement team.
1994–1998	Tool and die maker apprentice, Texas Metals, Inc., Dallas. Assisted senior tool and die makers during four-year training program. Worked on milling machines, jigs, punch presses, computer-assisted manufacturing, computer-assisted design (CAD/CAM).
Formal Education 1994–2000	Madagascar College, Dallas, Texas. Associate Degree in Business Administration; graduated with 3.16 grade point average. Courses in marketing, sales techniques, human relations, accounting, and statistics. President of Commuter's Club.
1990–1994	Big Horn High, Dallas. Honors student; academic major with vocational elective. Played varsity football and basketball. Earned part of living by selling magazine subscriptions.
Job-Related Skills	Professional sales representative. Able to size up customer manufacturing problem and make recommendations for appropriate machinery. Precise in preparing call reports and expense accounts. Good skill in gathering input from the field for market research purposes. Can contribute to development of E-commerce site.
Personal Interests and Hobbies	Information technology enthusiast (developed and installed own Web site), scuba diving, recreational golf player, read trade and business magazines. Auto enthusiast, including restoring a 1972 Corvette.
References	On file with placement office at Madagascar College.

Figure 15-2   A General Purpose Résumé

can be entered into the right place on the Web page. At other times an electronic résumé is printed and mailed to the employer, who in turn uses an optical scanner to enter the résumé in the company database. A distinguishing feature of an electronic résumé is that it contains key words that fit the requirements of a keyword search. The job seeker should isolate keywords (nouns and adjectives) by placing them right under the individual's name, address, and telephone numbers. Zane K. Quible recommends that key words be selected from among the following information:[7]

➤ Titles of jobs held by applicant

➤ Names of job-related tasks performed by the applicant

➤ Industry jargon such as "zero defects," "customer delight," or "just-in-time inventory management." Also use acronyms such as JIT for "just in time."

➤ Special skills or knowledge possessed by the applicant such as knowledge of enterprise software, including SAP and Oracle

➤ Degrees earned

➤ High school program or college major (For college graduates, information about the high school program can be deleted.)

➤ High schools or colleges attended

➤ Special awards or honors received

➤ Nature of interpersonal skills the applicant possesses

Most of this information, of course, should also be included in a conventional printed résumé. Figure 15-3 illustrates an electronic résumé.

In preparing either a print or electronic résumé, keep in mind that certain key words or references attract the attention of managers and specialists who scan résumés. In today's market these are as follows: *languages, computer, experience, achievement, hard working, overseas experience, flexible, task-oriented, Internet,* and *E-commerce.*[8] A sensible tactic would be to mention those words that apply to you. Except for *languages* and *overseas experience,* these terms are widely applicable.

The Cover Letter

A résumé should be accompanied by a cover letter explaining who you are and why you are applying for this particular position. The cover letter customizes your approach to a particular employer, whereas the résumé is a more general approach. Sometimes it is helpful to prepare an attention-getting cover letter in which you make an assertive statement about how you intend to help the employer deal with an important problem. A person applying for a credit manager position might state, "Let me help you improve your cash flow by using the latest methods for getting customers to pay on time, or even early."

Employment specialist Richard H. Beatty recommends a slightly different version of the attention-getting cover letter. He explains that an effective cover

Sara L. Adams
123 Elmwood Terrace
Framingham, MA 01701
(617) 555-1485 FAX (617) 555-4587
SLAdams@hmp.aol

Keywords: Accountant. Bookkeeper. Accounts receivable ledger. Accounts payable ledger. Financial reports. Business Administration. Lotus 1-2-3. Excel. Windows 95. Windows 2000. French. Supervision. President's Honor Roll. Superior oral communication skills. Superior written communication skills. Self-starter. Quick learner. Conscientious. Detail oriented. Reliable. Top 5 percent of class. IBM-compatible computers. Lakeville College, Framingham, MA.

Job objective: To work as accountant or bookkeeper for private or public business, with eventual goal of becoming supervisor of bookkeeping or accounting or office manager.

Education:	Lakeville College, Framingham, MA, 1999–2001 Accounting major. Associate's degree in Business Administration with High Honors. East Framingham High School, National Honor Society, 1995.
Experience:	London's Department Store, Framingham, MA, 1995–present. Full time for four years, part time while attending college. Performed bookkeeping and cashier activities. Maintained accounts receivable and accounts payable ledgers. Prepared variety of financial reports.
Key Accomplishment:	Developed a system of prompt payments that saved employer approximately $60,000 per year.
College Activities and Honors	President of Accounting Club for two years. Team Leader of Student Misconduct Committee. President's Honor Roll, each semester 1999–2001. Delta Phi Kappa Honorary, 1999–2001

Figure 15-3   Electronic Résumé

letter has five parts: an attention-grabbing introduction, a paragraph selling your value to the employer, a background summary paragraph, a compelling follow-up action statement, and an appreciative close. Beatty recommends mentioning a personal contact as part of the attention grabber.[9] An example: "John Kowolski, your computer operations manager, mentioned that you are looking for a talented person to manage your Web site. I would very much like to talk to you about this position."

PERFORMING WELL IN A JOB INTERVIEW

After a prospective employer has reacted favorably to your cover letter and résumé, the next step is a telephone screening interview or a more comprehensive job interview. The purpose of the telephone screening interview is generally to obtain some indication of the candidate's oral communication skills. Such an interview is most likely when one applies for a customer contact position or one that requires knowledge of a second language. Having passed the screening interview, the candidate is invited for an in-person job interview. Another type of screening interview is to respond to computerized questions, including a sample job problem. Your answers are printed for the interviewer to review. Candidates who get through the computer-assisted interview get to be interviewed by a company representative.[10]

Typically the applicant is interviewed by one person at a time, yet team interviews are becoming more commonplace. In this format, members of the team or department with whom you would be working take turns asking you questions. One justification for team interviews is to observe how the candidate fits in with the team.

A general guide for performing well in the job interview is to present a positive but accurate picture of yourself. Your chances of performing well in a job increase if you are suited for the job. Tricking a prospective employer into hiring you when you are not qualified is therefore self-defeating in terms of your career. Outright deception, such as falsifying one's educational or employment record, is widely practiced during interviews, on résumés, and in cover letters. If the person is hired and the deception is discovered later, he or she is subject to dismissal. Following is a list of some key points to keep in mind when being interviewed for a job you want:

1. *Be prepared, look relaxed, and make the interviewer feel comfortable.* Coming to the interview fully prepared to discuss yourself and your background and knowing key facts about the prospective employer will help you look relaxed. Many people today use company Web sites to gather background information about the prospective employer.

2. *Establish a link between you and the prospective employer.* A good way to build rapport between you and the prospective employer is to mention some plausible link you have with that firm. To illustrate, if being interviewed for a position at a Kmart, one might say, "It's fun to visit the office part of Kmart. Our family has been shopping here for years. In fact, I bought a CD player here last month. It works great."

3. *Ask perceptive questions.* The best questions are sincere ones that reflect an interest in the content of the job (intrinsic motivators) and job performance, rather than benefits and social activities. A good question to ask is "What would you consider to be outstanding performance in this job?" If the issue of compensation is not introduced by the interviewer, ask about such matters after first discussing the job and your qualifications.

4. *Be prepared to discuss your strengths and developmental opportunities.* Most interviewers will ask you to discuss your strengths and developmental opportunities. (These and other frequently asked questions are presented in Figure 15-4.) Knowledge of strengths hints at how good your

An effective way of preparing for job interviews is to rehearse answers to the types of questions you will most likely be asked by the interviewer. The following questions are a sampling of the types found in most employment interviews. Rehearse answers to them prior to going out on job interviews. One good rehearsal method is to role play the employment interview with a friend who asks these typical questions or to videotape yourself.

1. Why did you apply for this job?
2. What are your career goals?
3. What salary are you worth?
4. What new job skills would you like to acquire in the next few years?
5. Give me an example of how you displayed good teamwork.
6. Describe how you have shown leadership on the job or off the job.
7. What are your strengths (or good points)?
8. What are your weaknesses (or areas for needed improvement)?
9. Why should we hire you instead of other candidates for this position?
10. How well do you work under pressure?
11. What positions with other companies are you applying for?
12. What makes you think you will be successful in business?
13. What do you know about our firm?
14. Here is a sample job problem. How would you handle it?
15. What questions do you have for me?

Figure 15-4   Questions Frequently Asked of Job Candidates

potential job performance will be. If you deny having areas for improvement you will appear uninsightful or defensive. Some candidates describe developmental opportunities that could be interpreted as strengths. A case in point: "I have been criticized for expecting too much from myself and others." Do you think this approach is unethical?

5. *Be prepared to respond to behavioral interview questions.* A *behavioral interview* asks questions directly about the candidate's behavior in relation to an important job activity. The job candidate is expected to give samples of important job behaviors. The behavioral interview is therefore more applicable to candidates with substantial work experience. Two behavioral inquiries are "Tell me about a time in which your ability to work well on a team contributed to the success of a project" and "Give me an example of a creative suggestion you made that was actually implemented. In what way did it help the company?" To prepare for such questions, think of some examples of how you handled a few difficult job challenges. The idea is to document specific actions you took or behaviors you engaged in that contributed to a favorable outcome.

6. *Show how you can help the employer.* A prospective employer wants to know whether you will be able to perform the job well. Direct much of your conversation toward how you intend to help the company solve problems and get important work accomplished. Whatever the question, think about what details of your skills and experiences will be useful to the employer.

Skill-Building Exercise 15-2

THE JOB INTERVIEW

As described in Figure 15-4, a good way to prepare for a job interview is to rehearse answers to frequently asked questions. In this role play, one student will be the interviewer and one the interviewee (job applicant). The job in question is that of property manager for a large apartment complex in Phoenix, Arizona. Assume that the applicant really wants the job. The interviewer, having taking a course in human resource management, will ask many of the questions in Figure 15-4. In addition, the interviewer will ask at least one behavioral question, perhaps about teamwork. The interviewer might also have other questions, such as "Why do you want to live in Phoenix?"

Before proceeding with the role play, both people should review the information in this chapter about the job interview and in Chapter 3 about listening.

---

7. *Send a follow-up letter.* Mail a courteous follow-up letter several days after the interview, particularly if you want the job. A follow-up letter is a tip-off that you are truly interested in the position. You should state your attitudes toward the position, the team, and the company and summarize any conclusions reached about your discussion.

Now do Skill-Building Exercise 15-2 to practice the job interview.

THE VERTICAL AND HORIZONTAL CAREER PATHS

Career planning can begin at any point, including a kindergarten child saying, "I want to be an astronaut." Many other people think about developing their career after they have worked in a full-time professional position for several years. Planning and developing your career involves some form of goal setting. If your goals are laid out systematically to lead to your ultimate career goal, you have established a **career path**, a sequence of positions necessary to achieve a goal. Here we look at the more traditional career path with an emphasis on moving upward, along with the more contemporary path that emphasizes acquiring new skills and knowledge.

THE VERTICAL (TRADITIONAL) CAREER PATH

The vertical, or traditional, career path is based on the idea that a person continues to grow in responsibility with the aim of reaching a target position, such as becoming a top-level manager. The vertical career path is synonymous with "climbing the corporate ladder." The same path is based somewhat on the unwritten contract that a good performer will have the opportunity to work for one firm for a long time and receive many promotions in the process. However, a vertical career path can be spread out over several employers.

As the year 2000 approached, many employers had returned to the old-fashioned idea of cultivating corporate loyalty by emphasizing promotions for good performers. The reason for the change in attitude by top management was a shortage of workers to fill many positions. After an era of frequent downsizings, executives are now trying to send a new message to employees: "Don't leave. We need you. Work for us—you can build a career here."[11] Inducements for staying include helping workers develop skills to advance their careers and making it easier to change jobs with the company. Employees who are downsized in one unit of a firm are often transferred to another unit.

A career path should be related to the present and future demands of one firm or the industry. If you aspire toward a high-level manufacturing position, it would be vital to know the future of manufacturing in that firm and in the industry. Many U. S. firms, for example, plan to conduct more of their manufacturing in the Pacific Rim and Mexico. If you were really determined, you might study the appropriate language and ready yourself for a foreign position.

While laying out a career path, it is also helpful to list your personal goals. They should mesh with your work plans to avoid major conflicts in your life. Some life-styles, for example, are incompatible with some career paths. It would be difficult to develop a stable home life (spouse, children, friends, community activities, sports team, and garden) if a person aspired toward holding field positions in international marketing. Contingency ("what if") plans should also be incorporated into a well-designed career path. For instance, "If I am not promoted within two years, I will pursue an advanced degree."

Mary Gonzalez, an ambitious 20-year-old, formulated the career path shown in Figure 15-5 prior to receiving an associate degree in business management. After she presented her tentative career path to her classmates, several accused Mary of aiming too high. Mary's career goals are high, but she has established contingency plans.

A career path laid out in chart form gives a person a clear perception of climbing steps toward his or her target position. As each position is attained, the corresponding step can be shaded in color or cross-hatched. The steps, or goals, include a time element, which is helpful for sound career management even in work environments that are less predictable than they used to be. Your long-range goal might be clearly established in your mind (such as become regional manager of a hotel chain). At the same time, you must establish short-range (get any kind of job in a hotel) and intermediate-range (be manager of a hotel by age 27) goals. Goals set too far in the future that are not supported with more immediate goals may lose their motivational value.

THE HORIZONTAL CAREER PATH

In many organizations, the hope of staying for a long time and receiving a long series of promotions has vanished. Instead of climbing the ladder, the person is placed on a jungle gym in which he or she makes a series of moves in different directions. Each position in the company represents a rung on the jungle gym. Managers and others make their careers by scrambling over the frame or moving between positions.[12]

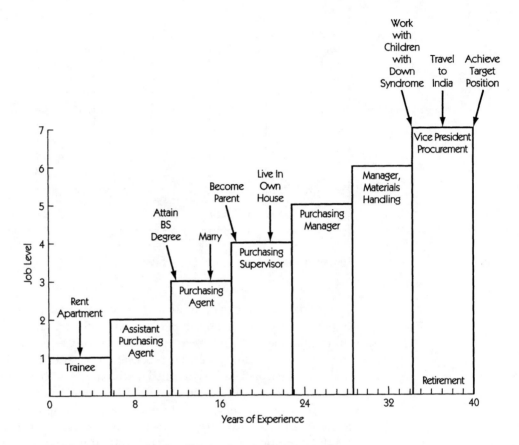

Figure 15-5   A Vertical (or Traditional) Career Path

Typically these moves in the modern organization are horizontal rather than vertical. A significant feature of the horizontal career path is that people are more likely to advance by moving sideways than by moving up. Or at least people who get ahead will spend a considerable part of their career working in different positions at or nearly at the same level. In addition, they may occasionally move to a lower-level position in order to gain valuable experience. With a horizontal career path, the major reward is no longer promotion, but the opportunity to gain more experience and increase job skills.

The horizontal career path is closely linked to the new employment contract that offers shared responsibility for career growth. The old employment contract was lifetime employment in exchange for corporate loyalty. Instead, today employees get a chance to develop new technical and professional skills. Instead of being offered job security, they become more employable because of the diversity of skills they acquire. The company provides the environment for learning, and the employees are responsible for developing their skills. (As mentioned earlier, many employers are reverting to the old promises of an opportunity to climb the organizational ladder. Furthermore, it is not unusual for workers to aspire toward holding higher-level, higher-paying positions.)

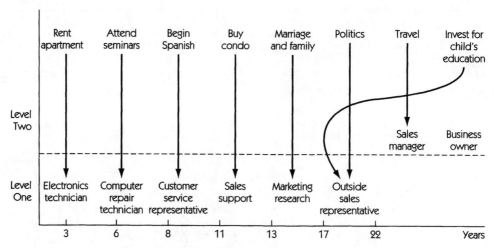

Figure 15-6 A Horizontal Career Path

A horizontal career path, as well as a traditional (or vertical) career path, does not necessarily mean the person stays with the same firm. For example, a worker might spend three years in one company as an electronics technician, three years in another as a sales representative, and then three years as a customer service specialist in a third company. All three positions would be approximately at the same level. The third company then promotes the individual to a much-deserved position as the marketing team leader. Figure 15-6 illustrates a horizontal career path for Larry Chang, a career school graduate who did attempt to make long-range predictions about his career. Notice that all the positions through year 17 are at the first level, and the positions for year 22 and beyond are at the second level. Chang's career contingency plans are as follows:

(1) If cannot obtain experience as a market research analyst, customer service rep, or sales rep, will continue to develop as electronics technician. (2) If cannot find employment as a sales manager, will attempt to become supervisor of electronic technicians. (3) If do not raise sufficient funds for starting own business, will continue in corporate job until retirement.

USING CAREER ADVANCEMENT STRATEGIES AND TACTICS

The many ways of improving interpersonal relationships described in this book can help advance and enhance a person's career. People who enhance their relationships with others are laying a foundation for career advancement. Here we will describe 12 other key strategies and tactics for career advancement, whether the advancement be vertical, horizontal, or a combination of the two. The first seven of the methods described deal more with controlling your own characteristics and behaviors, whereas the remaining five deal more with interacting with the environment.

Be Passionate About Your Work

Successful people in all fields are passionate about their work. Without passion, you rely too heavily on external rewards to sustain effort. Passion contributes to both your career growth and company productivity.[13] Effective leaders and business owners are usually passionate about their work. Being passionate is also important because it is linked to developing expertise and high job performance.

The surest path to career success is to identify your area of expertise and then build a career around it. The more passionate you are about your area of expertise, the better. Becoming wealthy and achieving recognition are by-products of making effective use of your talents. Expertise combined with passion helps you attain high job performance. Consistently good job performance is the foundation on which you build your career. Job competence is still the major success ingredient in all but the most political organizations (those where favoritism outweighs merit).

Develop a Code of Professional Ethics

Another solid foundation for developing a career is to establish a personal ethical code. An ethical code determines what behavior is right or wrong, good or bad, based on values. The values stem from cultural upbringing, religious teachings, peer influences, and professional or industry standards. As implied in Chapter 13, a code of professional ethics helps a worker deal with such issues as accepting bribes, backstabbing coworkers, and sexually harassing a work associate.

Develop a Proactive Personality

If you are an active agent in taking control of the forces around you, you stand a better chance of capitalizing on opportunities. Also, you will seek out opportunities such as seeing problems that need fixing. A **proactive personality** is a person who is relatively unconstrained by situational forces and who brings about environmental change. People who are highly proactive identify opportunities and act on them, show initiative, and keep trying until they bring about meaningful change. A health and safety specialist with a proactive personality, for example, might identify a health hazard others had missed. She would identify the nature of the problem and urge management to supply funding to control the problem. Ultimately her efforts in preventing major health problems would be recognized.

A study conducted with close to 500 men and women workers in diverse occupations examined the relationship between career success and a proactive personality. Proactive personality, as measured by a test, was related to salary, promotions, and career satisfaction.[14]

It may not be easy to develop a proactive personality, but a person can get started by taking more initiative to fix problems and attempt to be more self-starting. A proactive personality is close in meaning to having high perceived control over situations.

Keep Growing Through Continuous Learning and Self-Development

Given that continuous learning is part of the new employment contract, engaging in regular learning can take many forms, including formal schooling, attending training programs and seminars, and self-study, including using the Internet. It is particularly important to engage in new learning in areas of interest to the company, such as developing proficiency in a second language if the company has customers and employees in other countries. Many companies support continuous learning because they perceive themselves to be *learning organizations*. It may therefore be easy for you to implement the tactic of growth through continuous learning.

Document Your Accomplishments

Keeping an accurate record of what you have accomplished in your career can be valuable when being considered for reassignment, promotion, or applying for a position outside your company. The same log of accomplishments is useful for résumé preparation. It is preferable to point to tangible, quantifiable accomplishments than to another person's subjective impression of your performance. Let's assume that a retail store manager reduced inventory shrinkage by 30 percent in one year. It would be better to state that fact than to record a statement from the manager saying that "Kelly shows outstanding ability to reduce inventory shrinkage."

Documenting your accomplishments in a business field is similar to a person in the arts such as a photographer, interior designer, or architect developing a portfolio of work. When the person applies for a job or assignment, he or she carries along the portfolio of representative work.

Documentation enables you to promote yourself in a dignified, tactful way. When discussing work with key people in the company, let them know of your good deeds without taking too much credit for team accomplishments. If you distinguish yourself in the community, for example, by fundraising for a shelter for the homeless, let your manager know of your activities. The rationale is that most companies want their workers to be responsible community members.

Project a Professional Image

Your clothing, desk and work area, speech, and general knowledge should project the image of a professional, responsible person if you seek career advancement. Good grammar and sentence structure can give you the edge because so many people use highly informal patterns of speech. Being a knowledgeable person is important because today's professional businessperson is supposed to be aware of the external environment. Also, as noted by a human relations specialist, projecting a professional image hastens the development of trust and rapport in business relationships.[15]

A challenge in projecting a professional image is to figure out what constitutes a professional image in your particular environment. The information technology field in Silicon Valley, for example, is extremely informal. A programmer who wore a tank top and running shoes and brought a parrot to the office might be considered to project a professional image. Yet a marketing specialist for a health insurance provider behaving in the same way in Boston would be perceived as unprofessional.

Perceive Yourself as a Provider of Services

A useful perspective for upgrading your professional self-image and enhancing your feelings of job security is to perceive yourself as something other than a traditional employee. According to career specialist John A. Thomson, everyone should see himself or herself as a *personal service business entity*. Basically you are a business, offering the company (also your client from this perspective) a valuable service. You keep offering the service so long as the company keeps you on the payroll and you enjoy the work. Note the similarity to a high-level professional such as a dentist or information technology consultant. You are offering a service that many people need. Part of the same perception is that you own your skills, and that these are the service your business (you) offer to others.[16]

Another way of perceiving yourself as different from a traditional employee is to think of yourself as a professional-level temporary employee. Sometimes you will have a long stay with one employer, acting like a permatemp. At other times, you will move on to another company where your skills are more in need.

Develop Depth and Breadth

A continuing concern about career management is whether to acquire substantial depth in a specialty or to obtain broader experience. Is it better to be a specialist or a generalist? In general it pays to have good depth in one area of expertise, yet also acquire broad experience. A distribution specialist who helped set up shipping systems in an automobile supply company, an office supply company, and a hospital supply company would have excellent credentials. Yet some career specialists would argue that knowing one industry well has its merits.

If your goal is to become an executive, broadening your experience is a career enhancer. A person who held positions in sales and manufacturing would have broad experience. Breadth could come about also by experience in different industries, such as retailing and mining, or by holding positions in different companies. Being assigned to different teams, projects, and committees is another natural broadening experience. Another approach to broadening is to self-study different aspects of the business.

Rely on a Network of Successful People

Networking has already been described as a major assist to finding a job. Members of your network can also help you by assisting with difficult job problems, providing emotional support, buying your products or services, and offering you good prices on their products or services. The starting point in networking is to obtain an ample supply of business cards. You then give a card to any person you meet who might be able to help you now or in the future.

While first developing your network, be inclusive. Sandy Vilas says, "Remember the 3-foot rule—anyone within three feet of you is someone you can network with."[17] Later, as your network develops, you can strive to include a greater number of influential and successful people. Skill-Building Exercise 15-3 provides suggestions for systematically building your network.

Work with a Mentor

In Chapter 10 mentoring was presented as a way of helping people grow and develop. Mention also was made that minority group members who advanced in their careers attributed some of their success to mentors. Here we reemphasize that having a mentor can facilitate career advancement. Ideally a person should develop a small network of mentors who give advice and counsel on different topics such as job advancement opportunities and how to solve a difficult problem.

Many people who receive exceptional promotions within their own firms, or receive excellent job offers from other companies, are chosen by their mentors. At the root of mentoring is the ability to attract and build a relationship with a person who is more experienced and talented than yourself.

Find a Good Person–Organization Fit

Assuming that you have the luxury of selecting among different prospective employers, it is best to work for a company where your personality and style fit the organization culture. A **person–organization fit** is the compatibility of the individual and the organization. Job interviews represent a good opportunity for evaluating a person–organization fit for both the applicant and the employer.[18]

The compatibility often centers around the extent to which a person's major work-related values and personality traits fit major elements of the organization culture. Following this idea, a person who is adventuresome and risk taking would achieve highest performance and satisfaction in an organization in which adventuresome behavior and risk taking are valued. Conversely, a methodical and conservative individual should join a slow-moving bureaucracy. How much an organization emphasizes individual effort versus teamwork is another important area for person–organization fit. Workers who enjoy teamwork would fit better in a teamwork-oriented culture.

Person–organization fit can also include superficial aspects of behavior such as physical appearance and dress. For example, a person who dressed like a Wall Street investment banker might not feel comfortable working in a high-tech firm in California where jeans and sandals were standard work attire. As a consequence of not feeling comfortable in your work environment, you might not perform at your best.

Take Sensible Risks

People who make it big in their careers usually take sensible risks on their journey to success. Among these risks would be to work for a fledgling company that offers big promises but a modest starting salary, or to take an overseas assignment with no promise of a good position when you return. Purchasing stock in start-up companies is *sometimes* a sensible risk, if you do not absolutely

Skill-Building Exercise 15-3

BUILDING YOUR NETWORK

Networking can be regarded as the process of building a team that works with you to achieve success. You can start the following exercise now, but it will probably take your entire career to implement completely. To start networking, or make your present networking more systematic, take the following steps:

Step 1: Jot down your top three goals or objectives for the following three months, such as obtaining a new job or promotion, starting a small business, or doing a field research study.

1. _____

2. _____

3. _____

Step 2: List family members, friends, or acquaintances who could assist you in meeting your goals or objectives. Prepare a contact card, or database entry, for each person on your list, including as many details as you can about the person, the person's family, friends, employers, and contacts.

Step 3: Identify what assistance you will request of your contact, or contacts. Be realistic in light of your prior investment in the relationship. Remember, you have to be a friend to have a friend.

Step 4: Identify how you will meet your contact or contacts during the next month. Could it be for lunch, at an athletic field, night club, sports club, recreational facility on campus, cafeteria, and so forth? Learn more about your contacts during your face-to-face meetings. In some cases you may have to use the telephone or e-mail to substitute for an in-person meeting. Look for ways to mutually benefit from the relationship. At the beginning of each week, verify that you have made a small investment in building these relationships.

Step 5: Ask for the help you need. A network must benefit you. Thank the contact for any help given. Jot down on your planner a reminder to make a follow-up call, letter, or e-mail message to your contacts. In this way you will have less work to do before you make another request for help.

Step 6: For each person in your network, think of a favor, however small, you can return to him or her. Without reciprocity, a network fades rapidly.

Source: Adapted and expanded from Cheryl Kitter, "Taking the Work Out of Networking," Success Workshop, supplement to *The Pryor Report*, March 1998, pp. 1–2.

need the funds for living expenses. Industrial relations manager Michael Oliver offers this advice:

> If you want to achieve something really creative, thus enhancing your profession, then try a little risk taking. This doesn't mean you should pick up a lance and seek out a windmill. Balance your risk taking with good sense so you will be able to reach a new comfort level somewhere between the

role of a bureaucratic follower and leaper of tall buildings. The goal should be to develop credibility without perpetrating a maverick reputation.[19]

OVERCOMING CAREER BARRIERS

Another major aspect of career management is to be able to overcome career barriers or hurdles, as recognized in the chapter opener about adversity training. You may also recall from Chapter 8 that resiliency is an important leadership characteristic. People who are reslilient, or *psychologically hardy,* have developed the skills to overcome problems. They are able to overcome the emotional hurt associated with setback. After dealing with their emotions, they tackle the hurdle with a problem-solving approach.[20] Two representative barriers that many people face are overcoming the loss of employment and coping with hidden barriers to advancement.

COPING WITH JOB LOSS

Much has been written and said in recent years about coping with job loss because of the many downsizings in business, government, and education. Even during prosperous times, job loss can be a big emotional hurt and a major inconvenience. The best strategy for coping with job loss is to have good credentials, including a good reputation, and marketable skills. In addition, the following suggestions are in order:[21]

1. *Avoid panic.* Work hard at avoiding panic, because panic is a natural response to trauma that often immobilizes a person. The danger is that the person will run in the wrong direction such as grabbing a lower-paying job that does not fit his or her career plan. Talking over your job loss with a confidant (or confidante) will sometimes help control panic.

2. *Do a reality check.* Attempt to uncover what you might have done wrong that could have contributed to the job loss. Take stock of your assets and what you can offer prospective employers. Investigate the job market for a person of your background. Think through whether the network you have established will be helpful in finding new employment.

3. *Guard against depression and stay physically healthy.* Again we emphasize talking about your problems with one or two confidants. Get ample exercise and rest so you look your best when making contacts or going out on job interviews.

4. *Avoid bitterness and making angry statements about your past employer—especially to prospective employers.* Rehearse making whatever positive statements you can about your most recent employment, and practice smiling. Here is an example of a positive statement about a negative situation: "Although my job was eliminated, I am proud of what I accomplished during my stay. I am also thankful for how much I learned. My

only regret is that I was not able to continue contributing and learning."

5. *Give full-time attention to conducting a job campaign.* When unemployed your job is finding a job, and it should be a full-time, energetic activity including all the steps described in this chapter. A major mistake many job searchers make is to slow down or stop their efforts when the first warm job lead surfaces. Keep searching until you have reached an employment agreement. And don't discard the leads your job search has created until you are secure in your new position.

DEALING WITH THE GLASS CEILING

Many women and minority-group members complain that they may get off to a good start in their careers, but at some point the promotions stop. Outright discrimination may not be evident, but somehow a subtle barrier to further growth emerges despite all the progress women and minority-group members have made in business. A **glass ceiling** is an invisible but difficult-to-penetrate barrier to promotion based on subtle attitudes and prejudices. For example, less than 3 percent of senior executive positions in business are occupied by women and minorities combined.

Although the glass ceiling is difficult to crack, many women and minority-group members are making progress. A survey of Fortune 1000 CEOs, and the highest-ranking women in their companies, identified career-advancement strategies and tactics used by women to rise to the top.[22] (Notice that these women pursued a traditional career path.) The seven most effective strategies the women used are shown in Table 15-1. You will observe that the strategies chosen by the glass-ceiling breakers are similar to the career-advancement tactics described in this chapter. A later study by the career-research firm Catalyst investigated why minority-group women managers were not able to penetrate the glass ceiling. Nearly 50 percent of the women surveyed cited the lack of an influential mentor, in comparison to 29 percent of white women.[23]

An important conclusion is that workers in professional-level jobs who want to overcome hidden barriers to success should make effective use of sensible career-advancement strategies and tactics. Evidence presented here and in Chapter 10 emphasizes the importance of finding the right mentor to enhance your career.

SUMMARY

Recommended job-hunting tactics include the following:

1. Identify your job objectives.

2. Be aware of qualifications sought by employers.

3. Identify your skills and potential contribution.

4. Develop a comprehensive marketing strategy.

TABLE 15-1 Percentage of Women Using Seven Leading Strategies to Break the Glass Ceiling

Strategy	Critical	Fairly Important	Not Important	Did Not Use
Consistently exceed performance expectations	77	22	1	0
Develop style that men are comfortable with	61	35	3	1
Seek difficult or high-visibility assignments	50	44	2	4
Have an influential mentor	37	44	9	9
Network with influential colleagues	28	56	9	6
Gain line management experience	25	29	11	33
Move from one functional area to another (gain breadth)	23	34	20	22

Note: Not all percentages add to 100 because of rounding errors by researchers.

Source: Excerpted from Belle Rose Ragins, Bickely Townsend, and Mary Mattis, "Gender Gap in the Executive Suite," *Academy of Management Executive,* February 1998, p. 29.

5. Use networking to reach company insiders.

6. Use the Internet and résumé database services.

7. Smile at network members and interviewers.

8. Smooth out the rough spots in your background.

Job hunting almost always requires a résumé, with two pages in length recommended. A frequent requirement is to construct a résumé for an electronic database. Résumés should emphasize skills and accomplishments. A résumé should almost always be accompanied by a cover letter explaining how you can help the organization and why you are applying for this particular job.

Screening interviews, including computer-assisted ones, precede a full job interview. A general guide for performing well in an interview is to present a positive but accurate picture of yourself. More specific suggestions include the following:

1. Be prepared, look relaxed, and make the interviewer feel comfortable.

2. Establish a link between you and the employer.

3. Ask perceptive questions.

4. Be prepared to discuss your strengths and developmental opportunities.

5. Be prepared to respond to behavioral (examples of job behaviors) interview questions.

6. Show how you can help the employer.

7. Send a follow-up letter.

The vertical, or traditional, career path is based on the idea that a person continues to grow in responsibility with the aim of reaching a target position, such as becoming a top-level manager. A vertical path is based on the traditional employment contract. A vertical career path should be related to the present and future demands of one firm or the industry. The horizontal career path is less predictable; it resembles a jungle gym. A horizontal career path emphasizes lateral moves with an opportunity to gain more experience and increase job skills. A horizontal path is closely linked to the new employment contract that offers shared responsibility for career growth. Career paths should have contingency plans.

Improving interpersonal relationships assists career advancement. In addition, the following strategies and tactics are relevant:

1. Be passionate about your work.
2. Develop a code of professional ethics.
3. Develop a proactive personality.
4. Keep growing through continuous learning and self-development.
5. Document your accomplishments.
6. Project a professional image.
7. Perceive yourself as a provider of services.
8. Develop depth and breadth.
9. Rely on a network of successful people.
10. Work with a mentor.
11. Find a good person–organization fit.
12. Take sensible risks.

Another important aspect of career management is to be able to cope with barriers or problems. Being a resilient, or psychologically hardy, person is helpful. Two key career barriers are coping with job loss and, for some people, dealing with invisible barriers to promotion (the glass ceiling).

QUESTIONS FOR DISCUSSION AND REVIEW

1. Identify four situations in a career in which conducting a job campaign would be necessary.

2. Why do many employers look for signs of emotional intelligence when hiring candidates for professional-level positions?

3. As part of recruiting on the Internet, some human resource specialists hunt through the files of other companies to find résumés of employees who have certain key skills. (They gain access through a process called "flipping a Web site.") What is your opinion of the ethics of this approach to recruiting?

4. What is your evaluation of the ethics of a company firing a present employee when a company representative finds the employee's résumé on the Internet?

5. Why is a horizontal career path referred to as a *jungle gym*?

6. Give an example from your own life in which you behaved as if you were a proactive personality.

7. In the field you are in, or intend to enter, what are some of the characteristics of a professional image?

8. How would you rate the effectiveness of sending e-mail messages to people as a method of sustaining a network?

9. In your own words, what really is a *glass ceiling*? Why the choice or words, *glass ceiling*?

10. What is the most useful idea you picked up from this chapter about either conducting a job campaign or managing your career?

A Interpersonal Relations Case Problem

WHY ISN'T MY RÉSUMÉ GETTING RESULTS?

Billy Joe Wentworth was working in the family business as a manufacturing technician while he attended career school. Although he got along well with his family members, Billy Joe wanted to find employment elsewhere so he could build a career on his own. Billy Joe's job objective was a position in industrial sales. He compiled a long list of prospective employers. He developed the list from personal contacts, classified ads in newspapers, and job openings posted on the Internet. Billy Joe clipped a business card with a brief handwritten noted to each résumé. The note usually said something to the effect, "Job sounds great. Let's schedule an interview at your convenience." The résumé is shown in the accompanying exhibit.

After mailing out 200 résumés, Billy Joe still did not have an interview. He asked his uncle and mentor, the owner of the family business, "Why isn't my résumé getting results?"

Case Questions

1. What suggestions can you make to Billy Joe for improving his résumé? Or does it require improvement?

2. What is your evaluation of Billy Joe's approach to creating a cover letter?

(Continued)

Exhibit 1

RÉSUMÉ OF BILLY JOE WENTWORTH

BILLY JOE WENTWORTH
275 Birdwhistle Lane
Cleveland, Ohio 44131
(216) 555-7512(Please call after 7 PM weekday nights)
Billyjoe@wentworth.com

Objective

Long-range goal is Vice President of sales of major corporation. For now, industrial sales representative paid by with salary and commission.

Job Experience

Five years experience in Wentworth industries as manufacturing technician, tool crib attendant, shipper, and floor sweeper. Voted as "employee of the month" twice. Two years experience in newspaper delivery business. Distributed newspapers door to door, responsible for accounts receivable and development of new business in my territory.

Education

Justin Peabody Career College, business administration major with manufacturing technology minor. Expect degree in June 2001. 2.65 GPA. Took courses in sales management and selling. Received a B+ in professional selling course.
Cleveland Heights High School, business and technology major, 1994–1998. Graduated 45th in class of 125. 82% average.

Skills and Talents

Good knowledge of manufacturing equipment; friends say I'm a born leader; have been offered supervisory position in Wentworth Industries; real go getter.

References

Okay to contract present employer except for my immediate supervisor Jill Baxter with whom I have a personality clash.

Glossary

action plan A series of steps to achieve a goal.

active listener A person who listens intensely, with the goal of empathizing with the speaker.

aggressive personality A person who verbally, and sometimes physically, attacks others frequently.

assertiveness Being forthright in expressing demands, opinions, feelings, and attitudes.

behavior modification An attempt to change behavior by manipulating rewards and punishments.

brainstorming A group problem-solving technique that promotes creativity by encouraging idea generation through noncritical discussion.

brainwriting Brainstorming by individuals working alone.

burnout A condition of emotional, mental, and physical exhaustion in response to long-term stressors.

business etiquette A special code of behavior required in work situations.

career path A sequence of positions necessary to achieve a goal.

carpal tunnel syndrome A condition that occurs when repetitive flexing and extension of the wrist causes the tendons to swell, thus trapping and pinching the median nerve.

casual time orientation A cultural characteristic in which people view time as an unlimited and unending resource and therefore tend to be patient.

character trait An enduring characteristic of a person that is related to moral and ethical behavior that shows up consistently.

charisma A special quality of leaders whose purposes, powers, and extraordinary determination differentiate them from others. (However, people besides leaders can be charismatic.)

coaching A method of helping workers grow and develop and improve their job competence by providing suggestions and encouragement.

cognitive factors The collective term for problem-solving and intellectual skills.

cognitive restructuring Mentally converting negative aspects into positive ones by looking for the positive elements in a situation.

cognitive style Mental processes used to perceive and make judgments from situations.

collectivism A feeling that the group and society should receive top priority, rather than the individual.

communication The sending, receiving, and understanding of messages.

complementary transactions An exchange of words between two people that reduces tension and moves the two people toward a positive resolution.

compromise Settlement of differences by mutual concessions.

concern for others An emphasis on personal relationships and a concern for the welfare of others.

conflict A situation in which two or more goals, values, or events are incompatible or mutually exclusive.

conflict of interest A situation that occurs when a person's judgment or objectivity is compromised.

consensus General acceptance by the group of a decision.

cross-functional team A work group composed of workers from different specialties.

cultural fluency The ability to conduct business in a diverse, international environment.

cultural sensitivity An awareness of and willingness to investigate the reasons why people of another culture act as they do.

cultural training A set of learning experiences designed to help employees understand the customs, traditions, and beliefs of another culture.

cycle-of-service chart A method of tracking the moments of truth with respect to customer service.

defensive communication The tendency to receive messages in such a way that self-esteem is protected.

defining moment Choosing between two or more ideals in which one deeply believe.

denial The suppression of information a person finds uncomfortable.

developmental need A specific area in which a person needs to change or improve.

difficult person An individual who creates problems for others, even though he or she has the skill and mental ability to do otherwise.

disability A physical or mental condition that substantially limits an individual's major life activities.

diversity training (or valuing-differences training) Training that attempts to bring about workplace harmony by teaching people how to get along better with diverse work associates.

effort-to-performance expectancy The probability assigned by the individual that effort will lead to performing the task correctly.

electronic brainstorming Method of generating ideas with the aid of a computer. Group members simultaneously and anonymously enter their suggestions into a computer, and the ideas are distributed to monitors of other group members.

emotional intelligence Qualities such as understanding one's own feelings, empathy for others, and the regulation of emotion to enhance living.

empathy In communication, imagining oneself in the receiver's role, and assuming the viewpoints and emotions of that individual.

empowerment The process of managers transferring, or sharing, power with lower-ranking employees.

ethical screening Running a contemplated decision or action through an ethics test.

ethics The moral choices a person makes.

expectancy theory A motivation theory based on the premise that the effort people expend depends on the reward they expect to receive in return.

extinction Decreasing the frequency of undesirable behavior by removing the desirable consequence of such behavior.

feedback In communication, messages sent back and forth to the sender.

feeling-type individuals People who have a need to conform and adapt to the wishes of others.

femininity In the study of cultures, an emphasis on personal relationships and a concern for others.

fight-or-flight response The body's physiological and chemical battle against a stressor in which the person tries to cope with the adversity head-on or tries to flee from the scene.

formality A cultural characteristic of attaching considerable importance to tradition, ceremony, social rules, and rank.

frame of reference The fact that people perceive words and concepts differently because their vantage points and perspectives differ.

g (general) factor A factor in intelligence that contributes to the ability to perform well in many tasks.

glass ceiling An invisible but difficult-to-penetrate barrier to promotion based on subtle attitudes and prejudices.

group decision making The process of reaching a judgment based on feedback from more than one individual.

group norms The unwritten set of expectations for group members.

groupthink A deterioration of mental efficiency, reality testing, and moral judgment in the interest of group solidarity.

groupware Technology designed to facilitate the work of groups.

high-context culture A culture that makes extensive use of body language.

image exchanging A technique for resolving conflict in which two antagonists make it clear that they each understand the other person's point of view.

impression management A set of behaviors directed at enhancing one's image by drawing attention to oneself.

individual differences Variations in how people respond to the same situation based on personal characteristics.

individualism A mental set in which people see themselves first as individuals and believe that their own interests take priority.

informal learning The acquisition of knowledge and skills that take place naturally outside of a structured learning environment.

informality A cultural characteristic of a casual attitude toward tradition, ceremony, social rules, and rank.

intelligence The capacity to acquire and apply knowledge, including solving problems.

intermittent reward A reward that is given for good performance occasionally, but not always.

internal customers The people with whom a person interacts on the job.

interpersonal relations The technical term for relationships with people.

interpersonal skill training The teaching of skills in dealing with others so they can be put into practice.

intuitive-type individuals People who prefer an overall perspective, or the big picture.

job discrimination An unfavorable action brought against another person because of a characteristic unrelated to job performance.

law of effect Behavior that leads to a positive consequence for the individual tends to be repeated, whereas behavior that leads to a negative consequence tends not to be repeated.

leader-exchange model A theory explaining that group leaders establish unique working relationships with group members, thereby creating in-groups and out-groups.

leadership The ability to inspire support and confidence among the people who are needed to achieve common goals.

long-term orientation A cultural characteristic of maintaining a long-term perspective.

masculinity In the study of cultures, an emphasis on assertiveness and the acquisition of money and material objects.

materialism An emphasis on assertiveness and the acquisition of money and material objects.

mentor An individual with advanced experience and knowledge who is committed to giving support and career advice to a less experienced person.

message A purpose or idea to be conveyed.

metacommunicate To communicate about your communication to help overcome barriers or resolve a problem.

mirroring Subtly imitating someone.

moments of truth Situations in which a customer comes in contact with a company and forms an impression of its service.

moral intensity In ethical decision making, how deeply others might be affected by the decision.

motivation An internal state that leads to effort expanded toward objectives; an activity performed by one person to get another to accomplish work.

motivational state Any active needs and interests operating at a given time.

multiple intelligences A theory of intelligence contending that people know and understand the world in distinctly different ways and learn in different ways.

negative affectivity A tendency to experience aversive emotional states.

negative reinforcement (avoidance motivation) Rewarding people by taking away an uncomfortable consequence of their behavior.

negotiating Conferring with another person to resolve a problem.

networking Developing contacts with influential people, including gaining their trust and confidence.

noise Anything that disrupts communication, including the attitudes and emotions of the receiver.

nominal group technique (NGT) A group problem-solving technique that calls people together in a structured meeting with limited interaction.

nonverbal communication The transmission of messages through means other than words.

nurturing person One who promotes the growth of others.

organizational politics Gaining power through any means other than merit or luck.

paradigm A model, framework, viewpoint, or perspective.

participative leadership Sharing authority with the group.

perceived control The belief that an individual has at his or her disposal a response that can control the negative aspects of an event.

performance-to-outcome expectancy The probability assigned by the individual that performance will lead to outcomes or rewards.

personal productivity How much resources, including time, you consume to achieve a certain level of output.

personality Persistent and enduring behavior patterns that tend to be expressed in a wide variety of situations.

personality clash An antagonistic relationship between two people based on differences in personal attributes, preferences, interests, values, and styles.

person–organization fit The compatibility of the individual and the organization.

person–role conflict The situation that occurs when the demands made by the organization clash with the basic values of the individual.

positive gossip Unofficial information that does not attack others, is based on truth, and does not leak confidential information.

positive reinforcement Increasing the probability that behavior will be repeated by rewarding people for making the desired response.

power The ability or potential to control anything of value and to influence decisions.

power distance The extent to which employees accept the idea that members of an organization have different levels of power.

proactive personality A person who is relatively unconstrained by situational forces and who brings about environmental change.

procrastination Delaying action for no good reason.

protégé The less experienced person in a mentoring relationship who is helped by the mentor.

punishment The presentation of an undesirable consequence or the removal of a desirable consequence because of unacceptable behavior.

Pygmalion effect The phenomenon that people will rise (or fall) to the expectations that another person has of them.

role ambiguity A condition in which the job holder receives confusing or poorly defined expectations.

role conflict The situation that occurs when a person has to choose between two competing demands or expectations.

role overload Having too much work to do.

s (special) factors Specific components of intelligence that contribute to problem-solving ability.

self-efficacy The confidence in your ability to carry out a specific task.

self-managing work team A small group of employees responsible for managing and performing technical tasks to deliver a product or service to an external or internal customer.

sensation-type individuals People who prefer routine and order.

sexual harassment Unwanted sexually oriented behavior in the work place that results in discomfort and/or interference with the job.

short-term orientation A cultural characteristic characterized by a demand for immediate results.

social loafing Shirking individual responsibility in a group setting.

stress An adaptive response that is the consequence of any action, situation, or event that places special demands on a person.

stressor The external or internal force that brings about stress.

summarization The process of summarizing, pulling together, condensing, and thereby clarifying the main points communicated by another person.

support network A group of people who can listen to your problems and provide emotional support.

synergy A situation in which the group's total output exceeds the sum of each individual's contribution.

team A small number of people with complementary skills who are committed to a common purpose, set of performance goals, and approach for which they hold themselves mutually accountable.

technostress Stress caused by an inability to cope with computer technologies in a constructive manner.

thinking-type individuals People who rely on reason and intellect to deal with problems.

toxic person One who negatively affects others.

training The process of helping others acquire a job-related skill.

triarchic theory of intelligence An explanation of mental ability holding that intelligence is composed of three different subtypes: analytical, creative, and practical.

Type A behavior A behavior pattern in which the individual is demanding, impatient, and overstriving and therefore prone to negative stress.

uncertainty avoidance The extent to which people accept the unknown and tolerate risk and unconventional behavior.

universal training need An area for improvement common to most people.

urgent time orientation A cultural characteristic of perceiving time as a scarce resource and tending to be impatient.

valence The value, worth, or attractiveness of an outcome.

value The importance a person attaches to something.

virtual office A place of work without a fixed physical location, where the output is communicated electronically.

virtual team A small group of people who conduct almost all of their collaborative work by electronic communication rather that face-to-face meetings.

win-win The belief that after conflict has been resolved both sides should gain something of value.

workaholism An addiction to work in which not working is an uncomfortable experience.

References

CHAPTER 1

1. James C. Georges, "The Hard Reality of Soft-Skills Training," *Personnel Journal*, April 1989, p. 41.
2. The model presented here is an extension of the one presented in Thomas V. Bonoma and Gerald Zaltman, *Psychology for Management* (Boston: Kent Publishing Company, 1981), pp. 88–92.
3. Nancy Day, "Informal Learning Gets Results," *Workforce*, June 1998, pp. 30–36.
4. Morgan W. McCall, Jr., *High Flyers: Developing the Next Generation of Leaders* (Boston: Harvard Business School Press, 1998).

CHAPTER 2

1. Such is the theme of Kevin R. Murphy, *Individual Differences and Behavior in Organizations* (San Francisco: Jossey-Bass, 1996).
2. J. Madeline Nash, "The Personality Genes," *Time*, April 27, 1998, pp. 60–61; Dean Hamer, Living with Our Genes (New York: Doubleday, 1998).
3. Margaret A. McManus and Mary L. Kelly, "Personality Measures and Biodata: Evidence Regarding Their Incremental Predictive Value in the Life Insurance Industry," *Personnel Psychology*, Spring 1999, pp. 137–148; Murray R. Barrick and Michael K. Mount, "The Big Five Personality Dimensions and Job Performance: A Meta-Analysis," *Personnel Psychology*, Spring 1991, p. 11.
4. Jesus F. Salgado, "The Five Factor Model of Personality and Job Performance in the European Community," *Journal of Applied Psychology*, February 1997, pp. 30–43.
5. Adapted from John R. Schermerhorn, Jr., James G. Hunt, and Richard N. Osburn, *Managing Organi-* *zational Behavior*, 5th ed. (New York: John Wiley & Sons, 1994), p. 119.
6. Arthur R. Jensen, *The g Factor: The Science of Mental Ability* (Westport. CT: Praeger, 1998).
7. Robert J. Sternberg, *Beyond IQ: A Triarchic Theory of Human Intelligence* (New York: Cambridge University Press, 1985); Bridget Murray, "Sparking Interest in Psychology Class," *APA Monitor*, October 1995, p. 51.
8. Howard Gardner, *Leading Minds: An Anatomy of Leadership* (New York: Basic Books, 1996); www.funderstanding.com/multipleint.htm.
9. Daniel Goleman, "What Makes a Leader?" *Harvard Business Review*, November–December 1998, p. 95; Bridget Murray, "Does 'Emotional Intelligence' Matter in the Workplace?" *APA Monitor*, July 1998, p. 21.
10. Paul G. Stoltz, *Adversity Quotient—Turning Obstacles into Opportunities* (New York: Wiley, 1997).
11. David C. McClelland, "How Motives, Skills, and Values Determine What People Do," *American Psychologist*, July 1985, p. 815.
12. John B. Miner, *Organizational Behavior: Performance and Productivity* (New York: Random House, 1988), p. 83.

CHAPTER 3

1. Albert Mehrabian and M. Weiner, "Decoding of Inconsistent Communications," *Journal of Personality and Social Psychology*, 6, 1967, pp. 109–114.
2. Frederick Golden, "Lying Faces Unmasked," *Time*, April 5, 1999, pp. 52–53.
3. Jeffrey Jacobi, *The Vocal Advantage* (Upper Saddle River, NJ: Prentice Hall, 1996).
4. Roberta H. Krapels and Vanessa D. Arnold, "Speaker Credibility in Persuasive Work Situations," *Business Education Forum*, December 1997, p. 25.

5. Irene Hanson Frieze, Josephine E. Olson, and June Russell, "Attractiveness and Business Success: Is It More Important for Women or Men?" Paper presented at the Academy of Management, Washington, D.C., August 1989.

6. Suzette Haden Elgin, *Genderspeak* (New York: Wiley, 1993).

7. Mark Henricks, "Can We Talk? Speaking Up About the Value of Dialogue," *Entrepreneur,* January 1998, p. 82.

8. Sharon Lund O'Neil, "An Empowered Attitude Can Enhance Communication Skills," *Business Education Forum,* April, 1998, pp. 28–30.

9. Jimmy Calano and Jeff Salzman, "Persuasiveness: Make It Your Power Booster," *Working Woman,* October 1988, pp. 124–125; Krapels and Arnold, "Speaker Credibility," pp. 24–26; Gayle Theiss, "Say It Smart," *Aspire,* November–December 1998, pp. 3–4.

10. Jean Mausehund and R. Neil Dortch, "Communications—Presentation Skills in the Digital Age," *Business Education Forum,* April 1999, pp. 30–32.

11. Barry L. Reece and Rhonda Brandt, *Effective Human Relations in Organizations,* 5th ed. (Boston: Houghton Mifflin, 1993), p. 250.

12. Deborah Tannen, *Talking from 9 to 5* (New York: William Morrow, 1994); Tannen, *You Just Don't Understand* (New York: Ballantine, 1990); John Gray, *Men Are from Mars, Women Are from Venus* (New York: HarperCollins, 1992).

13. Deborah S. Roberts, "Communication + Stress = Breakdown," *Dartnell's Communication at Work,* sample issue, undated.

CHAPTER 4

1. Deborah Fineblum Raub, "Chief Mankiller to Talk Here on Power, Women," Rochester, New York, *Democrat and Chronicle,* May 1, 1994, p. 1F.

2. Jon R. Katzenbach and Douglas K. Smith, "The Discipline of Teams," *Harvard Business Review,* March–April 1993, p. 112.

3. Deal E. Yeatts and Cloyd Hyten, *High Performing Self-Managed Work Teams: A Comparison of Theory and Practice* (Thousand Oaks, CA: Sage, 1998), p. xiii.

4. Carla Johnson, "Teams at Work," *HR Magazine,* May 1999, p. 30.

5. James L. Creighton and James W. R. Adams, "The Cybermeeting's About to Begin," *Management Review,* January 1998, pp. 29–31.

6. Johnson, "Teams at Work," p. 32.

7. "When Committees Spell Trouble: Don't let Individuals Hide Within a Group," *WorkingSMART,* August 1998, p. 1.

8. Irving L. Janus, *Victims of Groupthink: A Psychological Study of Foreign Policy Decisions and Fiascos* (Boston: Houghton Mifflin, 1972); Glen Whyte, "Groupthink Reconsidered," *Academy of Management Review,* January 1989, pp. 40–56.

9. Martha A. Peak, "Treating Trauma in Teamland," *Management Review,* September 1997, p. 1.

10. Glenn M. Parker, *Team Players and Teamwork: The New Competitive Business Strategy* (San Francisco: Jossey-Bass, 1990), pp. 61–98; Thomas L. Quick, *Successful Team Building* (New York: AMACOM, 1992), pp. 40–52.

11. Pamela Lovell, "Healthy Teams Display Strong Vital Signs," *Teamwork,* sample issue, the Dartnell Corporation, 1997.

12. Glenn M. Parker, *Cross-Functional Teams: Working with Allies, Enemies, & Other Strangers* (San Francisco: Jossey-Bass, 1994), p. 170.

CHAPTER 5

1. Ryan K. Lahti, "Group Decision Making within the Organization: Can Models Help?" www.work-teams.unt.edu/reports/lahti.htm. Copyright 1996, University of North Texas. Accessed June 3, 1999.

2. Andrew E. Schwartz and Joy Levin, "Better Group Decision Making," *Supervisory Management,* June 1990, p. 4.

3. R. Brente Gallupe, William H. Cooper, Mary-Liz Grise, and Lana M. Bastianutti, "Blocking Electronic Brainstorms," *Journal of Applied Psychology,* February 1994, pp. 77–78;

4. R. Brent Gallupe and Associates, "Electronic Brainstorming and Group Size," *Academy of Management Journal,* June 1992, p. 352; R. Brent Galuppe, Lana M. Bastianutti, and William H. Cooper, "Unblocking Brainstorms," *Journal of Applied Psychology,* February 1991, pp. 137–142.

5. Keng L. Siau, "Electronic Brainstorming," *Innovative Leader,* April 1997, p. 3.

6. Allen C. Bluedorn, Daniel B. Turban, and Mary Sue Love, "The Effects of Stand-Up and Sit-Down Meeting Formats on Meeting Outcomes," *Journal of Applied Psychology,* April 1999, pp. 277–285.

7. Howard Baker, "Promoting Interaction and Teamwork with Electronic Mail," *Business Education Forum,* October 1994, pp. 30–31.

8. "Introduction to Groupware," www.usabilityfirst. com/groupware/intro.html. Accessed June 3, 1999.

CHAPTER 6

1. Adapted and excerpted from Rene Blank and Sandra Slipp, "Manager's Diversity Workbook," *HRfocus,* July 1998, p. S7.

2. Personal communication, January 1995.

3. Joan Crockett, "Winning Competitive Advantage Through a Diverse Workforce," *HRfocus,* May 1999, p. 9.

4. Arvind V. Phatak, *International Dimensions of Management* (Boston: Kent, 1983), p. 167.

5. Gillian Flynn, "White Males See Diversity's Other Side," *Workforce,* February 1999, p. 52.

6. Charlene Marmer Solomon, "Global Operations Demand That HR Rethink Diversity," *Personnel Journal,* July 1994, p. 50.

7. Geert Hofstede, *Culture's Consequences: International Differences in Work Related Values* (Beverly Hills, Calif.: Sage, 1980); updated and expanded in "A Conversation with Geert Hofstede," *Organizational Dynamics,* Spring 1993, pp. 53–61; Jim Kennedy and Anna Everest, "Put Diversity in Context," Personnel Journal, September 1991, pp. 50–54.

8. "Koreans Pitch In to Help In Crisis," Associated Press, syndicated story December 2, 1997.

9. Rick Borelli, "A Worldwide Language Trap," *Management Review,* October 1997, pp. 52–54.

10. The etiquette suggestion is from "Letitia Baldrige: Arbiter of Business Manners and Mores," *Management Review,* April 1992, p. 50.

11. Roger E. Axtell, *Gestures: The Do's and Taboos of Body Language around the World* (New York: Wiley, 1990).

12. Chris Sandlund, "There's a New Face to America," *Success,* April 1999, p. 42.

13. Marcia Forsberg, "Cultural Training Improves Relations with Asian Clients," *Personnel Journal,* May 1993, pp. 79–89. The quotes are from the same source.

14. Valerie Frazee, "Culture & Language Training: Send Your Expats Prepared for Success," *Global Workforce,* March 1999, p. 7. (The list of facts was compiled from 10 different sources by Frazee.)

15. R. Roosevelt Thomas, Jr., *Beyond Race and Gender: Unleashing the Power of Your Total Work Force by Managing Diversity* (New York: AMACOM, 1991), p. 25.

16. Gillian Flynn, "The Harsh Reality of Diversity Programs," *Workforce,* December 1998, p. 29.

CHAPTER 7

1. Richard J. Mayer, *Conflict Management: The Courage to Confront* (Columbus, Oh.: Batelle Press, 1990).

2. Dominic A. Infante, *Arguing Constructively* (Prospect Heights, Ill.: Waveland Press, 1992).

3. Survey reported in Jessica Guynn, "Bullying Behavior Affects Morale as Well as the Bottom Line," Knight Ridder, syndicated story November 2, 1998.

4. Michael D. Kelleher, *Profiling the Lethal Employee: Case Studies of Violence in the Workplace* (Westport, CT: Praeger, 1997), p. 112.

5. Kenneth Thomas, "Conflict and Conflict Management," in Marvin D. Dunnette (ed.), *Handbook of Industrial and Organizational Psychology* (Chicago: Rand McNally College Publishing, 1976), pp. 900–902.

6. Simon, cited in Mark Liu, "You Can Learn to Be Less Accommodating—If You Want To," Rochester, New York, *Democrat and Chronicle,* April 25, 1999, p. 1C.

7. Catherine Tinsley, "Models of Conflict Resolution in Japanese, German, and American Cultures," *Journal of Applied Psychology,* April 1998, p. 317.

8. Robert R. Blake and Jane S. Mouton, *The Managerial Grid III* (Houston: Gulf Publishing, 1985), p. 101.

9. The first three suggestions are from Connirae Andreas and Steve Andreas, *Heart of the Mind* (Moab, Ut.: Real People Press, 1991).

10. Kenneth Kaye, *Workplace Wars and How to End Them: Turning Personal Conflicts into Productive Teamwork* (New York: AMACOM, 1994).

11. Kimberly T. Schneider, Suzanne Swan, and Louise F. Fitzgerald, "Job-Related and Psychological Effects of Sexual Harassment in the Workplace: Empirical Evidence from Two Organizations," *Journal of Applied Psychology,* June 1997, p. 406; Joanne Cole, "Sexual Harassment: New Rules, New Behavior," *HRfocus,* March 1999, p. 1.

12. Jennifer Laabs, "What You're Liable For Now," *Workforce,* October 1998, pp. 34–42; Gillian Flynn, "Sexual Harassment Interpretations Give Cause for New Concerns," *Workforce,* May 1999, pp. 105–106.

13. Schneider, Swan, and Fitzgerald, "Job-Related and Psychological Effects," pp. 412–413.

14. Theresa M. Glomb, Liberty J. Munson, and Charles L. Hulin, "Structural Equation Models of Sexual Harassment: Longitudinal Explorations and Cross-Sectional Generalizations," *Journal of Applied Psychology,* February 1999, pp. 14–28.

15. Kathleen Neville, *Corporate Attractions: An Inside Account of Sexual Harassment with the New Sexual Roles for Men and Women on the Job* (Reston, Va.: Acropolis Books, 1992; Joanne Cole, "Sexual Harassment: New Rules, New Behavior," *HRfocus,* March 1999, pp. 1, 14–15.

16. Robert McGarvey, "Hands Off! How Do the Latest Supreme Court Decisions On Sexual Harassment Affect You?" *Entrepreneur,* September 1998, p. 86; Cole, "Sexual Harassment: New Rules," p. 14.

CHAPTER 8

1. Bill Bradley, "Whatever the Score—Bounce Back," *Parade Magazine,* October 18, 1998, p. 6.

2. Shelley A. Kirkpatrick and Edwin A. Locke, "Leadership: Do Traits Matter?" *The Executive,* May 1991, pp. 26–27; Nathaniel Brandon, *Self-Esteem at Work: How Confident People Make Powerful Companies* (San Francisco: Jossey-Bass, 1998).

3. Dale E. Zand, *The Leadership Triad: Knowledge, Trust, and Power* (New York: Oxford University Press, 1997).

4. Reported in "Developing Trust Pays Off," *Managers Edge,* April 1999, p. 9.

5. Richard Mullins, "Big Job—Fast Track," *Rochester, New York, Democrat and Chronicle,* April 18, 1999, p. 1E.

6. Anthony Bianco, "The Rise of a Star," *Business Week,* December 21, 1998, p. 63.

7. Bruce J. Avolio, Jane M. Howell, and John J. Sosik, "A Funny Thing Happened on the Way to the Bottom Line: Humor as a Moderator of Leadership Style Effects," *Academy of Management Journal,* April 1999, pp. 219–227.

8. Zand, *The Leadership Triad,* p. 8.

9. Keith Bradsher, "Saturn's New Boss Rose to the Top from the Factory Floor," *The New York Times,* syndicated story, December 27, 1998.

10. Daniel Goleman, "What Makes a Leader?" *Harvard Business Review,* November–December 1998, p. 92.

11. Jay A. Conger, *The Charismatic Leader: Behind the Mystique of Exceptional Leadership* (San Francisco: Jossey-Bass, 1989).

12. Elizabeth Weil, "Every Leader Tells a Story," www.fastcompany.com/online/15/rftf.html. (Accessed May 6, 1999).

13. Suggestions 7, 9, and 10 are from Roger Dawson, *Secrets of Power Persuasion* (Upper Saddle River, N.J.: Prentice-Hall, 1992), pp. 181–183.

14. Jon R. Katzenbach and Douglas K. Smith, "The Discipline of Teams," *Harvard Business Review,* March–April 1993, p. 118.

15. Terri A. Scandura and Chester A. Schrieisheim, "Leader-Member Exchange and Supervisor Career Mentoring as Complementary Constructs in Leadership Research," *Academy of Management Journal,* December 1994, pp. 1588–1602; George Graen and J. F. Cashman, "A Role Making Model of Leadership in Formal Organizations: A Developmental Approach," in J. G. Hunt and L. L. Larson (eds.), Leadership Frontiers (Kent, Ohio: Kent State University Press, 1975), pp. 143–165.

16. Francis J. Yammarino, Alan J. Dubinsky, Lucette B. Comer, and Marvin A. Jolson, "Women and Transformational and Contingent Reward Leadership: A Multiple-Levels-of-Analysis Perspective," *Academy of Management Journal,* February 1997, pp. 205–222.

17. Jon R. Katzenbach and Jason A. Santamaria, "Firing Up the Front Line," *Harvard Business Review,* May–June 1999, pp. 116–117.

18. William D. Hitt, *The Model Leader: A Fully Functioning Person* (Columbus, Oh.: Battelle Press, 1993).

19. Michael E. McGill and John W. Slocum, Jr., "A *Little* Leadership Please?" *Organizational Dynamics,* Winter 1998, p. 48.

CHAPTER 9

1. Gerald Kushel, *Reaching the Peak Performance Zone: How to Motivate Yourself and Others to Excel* (New York: AMACOM, 1994), p. 66.

2. Research summarized in "One of These Seven Things Will Motivate Any Employee in the Company," *The Motivational Manager,* sample issue, 1998 (Lawrence Ragan Communications, Inc.)

3. Jennifer J. Laabs, "Targeted Rewards Jump-start Motivation," *Workforce,* February 1998, p. 90.

4. cited in Shari Caudron, "Motivating Creative Employees Calls for New Strategies," *Personnel Journal,* May 1994, p. 105.

5. Fred Luthans and Alexander D. Stajkovic, "Reinforce for Performance: The Need to Go Beyond Pay and Even Rewards," *Academy of Management Executive,* May 1999, p. 52.

6. Steven Kerr, *Ultimate Rewards: What Really Motivates People to Achieve* (Boston: Harvard Business School Publishing, 1997).

7. Jennifer Laabs, "Satisfy Them with More Than Money," *Workforce,* November 1998, p. 43.

8. The original version of expectancy theory applied to work motivation is Victor Vroom, *Work and Motivation* (New York: Wiley, 1964).

9. Alexander D. Stajkovic and Fred Luthans, "Social Cognitive Theory and Self-Efficacy: Going Beyond Traditional Motivational and Behavioral Approaches," *Organizational Dynamics,* Spring 1998, p. 66.

CHAPTER 10

1. Jeffrey Keller, "Associate with Positive People," A Supplement to the *Pryor Report,* 1994.

2. Ibid.

3. Erik J. Van Slyke and Bud Van Slyke, "Mentoring: A Results-Oriented Approach," *HRfocus,* February 1998, p. 14.

4. Based mostly on Kathy E. Kram, *Mentoring at Work: Developmental Relationships in Organizational Life* (Glenview, Ill.: Scott, Foresman, 1985), pp. 22–39; Van Slyke and Van Slyke, "Mentoring," 1998, p. 14.

5. Jerry Langdon, "Minority Executives Benefit from Mentors," Gannett News Service, December 7, 1998. See also Letty C. Hardy, "Mentoring: A Long-term Approach to Diversity," *HRfocus,* July 1998, p. S11.

6. Hal Rosenbluth and Diane McFerrin Peters, *Good Company: Caring as Fiercely as You Compete* (Reading, MA: Addison Wesley, 1998).

7. "Coach with 'Could,' not 'Should,'" *Executive Strategies,* April 1998, p. 1.

8. Ian Cunningham and Linda Honold, "Everyone Can Be a Coach," *HRMagazine,* June 1998, pp. 63–66.

9. *Career Track* seminar, How to Deal with Difficult People, 1995; Kenneth Kaye, *Workplace Wars and How to End Them: Turning Personal Conflicts into Productive Teamwork* (New York: AMACOM, 1994);

"Tame the Best Within You: How to Cope with Mood Swings in Yourself and Others," *WorkingSMART,* April 1999, p. 1.

10. Quoted in Jessica Guynn, "Bullying Behavior Affects Morale as Well as the Bottom Line," Knight Ridder syndicated story, November 2, 1998.

CHAPTER 11

1. Andrew J. DuBrin, "Sex Differences in the Use and Effectiveness of Tactics of Impression Management," *Psychological Reports,* 1994, 74, pp. 531–544.

2. William L. Gardner III, "Lessons in Organizational Dramaturgy: The Art of Impression Management," *Organizational Dynamics,* Summer 1992, p. 45.

3. Jim Rucker and Jean Anna Sellers, "Changes in Business Etiquette," *Business Education Forum,* February 1998, p. 45.

4. This section of the chapter is based on Annette Vincent and Melanie Meche, "It's Time to Teach Business Etiquette," *Business Education Forum,* October 1993, pp. 39–41; "Business Etiquette: Teaching Students the Unwritten Rules," *Keying In,* January 1996, pp. 1–8; Rucker and Sellers, "Changes in Business Etiquette," pp. 43–45; "Culture Shock?" *Entrepreneur,* May 1998, p. 46. The quotes are from the same source.

5. "Hardball Office Politics," *WorkingSMART,* September 1993, p. 5.

6. Research reported in Laura Lippman, "The Age of Obsequiousness: Flattering Your Way Up the Corporate Ladder," Baltimore, Maryland, *The Sun,* October 24, 1994.

7. Unpublished research reported in Kathleen Kelleher, *Los Angeles Times,* February 24, 1997.

8. Quoted in Mildred L. Culp, "Work Productively: Buddy-Up with Tech Fixers," *WorkWise*®, a syndicated column, January 10, 1999.

CHAPTER 12

1. Mike Miller, "Customer Service Drives Reengineering Effort," *Personnel Journal,* November 1994, pp. 87–91.

2. Anthony J. Rucci, Steven P. Kirn, and Richard T. Quinn, "The Employee-Customer-Profit Chain at Sears," *Harvard Business Review,* January–February 1998, pp. 82–97.

3. Barry M. Stow and Jerry Ross, "Stability in the Midst of Change: A Dispositional Approach to Job Attitudes," *Journal of Applied Psychology*, August 1985, p. 471.

4. Adrian J. Slywotzky and David J. Morrison, "Forget the Product: Focus on the Customer," *Leadership* (Newsletter of the American Management Association International), February 1999, p. 2.

5. Karl Abrecht, *The Only Thing That Matters* (New York: HarperCollins, 1992).

6. Susan Okula, "Customer Service: New Tools for a Timeless Idea," *Business Education Forum*, December 1998, p. 7; Robert F. Gault, "Managing Customer Satisfaction for Profit," *Management Review*, April 1993, p. 23.

7. Okula, "Customer Service," p. 9.

8. Joyce E. Santora, "Alamo's Drive for Customer Service," *Personnel Journal*, April 1991, p. 43.

9. Dot Yandle, "Helping Your Employees Give Customers What They Want," *Success Workshop* (A supplement to *Managers Edge*), November 1998, p. 1.

10. "Supermarket Smiles Misread in the Aisles," Associated Press, September 3, 1998.

11. Research cited in "Service Facts," *Customer Service Professional*, October 1997, p. 1.

12. Donna Deeprose, "Helping Employees Handle Difficult Customers," *Supervisory Management*, September 1991, p. 6; Chip R. Bell and Ron Zemke, "Service Breakdown-The Road to Recovery," in *Service Wisdom: Creating and Maintaining the Customer Service Edge* (Minneapolis, Minn.: Lakewood Books, 1992).

13. "Customer Problem Clinics," in *Making . . . Serving . . . Keeping Customers,* published by Dartnell, 4660 Ravenswood Avenue, Chicago, IL 60640.

14. Excerpted and paraphrased from Scott Hays, "Exceptional Customer Service Takes the 'Ritz' Touch," *Workforce*, January 1999, pp. 99–102.

CHAPTER 13

1. Linda K. Treviño and Katherine A. Nelson, *Managing Business Ethics: Straight Talk About How to Do It Right* (New York: Wiley, 1995), pp. 24–35; "Why Have a Code of Ethics?" *The Fact Finder*, January 1995, p. 3; Ralph Estes, *Tyranny of the Bottom Line: Why Corporations Make Good People Do Bad Things* (San Francisco: Berrett-Koehler, 1996).

2. Thomas M. Jones, "Ethical Decision Making by Individuals in Organizations: An Issue Contingent Model," *Academy of Management Review*, April 1991, p. 391.

3. Samuel Greengard, "50% of Your Employees Are Lying, Cheating, and Stealing," *Workforce*, October 1997, pp. 44–53.

4. Treviño and Nelson, *Managing Business Ethics*, pp. 47–64.

5. The concept of the game is from Karen Ireland, "The Ethics Game," *Personnel Journal*, March 1991, p. 74. The scenarios are original.

6. Joseph L. Badaracco, Jr., "The Discipline of Building Character," *Harvard Business Review*, March–April 1998, pp. 114–124.

7. Michael S. Josephson, "Does Character Still Count?" *USA Weekend*, September 23–25, 1994, p. 20.

8. "Extolling the Virtues of Hot Lines," *Workforce*, June 1998, pp. 125–126. For the original article, go to: www.depaul.edu/ethics/inter1.html.

9. Treviño and Nelson, *Managing Business Ethics*, pp. 71–75.

10. Daniel J. Brass, Kenneth D. Butterfield, and Bruce C. Skaggs, "Relationships and Unethical Behavior: A Social Network Perspective," *Academy of Management Review*, January 1998, pp. 14–31.

CHAPTER 14

1. Daniel Eisenberg, "Offices by the Hour," *Time*, February 1, 1999, p. 40.

2. Robert Boice, *Procrastination and Blocking: A Novel, Practical Approach* (Westport, CT: Greenwood Publishing Group, 1996).

3. The term *WIFO* has been contributed by Shale Paul, as cited in "Tips to Keep Procrastination Under Control," Gannett News Service syndicated story, November 9, 1998.

4. Dru Scott, *How to Put More Time in Your Life* (New York: New American Library, 1980), p. 1.

5. Mildred L. Culp, "Looking for Harmony? Swat the Clutter Bug for Greater Efficiency," syndicated column, Passage Media, 1998.

6. Meni Koslowky and Abraham Sagie, "Correlates of Employee Lateness: Some Theoretical Considerations," *Journal of Applied Psychology*, February 1997, pp. 79–88.

7. Mildred L. Culp, "Working Productively with Workaholics While Minimizing Legal Risks," *Passage Media* syndicated story, 1997.

8. Odette Pollar, "Tame Your In-Basket Once and for All," *Managers Edge*, September 1998, p. 11.

9. Amy Dunkin, "Saying 'Adios' to the Office," *Business Week*, October 12, 1998, p. 153; Heather Page, "Remote Control," Entrepreneur, October 1998, p. 148; Jenny C. McCune, "Telecommuting Revisited," February 1998, p. 14; E. Jeffrey Hill, Brent C. Miller, Sara P. Weiner, and Joe Colihan, "Influences of the Virtual Office on Aspects of Work/Life Balance," *Personnel Psychology*, Autumn 1998, pp. 667–683.

10. John J. Fried, "Be a Sharp Web Detective," Knight Ridder syndicated story, June 27, 1999.

11. Richard S. DeFrank and John M. Ivancevich, "Stress on the Job: An Executive Update," *Academy of Management Executive*, August 1998, pp. 55–56.

12. Jeffrey R. Edwards, "A Cybernetic Theory of Stress, Coping, and Well-Being in Organizations," *Academy of Management Review*, April 1992, p. 248.

13. Quoted in "An Ounce of Prevention Beats Burnout," *HRfocus*, June 1999, p. 1.

14. Christina Maslach, *The Truth About Burnout* (San Francisco: Jossey-Bass, 1997). See also Dirk van Dierendonck, Wilmar B. Schaufeli, and Bram P. Buunk, "The Evaluation of an Individual Burnout Intervention Program: The Role of Equity and Social Support," *Journal of Applied Psychology*, June 1998, pp. 392–407.

15. M. Afalur Rahim, "Relationships of Stress, Locus of Control, and Social Support to Psychiatric Symptoms and Propensity to Leave a Job: A Field Study with Managers," *Journal of Business and Psychology*, Winter 1997, p. 159.

16. Steve M. Jex and Paul D. Bliese, "Efficacy Beliefs as a Moderator of the Impact of Work-Related Stressors," *Journal of Applied Psychology*, June 1999, pp. 349–361.

17. Jeffrey R. Edwards and A. J. Baglioni, Jr., "Relationships between Type A Behavior Pattern and Mental and Physical Symptoms: A Comparison of Global and Component Measures," *Journal of Applied Psychology*, April 1991, p. 276.

18. Peter Y. Chen and Paul E. Spector, "Negative Affectivity as the Underlying Cause of Correlations between Stressors and Strains," *Journal of Applied Psychology*, June 1991, p. 398.

19. "Too Much Work Causes Stress," *Management Review*, March 1995, p. 6.

20. Craig Bond, *Technostress: The Human Cost of the Computer Revolution* (Reading: Mass.: Addison-Wesley, 1984), p. 16.

21. DeFrank and Ivancevich, "Stress on the Job," pp. 56–57.

22. DeFrank and Ivancevich, "Stress on the Job," pp. 57–58.

23. Harriet Johnson Brackey, "Snoozing Studies Alarm Experts," Knight Ridder syndicated story, July 6, 1998; Donald J. McNerney, "Napping at Work: You Snooze, You Win!" *HRfocus*, March 1995, p. 3.

CHAPTER 15

1. "Turn Passive Workers into 'Climbers'" *The Washington Post* syndicated story, June 29, 1998.

2. "CEOs Speak Out: What Is Needed to Work in Today's Ever-changing Business World," *Keying In*, November 1996, pp. 1–2; Brien N. Smith, Carolee Jones, and Judy Lane, "Employers' Perceptions of Work Skills," *Business Education Forum*, April 1997; Claudio Fernandez-Araoz, "Hiring without Firing," *Harvard Business Review*, July–August 1999, p. 113.

3. Quoted in Jerry Useem, "Cyberspace Is a Job Jungle: Read This Before You Put a Résumé Online," *Fortune*, May 24, 1999, p. 290.

4. Cited in Anitia Bruzzese, "Dangers Lurk for Job Hunters Online," Gannett News Service syndicated story, January 11, 1999.

5. Quoted in "Job Hunt," *Business Week Careers*, February 1987, p. 77.

6. Edward A. Robinson, "Beware—Job Seekers Have No Secrets," *Fortune*, December 29, 1997, p. 285.

7. Zane K. Quible, "Job Seeking Process," in *The Changing Dimensions of Business Education* (Reston, Va.: National Business Education Association, 1997), p. 176.

8. Quoted and updated July 1999 from Carol Kleiman, "Key Words Bosses Seek When Scanning Résumés," *Chicago Tribune* syndicated story, October 27, 1997.

9. Richard H. Beatty, *The Perfect Cover Letter* (New York: Wiley, 1997).

10. Linda Thornburg, "Computer-Assisted Interviewing Shortens Hiring Cycle," *HRMagazine*, February 1998, pp. 73–79.

11. Aaron Bernstein, "We Really Want You to Stay, Really," *Business Week*, June 22, 1998, p. 68.

12. Hugh P. Gunz, R. Michael Jalland, and Martin G. Evans, "New Strategy, Wrong Managers? What You Need to Know about Career Streams," *Academy of Management Executive*, May 1998, p. 22.

13. Such is the theme of James R. Lucas, *The Passionate Organization: Igniting the Fire of Employee Commitment* (New York: AMACOM, 1999).

14. Scott E. Seibert, Michael Crant, and Maria L. Kraimer, "Proactive Personality and Career Success," *Journal of Applied Psychology*, June 1999, pp. 416–427.

15. Philip L. Hunsaker, "Projecting the Appropriate Image," *Supervisory Management*, May 1989, p. 26.

16. "Taking Charge in a Temp World," *Fortune*, October 21, 1998, pp. 247–248.

17. Quoted in "Network Your Way Up," *WorkingSMART*, February 1997, p. 4.

18. Daniel L. Cable and Timothy A. Judge, "Interviewers' Perceptions of Person–Organization Fit and Organizational Selection Decisions," *Journal of Applied Psychology*, August 1997, pp. 546–561.

19. Michael Oliver, "Taking Risks Will Get You Moving," *Personnel Journal*, April 1983, p. 319.

20. This theme pervades Manuel London, *Career Barriers: How People Experience, Overcome, and Avoid Failure* (Mahwah, N.J.: Lawrence Erlbaum, 1998).

21. Gloria Dunn, "What to Do After You've Lost Your Job," *Workforce Extra* (supplement to the April 1999 *Workforce*), April 1999, pp. 2–3.

22. Belle Rose Ragins, Bickley Townsend, and Mary Mattis, "Gender Gap in the Executive Suite: CEOs and Female Executives Report on Breaking the Glass Ceiling," *Academy of Management Executive*, February 1998, pp. 28–42.

23. "Advancement for Minority Women Slow," The Associated Press syndicated story, July 14, 1999.

Index

360-degree survey for leadership, 172

A

Action plan for interpersonal skills, 4
Active listening, 53–54
Adversity quotient, 29
Aggressive personalities, 133
Assertiveness, 157–158
Attendance and punctuality for productivity, 296

B

Badaracco, Joseph L., 277
Balance in life, 296
Baldrige, Letitia, 117
Beatty, Richard H., 323
Behavior modification, 182–187
    extinction strategy, 183
    intermittent rewards, 185–186
    law of effect, 181
    negative reinforcement (avoidance motivation), 183
    positive reinforcement, 183
    punishment list, 183
    reward changing, 184
    reward list, 185
    rules for application, 184–187

    visibility of rewards, 186–187
Behavioral interview, 326
Big Five personality factors, 17–23
"Big picture," seeing, 81–82
Bonds with customer, 256–258
    care and concern, 257
    exceptional service, 257
    invitation to return, 258
    making buyer feel good, 257
    personal relationship building, 257–258
    welcoming attitude, 256
Brainstorming, 92–96
Brainwriting, 94
Broad experience, 171, 333
Bullies in workplace, 133
Bridge burning, 241

C

Career advancement strategies and tactics, 10, 330–336
    code of professional ethics, 331
    continuous learning and self-development for, 332
    depth and breadth for, 333
    document accomplishments, 332
    mentor for, 334
    networking for, 333–334

Career advancement strategies and tactics *(Cont.)*
   passion for work, 331
   person–organization fit, 334
   personal service business entity, 333
   proactive personality for, 331–332
   professional image for, 332–333
   risk taking and, 334
   as universal need, 10
Career barriers, 336–337
   glass ceiling problem, 337
   job-loss coping, 336–337
   mentor for, 337
Career paths, 327–330
   horizontal, 328–330
   vertical (traditional), 327–328
Carpal tunnel syndrome, 306
Character traits for ethics, 280–281
Charisma, 163–166
Coaching, 204, 205–210
   advice giving, 207
   barrier busting, 208
   emotional support in, 207
   fallacies about, 208, 210
   interpretation of events, 208
   mentoring and, 204
   modeling of behavior, 208
   skills and techniques for, 206–208
Cognitive restructuring, 139–140
Cognitive skills, 162–163
Cognitive styles and personality types, 19–21
Collaborative work place, 64
Communication, 7, 39-62, 115–118
   cross-cultural barriers, 115–118
   gender differences, 57–59
   as interpersonal skill, 7
   nonverbal type, 42–47
   overcoming problems and barriers, 48–59
   steps in process, 40–42
   universal needs and, 7
Communication problem handling, 48–59
   active listening, 53–54
   complementary transactions, 54–57
   defensive communication, 50
   empathy and, 48
   frame of reference, 49
   gender differences, 57
   metacommunications, 59
   multiple channels and, 50
   paradigm differences, 49–50
   persuasive communication, 51–53
   positive attitude and, 51
   understand receiver, 48–49
   verbal and nonverbal feedback, 51

Competition for limited resources, 128–129
Complementary transactions, 54
Compromise in negotiation, 143
Conflict of interest, 276
Conflict of interest and ethics, 276
Conflict-management styles, 133–135
Conflict resolution, 9, 127–152
   aggressive personalities and bullies, 133
   cognitive restructuring, 139
   competition for limited resources, 128–129
   compromise, 142–143
   conflict-management styles, 133–135
   confrontation and problem solving, 136
   criticism handling, 137–138
   development of allies, 291
   disarm the opposition, 137–138
   guidelines and techniques for, 135–144
   image exchanging, 138–139
   negotiating and bargaining, 139–144
   personality clashes, 132
   role conflict, 131–132
   sexual harassment, 144–148
   sources of conflict, 128–133
   stone wall building, 132
   as universal need, 9
   win–win (collaborative) style, 134–135
Confrontation and problem solving, 136–137
Conscientiousness and personality, 18
Consensus in groups, 82
Continuous learning and self-development, 332
Corporate ethics programs, 281–282
Cover letter for job search, 323–324
Coworker relationships, 235–239
   advice asking, 237–238
   ally development, 236
   diplomacy, 237
   exchange of favors, 237
   gossip sharing, 238
   group standards of conduct, 238
   honest and open relationships, 235–236
   interest expression, 236
   tech fixer alliance, 238
Criticism handling, 80, 137–138, 168–169, 216
   conflict and, 137–138
   difficult people and, 216
   team leadership and, 168–169
   of team members, 80
Cross-cultural communication barriers, 115–118
Cross-cultural relations and diversity, 9, 105–126
   business implications of differences, 118–119
   communication barriers, 115–118
   cultural bloopers, 113–115
   cultural fluency, 110

cultural sensitivity, 108–110
cultural training, 119–120
diversity training, 122–123
diversity umbrella, 106, 108
language training, 120–121
respect for workers and cultures, 110, 115
techniques for improving, 119–123
understanding cultural differences, 118–119
as universal need, 9
value dimensions of cultures, 110–113
Cross-functional teams, 67
Cultural bloopers, 113–115
Cultural differences, understanding, 108–115
competence goals, 108–110
cultural bloopers, 113–115
dimensions of values, 110–113
Cultural fluency, 110
Cultural sensitivity, 108, 110
Cultural training, 119–120
Customer dissatisfaction, handling, 258–261
involvement of customer in solution, 261
unreasonable request handling, 262
Customer satisfaction principles, 9, 245–266
customer needs understanding, 250–251
customer retention value, 248
cycle-of-service chart, 252
employee satisfaction importance, 248–250
empowerment of employees, 252–253
information technology role, 253
moments of truth, 252
problem-solving approach, 251
rudeness avoidance, 254
satisfaction levels, 248
as universal need, 9
Customer service training, at Ritz Carlton, 262–264
Cycle-of-service chart, 252

D

Defensive communication, 50
Defining moments in ethics, 277, 280
Deluga, Ronald, 233
Developmental experiences, 11
Developmental need identification, 6–7
Difficult people helping, 215–217
bully busting, 216
tactics for dealing with, 215–217
types of, 213
Diplomacy, 237
Disability explanation, 274
Disarming the opposition, 138
Diversity training, 122
Diversity umbrella, 106–108
Documenting accomplishments for career, 332

E

Electronic brainstorming, 95–96
E-mail for group decision making, 100
Emotional expressiveness, 165
Emotional intelligence, 28, 163
Emotional stability, 18, 158
Emotional support in coaching, 207
Empathy in communication, 48
Empowerment of employees, 252–253
Environment and communication, 43
Ethical behavior, 9, 269–289, 331
character traits for, 280–281
choosing between two rights, 277, 279
close interpersonal relationships and, 286–287
code for advancement, 331
common ethical problems, 273–277
computer ethics, 277
confidential information, 276
conflict of interest, 276
corporate ethics programs, 281–282
corporate resource use, 276
defining moments, 277, 280
eight-step guide for decision making, 282–285
ethical screening, 282
extent of problems, 273
guidelines for behaving ethically, 280–281
job discrimination, 274
reasons for concern, 270, 272–273
software copying, 274, 275
as universal need, 9
Ethical code for career advancement, 331
Ethical screening, 282
Ethics hot line, 282
Etiquette for business, 225–231
cross-cultural, 231
dining, 230
electronic devices, 231
hard-copy and e-mail correspondence, 230
meeting people, 229–230
telephone, 230
work behavior and clothing, 227
Exchange of favors, 237
Expectancy theory, 189–195
basic components, 190–193
diagnosing motivation, 193–195
effort-to-performance expectancy, 190
guidelines for application, 194
overview, 189–190
Pygmalion effect, 194
self-efficacy and, 191, 194
violence, 191–193
Expert power, 234
External versus internal customers, 246

Extinction in motivation, 183
Extraversion in personality, 17

F

Facial expressions, 44–45
Feedback
    behavior modification and, 184
    coaching and, 207
    communication problems and, 51
    interpersonal communication and, 42
    interpersonal skill development and, 5
Fight-or-flight response, 301
Flattery, 233
Formality vs. informality, 113
Frame of reference, 49
Free riding in groups, 95

G

Gender differences in communication, 57
General problem-solving groups, 89–94
Gestures, 44
Glass ceiling, 337
Goals, 3–4, 184
    behavior modification and, 184
    interpersonal skills training and, 3–4
Gossip for relationship building, 238
Gray, John, 57
Gretsky, Wayne, 80
Group decision making, 87
Group norms, 238
Group problem solving, 9, 86–104
    brainstorming, 92–96
    brainwriting, 94
    electronic brainstorming, 95–96
    e-mail and groupware, 100–101
    free-riding, 95
    general problem-solving groups, 89–92
    as interpersonal skill, 9
    nominal group technique, 96–98
    rational model of decision making, 87–89
    rational vs. political decision making, 87–89
    stand-up meetings, 98–99
    topics for work teams, 90
    as universal need, 9
Groupthink, 69–70
Groupware, 101
Growth and development of others, 9, 199–220
    bully busting, 216
    coaching others, 205–210
    difficult people helping, 212–217
    growth needs recognition, 202
    mentoring others, 203–205

    nurturing, positive person, 200, 202
    protégé role, 203
    training others, 211–212
    as universal need, 9
Growth needs, 202

H

High- vs. Low-context cultures, 113
Hitt, William D., 172
Humor, 158, 161, 216–217
    difficult people and, 216–217
    leadership and, 158, 161

I

Image exchanging, 138–139
Impression management, 225
Individual differences, 7, 15–38
    cognitive styles and personality types, 19–21
    emotional intelligence, 28–29
    mental ability, 23–28
    multiple intelligences, 27–28
    personality, 16–19
    practical intelligence, 25, 27
    psychological types and cognitive styles, 19–21
    traditional intelligence, 24–25
    values and, 30–34
Individualism vs. collectivism, 111–112
Informal learning, 10–11
Information power, 234
Information technology, 253–254
    customer service, 253–254
    ethical considerations, 277
Ingroups vs. outgroups, 170–171
Integrated human being, 172–173
Intelligence, 23–30
    adapting to different types, 29–30
    emotional type, 28
    multiple intelligences, 27–28
    practical type, 25, 27
    traditional intelligence components, 24–25
    triarchic theory, 25
Intermittent rewards, 185–186
Internet, 122, 299, 318–320
    foreign language skill development, 122
    job search and, 318–320
    search skills, 299
Interpersonal distance, 43
Interpersonal relations, 2
Interpersonal skill development on the job, 10–12
Interpersonal skills model, 3–5
Intuition for ethics, 285

J

Jaccobi, Jeffrey, 45
JCPenny, 118
Job discrimination, 274
Job-hunting tactics, 315–321
Job insecurity, 306
Job interview performance, 324–327
Job-loss coping, 336–337
Job objectives, 316
Job résumé (*see* Résumé for job)
Job satisfaction, 248–250
Job search, 10, 315–327
    background investigation and, 320
    behavioral interview, 326
    comprehensive marketing strategy, 316
    cover letter for, 323–324
    Internet and résumé database services, 318–320
    job-hunting tactics, 315–321
    job interview performance, 324–327
    job-objective identification, 316
    networking to reach insiders, 317–318
    qualifications sought by employers, 316
    questions asked by applicants, 326
    résumé for job, 321–323
    skill and contribution identification, 316
    smiling technique, 320
    as universal need, 10
    Web sites for, 319
Job search Web sites, 319

K

Kushel, Gerald, 180

L

Language training, 120–121
Law of effect, 181
Leader-exchange model, 170
Leadership, 9, 153–176
    charisma development, 163–166
    leader–member exchange model, 170–171
    team leadership skills, 166–170
    teamwork development, 166–170
    as universal skill, 9
    vision communication, 164
Leadership development, 171–173
    360-degree survey, 172
    broad experience, 171
    integrated human being, 172
    modeling leaders, 171
    practice "little" leadership, 173
    self-development of traits and behaviors, 172
Leadership traits, 154–163

    assertiveness, 157–158
    cognitive skills, 162–163
    emotional intelligence, 163
    emotional stability, 158
    self-awareness and self-objectivity, 162
    self-confidence, 156–157
    sense of humor, 158, 161
    trustworthiness, 157
Listening, 53-54, 75–76, 297
    coaching and, 297
    communication and, 53–54
    team player and, 75–76
Lovel, Pamela, 80
Low perceived control, 304

M

Mankiller, Wilma, 64
Materialism vs. concern for others, 112
Mehrabian, Albert, 42
Mental ability (*see* Intelligence)
Mentor, 203–205, 334, 337
    career advancement and, 334
    career barrier breaking and, 337
    helping others grow, 203–205
Metacommunications, 59
Mirroring, 47
Mission statement for productivity, 166
Moments of truth, 252
Motivation, 9, 177–198
    behavior modification for, 181–187
    expectancy theory for, 189–195
    as interpersonal skill, 9
    Pygmalion effect, 194
    recognition strategy, 188–189
    as universal skill, 9
    "What's in it for me?" (WIIFM), 178–181
Motivational state for communication, 49
Multiple intelligences, 27–28
Myers-Brigg type indicator, 19

N

Needs in motivation, 181
Negative affectivity, 305
Negative reinforcement (avoidance motivation), 183
Negotiating and bargaining, 140–143
    BATNA, 143–144
    compromise, 142–143
    concession granting, 143
    focus on interests, not positions, 140, 142
    plausible demand or offer, 143
Nelson, Katherine A., 224

Networking, 231–232, 317–318, 333–334
    career advancement and, 333–334
    job hunt and, 317–318
    relationship building with superiors, 231–232
Nominal group technique, 96–98
Nonverbal communication, 42–47, 118
    cross-cultural differences in, 118
    emotional impact of messages, 42–43
    guidelines for improving, 46–47
    modes of transmission, 43–45
Nurturing person, 200–202

O

Office at home, 298–299
O'Neil, Sharon Lund, 51

P

Paradigms in communication, 49
Participative leadership, 166, 167
Passion for work, 331
Peer evaluations, 169–170
Perceived control, 304
Person–organization fit, 334
Person–role conflict, 32
Personal appearance, 45
Personal productivity, 10, 291–301
    attendance and punctuality, 296
    attitudes and values for, 294–296
    balanced life for, 296
    Internet search skills, 299
    mission and goals for, 294
    office at home, 298
    paper work and electronic work control, 298
    procrastination coping, 292–294
    time waster overcoming, 299–301
    to-do list and priorities, 297
    as universal need, 10
    value orderliness and cleanliness, 296
    virtual office, 298
    work smarter, not harder, 294
    work streamlining, 297
    workaholic avoidance, 296
Personal service business entity, 333
Personality, 16–23
    agreeableness, 18
    Big Five factors, 17–23
    conscientiousness, 18
    emotional stability, 18
    extraversion, 17
    feeling type, 21
    genetic factors, 17
    guidelines for dealing with types, 21–23
    intuitive type, 23
    openness to experience, 18
    psychological types and cognitive styles, 19–21
    self-monitoring of behavior, 19
    sensation type, 19
    thinking type, 21
Personality clashes, 132
Persuasive communication, 51–53
Physical exercise and stress, 307–308
Political blunders, 239–241
Political skills, 9, 221–244
    blunder avoidance, 239–241
    business etiquette, 225–231
    impression management, 225, 226–227
    politics→power→influence, 222
    relationships with managers, 231–235
    relationships with work associates, 235–239
    as universal need, 9
Positive attitude and communication, 51
Positive reinforcement, 183
Posture and communication, 43–44
Power distance, 112
Practical intelligence, 25–27
Proactive personality, 331–332
Procrastination problem, 292–294
    calculate cost, 292
    commitment to others, 293
    manageable chunks, 292
    seriousness of problem, 292
    uncluttering the mind, 293
    worst in, first out, 292
Professional image, 332
Protégé role, 204
Punishment, 183
Pygmalion effect, 194

Q

Qualifications sought by employer, 316
Quible, Zane K., 323

R

Recognition for motivation, 188–189
Relationships with managers, 231–235
    coolness under pressure, 235
    expert power, 234
    flattering influentials, 233–234
    information power, 234
    laughing at humor, 235
    networking with influentials, 231–232
    success assistance, 233
    volunteering for assignments, 233
Repetitive motion disorder, 306

Respect for others, 110, 115
Responsibility assuming in teams, 81
Résumés for job, 321–323
    electronic type, 321, 323
    format, 321, 323
    length, 321
    purpose, 321
Rewards and punishments as motivators, 184
Risk taking in career, 334–336
Ritz-Carlton customer service training, 262–264
Role ambiguity, 306
Role conflict, 131–132
Role conflict and stress, 306
Role overload, 305

S

Sears Roebuck & Co., 282
Self-assessment quizzes
    adversity quotient, 29
    assertiveness scale, 159–160
    business etiquette, 228–229
    conflict management styles, 129–131
    cross-cultural skills and attitudes, 107
    cultural value profile, 114
    customer responsiveness, 247
    developmental needs, 8
    difficult people handling, 214–215
    effective coach characteristics, 209
    ethical reasoning inventory, 271–272
    helping others, 201
    impression management tactics, 226
    leadership skills, 155
    leadership style, 167
    listening traps, 56
    motivating others, 179–180
    negotiator quiz, 141
    numerical information attitudes, 26
    organizational politics questionnaire, 223–224
    political blunders, 240
    problem-solving tendencies, 88
    procrastination tendencies, 293
    qualifications sought by employers, 317
    rudeness survey, 225
    self-monitoring scale, 20
    team player attitudes, 65
    team player roles, 72
    team skills, 66
    value clarification, 33
    voice quality checkup, 46
Self-awareness and self-objectivity, 162
Self-confidence for leadership, 156–157
Self-efficacy, 191, 303
    motivation, 191

stress and, 304
Self-esteem and job satisfaction, 250
Self-image and job satisfaction, 250
Self-managing work teams, 64
Self-monitoring of behavior, 19
Sexual harassment, 144–148
    adverse effects of, 146
    guidelines for prevention and dealing with, 146–148
    Supreme Court rulings, 145–146
    types and frequency, 144–145
Skill-building exercises
    behavior modification role plays, 187
    bonding with customer, 259
    brainstorming (1-800-INSIGHT), 94
    brainstorming vs. brainwriting, 95
    business etiquette, 232
    coaching good performer, 210
    cognitive restructuring, 140
    complementary vs. crossed transactions, 57
    coworker relationships, 239
    cross-cultural role play, 121
    cultural mistakes, 116
    cultural sensitivity development, 111
    defining moments for ethics, 280
    difficult customer dealing, 263
    difficult people dealing, 218
    disarming the opposition, 138
    empathy for differences, 124
    ethical decision making, 286
    ethics game, 278–279
    expectancy theory application, 195
    flattering influential person, 234
    general problem-solving group, 92
    Habitat for homeless team building, 83
    Internet for language skills, 122
    Internet productivity, 300
    job hunting on the Web, 320
    job interview, 327
    mental ability differences, 30
    mirroring technique, 48
    mission statement for work habits, 295
    moments of truth, 253
    network building, 335
    nominal group technique, 99
    nonverbal communication e-mail skills, 62
    nurturing person role play, 203
    personality role plays, 24
    protégé selection, 206
    sexual harassment combatting, 149
    team member roles, 78
    team mission statement, 169
    training program design, 212
    trust fall, 79

Skill-building exercises *(Cont.)*
    valence estimations, 192-193
    value-conflict role play, 34
    vision creation, 164
    visualization for stress reduction, 309
    WIIFM investigation, 182
    win–win conflict resolution, 135
    witty leader, 161
Smiling at customers, 256
Smiling for job hunt, 320
Social loafing, 69
Stand-up meetings, 98–99
Stress, 300–309
    burnout as consequence, 303
    carpal tunnel syndrome, 306
    job insecurity, 306
    job performance and, 302–303
    job source, 305–307
    low perceived control, 304
    low self-efficacy and, 304
    negative affectivity, 305
    personality factors related to, 304–305
    physiological reactions, 302
    repetitive motion disorder, 306
    role ambiguity, 306
    role conflict, 306
    role overload, 305
    symptom chart, 303
    symptoms and consequences, 300–304
    technostress, 306
    Type A behavior, 304
    workplace violence, 306
Stress busters, 309
Stress management, 307–308
    everyday methods, 308
    modifying or eliminating stressor, 307
    physical exercise, 307
    rest contribution, 308
    stress busters, 309
    support network, 308
    as universal need, 10
    visualization, 308
Support network, 308

T

Tannen, Deborah, 57
Team development by leader, 166–171
    criticism encouragement, 168–169
    high performance standards, 166, 168
    ingroup vs. outgroups, 70
    mission statement, 166
    peer evaluations for, 169
    sense of urgency, 166

    symbol utilization, 169
Team member roles, 71–76
Team symbols, 169
Teamwork skills, 9, 63–85
    advantages of teams, 68–69
    assistance to members, 82
    big picture seeing, 81–82
    consensus approach, 82
    cooperation and collaboration, 77–79
    cross-functional teams, 67
    disadvantages of teams, 69–70
    groupthink, 69–70
    helpful criticism, 80
    interpersonal aspects, 77–80
    raining on parade, 80–81
    recognition of others, 79–80
    responsibility assuming, 81
    roles for team members, 70–77
    self-managing work team, 65–68
    social loafing, 69
    task aspects, 81–82
    technical expertise, 81
    trusting team members, 77
    types of teams, 64–68
    as universal need, 9
    virtual teams, 67–68
Technostress, 306
Technical expertise, 81
Thomson, John A., 333
Time orientation, 113
Time wasters, 299–300
To-do list and priorities, 297
Toxic person, 200
Training principles, 211–212
Treviño, Linda K., 274
Triarchic theory of intelligence, 25
Trust and teamwork, 77
Trustworthiness, 157
Type A behavior, 304

U

Uncertainty avoidance, 112
Universal needs for training and development, 7–10
Urgent vs. casual time orientation, 113

V

Valence in motivation, 191–193
Values, 30–34
    clarification, 31
    guidelines for interpersonal relations, 32–34
    individual vs. job values, 32
    learning of, 31

person–role conflict, 32
Valuing-differences training (*see* Diversity training)
Violence in workplace, 306
Virtual office, 298
Virtual teams, 67-68
Vision communication, 164
Vision creation, 64
Visualization for stress, 308
Voice quality, 45

W

WIIFM ("What's in it for me?") principle, 178, 180
Win–win conflict resolution, 134–135

Work habits and time management (*see* Personal
    productivity)
Work smarter, not harder, 294–295
Work streamlining, 297
Workaholic, 296

X

Xerox Corp., 118

Z

Zand, Dale, 157